Politics and Society
in Soviet Ukraine
1953–1980

POLITICS AND SOCIETY
IN SOVIET UKRAINE
1953–1980

by

Borys Lewytzkyj

Canadian Institute of Ukrainian Studies
University of Alberta
Edmonton   **1984**

THE CANADIAN LIBRARY IN UKRAINIAN STUDIES

A series of original works and reprints relating to Ukraine, issued under the editorial supervision of the Canadian Institute of Ukrainian Studies, University of Alberta, Edmonton.

Editorial Board:
Bohdan Bociurkiw, Carleton University (Social Sciences)
Manoly R. Lupul, University of Alberta (Ukrainians in Canada)
Bohdan Rubchak, University of Illinois at Chicago Circle (Humanities)
Ivan L. Rudnytsky, University of Alberta (History)

Canadian Cataloguing in Publication Data
Lewytzkyj, Borys.
  Politics and society in Soviet Ukraine, 1953–80

(The Canadian library in Ukrainian studies)

Includes index.
ISBN 0-920862-31-4 (bound). — ISBN 0-920862-33-0 (pbk.)

1. Ukraine—Politics and government—1917– 2. Ukraine—Social conditions. I. Canadian Institute of Ukrainian Studies. II. Title. III. Series.
DK508.8.L49 1984   947'.71085   C83–091489–7

Cover design: Sherryl Petterson

Index: Lubomyr Szuch

Printed in Canada by Printing Services, University of Alberta
Distributed by the University of Toronto Press
5201 Dufferin St.
Downsview, Ontario
Canada M3H 5T8

Contents

Preface

Among the fifteen republics which constitute the Union of Soviet Socialist Republics, the Ukrainian Soviet Socialist Republic is second only to the Russian Soviet Federated Socialist Republic in importance. With only 3 per cent of Soviet territory, Ukraine, according to the latest census results, accounts for 19 per cent of the Soviet Union's population. Ukraine plays a leading economic role in the multinational state, accounting for one-fifth of Soviet national income. Its per capita output of coal, gas, ferrous metals, diesel locomotives, tractors and combine harvesters is higher than that of any Western European country. It produces over 50 per cent of the Soviet Union's iron ore, about half of its coke and iron, 40 per cent of its steel and about one-third of its coal. Over 20 per cent of the Soviet Union's agricultural produce is produced by Ukrainian farmers including more than 23 per cent of field crops and 21 per cent of livestock. In grain and milk production Ukraine is second in the USSR. In this study, however, economic issues, though not ignored, are secondary to the republic's political, social and cultural development in the twenty-five-year period after Stalin's death in 1953.

Soviet leaders maintain that the nationality problem has been solved satisfactorily and even recommend their treatment of the non-Russian peoples as a model for other multinational states. So far no country in the socialist camp has accepted this "export offer." Czechoslovakia follows its own nationality policy and the Yugoslav solution is almost the antithesis of the Soviet model. Undeterred, Soviet propaganda proclaims that Moscow's example is being emulated with great success in the Third World. In Biafra the Soviet Union did all it could to annihilate the separatist movement. In Iraq it helped to "solve" the perennial Kurdish problem by supplying weapons to crush the rebels. In Ethiopia the battle against the Eritrean liberation movement is being fought with Soviet aid. In each case the Soviet Union has tried to subjugate the national groups within its unitary client-states to the central pro-Soviet regimes. Clearly it has not promoted national self-determination and independent development. This book analyzes Moscow's nationality policy in the Ukrainian republic in recent years.

Part one covers three distinct historical phases. The first phase (1953–64) coincides approximately with the period when Nikita Khrushchev enjoyed supreme power. It analyzes the consequences of Khrushchev's policies for the Ukrainian SSR. The second phase began with the period preceding Khrushchev's fall (in October 1964) and lasted until 1972. It encompasses the leadership of Petro Shelest, who was elected first secretary of the Central Committee of the Communist Party of Ukraine (CC CPU) in 1963. The third phase, beginning with Shelest's fall in 1972, saw the ascendancy of hard-line policies and increased centralism and Russification. This shift to the right in Soviet policy emerged with particular clarity after the invasion of Czechoslovakia in 1968. It was symbolized by the much-quoted concept of the "Soviet people" as a new historical national entity: an idea that is used to promote the assimilation of the peoples of the USSR.

Part two analyzes events and developments in the social, economic and cultural life of contemporary Ukraine. Part three reviews and summarizes parts one and two.

Many aspects of Ukrainian history have been treated only briefly, and some topics have been omitted altogether. The course taken by the Ukrainian economy from 1953–78, for example, justifies a separate study. I have merely highlighted the main developments in this field.

This study is based mainly on Soviet source material from the author's archives rather than the works of Western specialists. I wish to thank my assistant, Elwine Sprogis, my translator, Roy Glashan, Dr. Bohdan Krawchenko, David Marples and Peter Matilainen of the Canadian Institute of Ukrainian Studies, and many colleagues who have given me the benefit of their professional advice and helped me to obtain additional source material.

Borys Lewytzkyj
Munich,
January 1982

Chapter One

From Stalin's Death to the Twentieth Congress of the CPSU (1953–6)

The Situation in Ukraine, March 1953

Until Stalin's death in March 1953, a hard-line ideological policy was in force aimed at eradicating all possible Western influence in the arts and sciences, in education and literature, and in other fields. The policy was enunciated by Stalin's close associate, Andrei Zhdanov, immediately after the Second World War, and thus bore the name *Zhdanovshchina*. Although Zhdanov died in 1948, the course he charted continued up to Stalin's death. The policy was justified as follows:

> During the war years several million people lived in the territory temporarily occupied by the enemy. Millions were deported to Germany by Hitler's fascists. Many members of the Soviet Army were prisoners of war. The Hitlerite fascists tried to influence these people ideologically. During the anti-fascist liberation campaign Soviet troops advanced far into the West, and elements of the armed forces remained on the territory of capitalist states, where the forces of reaction strove to influence the Soviet soldiers by all manner of methods. The Hitlerite fascists left behind bourgeois-nationalist groups in the western regions of Ukraine and Belorussia and in the Baltic republics to conduct anti-Soviet agitation among the population. A pernicious ideological influence was exerted on the Soviet people through all these and

other channels. The majority spurned the reactionary bourgeois views that such elements tried to impose on them, but part of the population lacked ideological education and displayed an uncritical attitude toward capitalist conditions.[1]

Since the Germans had occupied virtually all Ukraine, the campaign to eradicate "Hitlerite" influence in the republic was widespread. The Zhdanov policy was implemented through several decrees of the Communist Party of the Soviet Union (CPSU).[2] Similar decrees approved by the Ukrainian central party organs in 1946–8 criticized national deviation in literature, drama, music and historical scholarship.[3] In consequence, hundreds of intellectuals were persecuted, among them such outstanding literary figures as Maksym Rylsky, Volodymyr Sosiura and Ostap Vyshnia.[4]

Integral to *Zhdanovshchina* was the concept of the Russian people as the "master race." This was initiated on 24 May 1945 during a Kremlin reception for officers at which Stalin offered a "historic" toast: "I drink to the health of the Russian people not only because it is a leading people but also because it possesses a clear understanding, a steadfast character and patience."[5] During *Zhdanovshchina* a wave of "Great-Russian chauvinism" acquired grotesque forms and elicited considerable derision abroad. The party ordered Soviet scientists to prove that the most important discoveries in human history were made by Russians. Soviet historians were forced to glorify tsarist policies and colonial conquests and to label reactionary the movements against Russification. Historians in the national republics were obliged to maintain that annexation by tsarist Russia represented not imperialist expansion but "voluntary union."

In the last years of *Zhdanovshchina*, the campaigns against "cosmopolitans," "bourgeois nationalists" and "Zionists" intensified. The number of Jews in Ukraine was then relatively high (840,300 according to the 1959 census), and exhortations to "struggle against Jewish bourgeois nationalists and Zionists" fell on fertile soil. Agitation against Zionists soon turned into anti-Semitism, with purges of alleged Zionists in government and the persecution of Ukrainian Jews. Prominent victims of this "struggle" were L. S. Pervomaisky, S. O. Holovanivsky and I. I. Stebun. Unfortunately, a number of Ukrainian writers and scientists participated in the anti-Semitic campaigns. Some wanted to deflect the wrath of party leaders onto Jews to save the Ukrainian intelligentsia from the full force of party measures. Others were merely following orders. But the anti-Semitic policy failed to gain widespread support in the population at large.

The campaign against Jews, increasing Russification and attacks on Ukrainian cultural figures caused panic among the Ukrainian intelligentsia and party rank and file. This fear increased when L. M. Kaganovich replaced Khrushchev as first secretary of the CPU in March 1947 with a commission from Stalin to intensify the ideological struggle in Ukraine. Khrushchev retained his position as chairman of the Council of Ministers, but everything pointed to an imminent mass purge and a wave of arrests. This, however, did not materialize. Kaganovich was ordered back to Moscow in December of the same year. Khrushchev was reappointed first party secretary while the chairmanship of the Council of Ministers was given to D. S. Korotchenko, a Central Committee secretary renowned as an organizer of the partisan movement in the occupied regions of Ukraine. Khrushchev was subsequently recalled to Moscow, where he became a secretary of the CC CPSU and first secretary of the Moscow oblast committee. From the Nineteenth Party Congress (1952) to his fall in October 1964 he was a member of the Presidium (later Politburo) of the CC CPSU.

Melnikov's Fall and the Promotion of Ukrainian Cadres

Developments in the Ukrainian party leadership took a course somewhat different from those in the Moscow leadership after Stalin's death in March 1953. Whereas uncertainty, mistrust and political infighting prevailed in Moscow, the situation in the Kiev party leadership was marked by a process of consolidation. The Ukrainian party leaders realized that they were no longer in danger and demonstratively supported Khrushchev. Khrushchev's successor as first secretary of the CC CPU was Leonid Melnikov. It is possible that Kaganovich proposed this appointment because he believed that Melnikov was the right man to continue his and Stalin's course. In spite of his experience (first secretary of the Donetsk [Stalino] oblast and city committees of the CPU, 1945–7, second secretary of the CC CPU, 1947–50), Melnikov proved to be a weak leader. He was removed from office in 1953 allegedly for violating nationality policy. One version of the events that led to Melnikov's fall reads as follows:

> In the last few days a plenary session of the Central Committee of the CPU was held. The plenum deliberated the question of shortcomings in political work and in the leadership of economic and cultural development.
>
> The plenum pronounced unsatisfactory the leadership of the Central Committtee of the CPU and the Council of Ministers of the Ukrainian SSR in the western oblasts of Ukraine.
>
> The plenum noted that the Bureau of the Central Committee and the Secretary of the Central Committee of the CPU, Comrade Melnikov, in their practical work, were guilty of deviations from the Leninist-Stalinist nationality policy of our party that found expression in the erroneous practice of giving preference when filling posts in Western Ukraine to workers from other regions of the Ukrainian SSR, and also in a virtual changeover to lecturing in the Russian language in institutions of higher learning. The plenum discovered serious errors in the organizational-economic consolidation of the collective farms of the western oblasts of Ukraine.

The plenum of the Central Committee of the CPU announced practical measures for the intensification of political work, the consistent execution of Leninist-Stalinist norms in nationality policy and the removal of shortcomings in the leadership of economic and cultural development. The plenum of the Central Committee of the CPU adopted resolutions on organizational questions. The plenum released from the post of first secretary, and removed from the Bureau of the Central Committee of the CPU, L. G. Melnikov, on charges of having failed to provide leadership, allowing grave errors in the selection of cadres and in the implementation of the party's nationality policy.

The plenum appointed Comrade O. I. Kyrychenko as first secretary of the Central Committee of the CPU, having released him from his responsibilities as second secretary of the Central Committee of the CPU. The plenum elected as a member of the Bureau of the Central Committee of the CPU the First Deputy-Chairman of the Council of Ministers of the Ukrainian SSR, Comrade O. Ie. Korniichuk.[6]

The charges against Melnikov were largely unfounded. The degree of Russification (especially in post-secondary education) was much greater in Eastern than in Western Ukraine and had increased since the *Zhdanovshchina*.[7] Thus the dismissal was a psychological move; indeed, Melnikov's career suffered little as a result of his recall from Kiev.[8] Moreover, according to V. Malanchuk, the official reasons for Melnikov's dismissal were not taken seriously in Soviet publications.[9]

The change in leadership consolidated the party and boosted the self-confidence of the Ukrainian leaders, whose sphere of competence was steadily increased. It formed the background for personnel changes, including the election of the writer Oleksandr Korniichuk to the Presidium of the CPU Central Committee, and S. V. Stefanyk, son of the famous West Ukrainian writer Vasyl Stefanyk, to the post of deputy chairman of the Ukrainian Council of Ministers. There was also a strengthening of Ukrainian representation in the party apparatus. In Lviv, for example, a former leader of the not yet fully rehabilitated Communist Party of Western Ukraine (CPWU), B. Dudykevych, was elected second secretary of the oblast committee.[10]

In July 1953 *Pravda* reported the dismissal of USSR Interior Minister L. P. Beria, who was sentenced to death in December together with P. Ia. Mishik, a former NKVD department director and interior minister of the Ukrainian SSR, and others. The reason given for the sentence was that Beria had tried to attract the non-Russian peoples to his "treasonous undertakings."[11] Beria's "divisive activity" in Ukraine has remained a much-discussed issue. The recent edition (1977) of *Ocherki istorii Kommunisticheskoi partii Ukrainy* denounces his activities: "He strove to undermine the foundation of our multinational state and the friendship of peoples of the USSR, to sow discord among them, and to activate bourgeois-nationalist elements in the Union republics, including Ukraine."[12]

During the investigation against Beria, the Ukrainian political leadership emphasized (in what was evidently a compromise formulation) that serious violations of "socialist legality" had been revealed.[13] Accordingly, many Ukrainians anticipated a more rapid rehabilitation of the victims of the Stalinist terror. The party was interested in the rehabilitation of its cadres, while other circles wanted the rehabilitation of scholars and cultural figures. Many welcomed the announcement that the security organs would henceforth be subject to party control.

Ukraine: Secunda inter pares

In order to consolidate its position, the new Soviet leadership wooed the Ukrainians, the second most populous national group. Thus in 1954 the three-hundredth anniversary of the Pereiaslav agreement, Ukraine's union with Russia, was used to invoke "the eternal and unshakeable friendship between Russians and Ukrainians." In a joint statement, the Presidium of the USSR Supreme Soviet, the USSR Council of Ministers and the CC CPSU declared:

> The experience of history has shown that the way of fraternal union and alliance chosen by the Russians and Ukrainians was the only true way. The union of two great Slavic peoples multiplied their strength in the common struggle against all external foes, against the serf owners and the bourgeoisie, against tsarism and capitalist slavery. The unshakeable friendship of the Russian and Ukrainian peoples grew and strengthened in this struggle. . . . [14]

In honour of the occasion, the Russian republic ceded to Ukraine an impressive "gift," the Crimea. The Presidium of the USSR Supreme Soviet cited economic dependence, territorial proximity and the cultural and economic ties between the Crimea and Ukraine as the reasons for this action.

The theses of the CC CPSU marking the Pereiaslav anniversary proclaimed the tercentenary to be "a great festive day not only for the Ukrainian and Russian peoples but also for all the peoples of the Soviet Union." During the Seventeenth Congress of the CPU, held at the end of March 1954, political discussions were eclipsed by the celebrations, which continued throughout most of the year. The Russian republic, Ukraine and the city of Kiev were awarded the Order of Lenin.

Numerous articles on the "union" in scholarly journals and in the party press followed the party line developed during the *Zhdanovshchina*. Bohdan Khmelnytsky, it was claimed, had tried to convince the Ukrainian Cossacks of the advantages of the 1654 union with Russia. (In truth, although these advantages had been guaranteed by the Pereiaslav agreement, the Russians had not respected them. The promised Cossack autonomy did not materialize and the Ukrainian language was eventually banned.) Soviet interpretations of the union during the jubilee year contrasted with the treatment it received from Marxist historians in the 1930s, especially those of the Pokrovsky school, who mercilessly attacked the distorters of "historical reality." A reference work published in the early 1930s, *Malaia sovetskaia entsikopediia*, reflecting the views of the Pokrovsky school, criticized the "Russian chauvinist" view of history:

> Great-power chauvinist historiography viewed the so-called annexation of Ukraine to Russia in 1654 as the "reunification" of the two parts of a homogeneous "Russian" nation.... Ukraine, now incorporated into the Russian state as a province, developed into a Russian colony in the nineteenth century—a colony in which the Russian government began to eradicate all traces of national character. The Ukrainian people were finally subjugated, stifled by national oppression and serf laws.[15]

This materialist interpretation of Ukrainian-Russian relations, written in the early years of the Soviet state, contrasts with the later historiography.

In connection with the three-hundredth anniversary, the theoretical journal of the CC CPSU, *Kommunist*, published an article by Mykola Pidhorny [Nikolai Podgorny], in which the then secretary of the CPU Central Committee (quoting Stalin) denounced the "lackeys of imperialism—the Ukrainian bourgeois nationalists" as the enemies of co-operation with the "fraternal" Russian people. Their aim, he alleged, was to deliver "the Ukrainian people into the colonial slavery of foreign conquerors." He listed the famous communists who had "defended" Ukraine, many of whom were soon to become *personae non gratae*:

> Commissioned by the party of V. I. Lenin, his closest disciples and companions—I. V. Stalin, V. M. Molotov, M. I. Kalinin, Ia. M. Sverdlov, F. E. Dzerzhinsky, K. E. Voroshilov, M. V. Frunze, N. S. Khrushchev and L. M. Kaganovich—made several visits to Ukraine and rendered invaluable assistance to the Ukrainian Soviet state and the Communist Party of Ukraine by personal involvement in the work of the state and Party *apparat*, in the command of the armed forces on the Ukrainian fronts and in the partisan movement.[16]

In addition, Pidhorny expressed loyalty to Khrushchev. He described the "gift" of the Crimea as:

> yet another affirmation of the great fraternal love and trust of the Russian people for Ukraine. The transfer of the Crimean oblast to Ukraine will contribute to the swift flourishing of our republic and to a strengthening of

the unshakeable friendship of the Ukrainian and great Russian peoples and of the other peoples of the USSR.[17]

According to Pidhorny, the union of the Crimea with Ukraine would boost economic development. In reality, it generated major problems. The Crimean Tatars, who accounted for 25 per cent of the population of the former autonomous republic, had been deported during the war. As a result, the fruit harvest declined drastically, from 40,400 metric tons in 1940 to 18,400 metric tons in 1955, a year in which measures for the reconstruction of the Crimean economy were already in effect.

The 1959 census states that there were about 858,000 Russians and 268,000 Ukrainians in the Crimea. The authorities made various efforts to settle Ukrainians there and offered material incentives, but the 1970 census figures show that these efforts were not successful. Although there were now said to be 480,733 Ukrainians in the Crimea, the number of Russians had increased to 1,220,484. Many Crimean Russians glorify the territory's "heroic past" as an important naval base in tsarist times. They have resisted Ukrainization and try to control immigration, thereby ensuring the territory's "Russian character." At the same time they oppose the Crimean Tatars' efforts to return to their homeland and restore their national autonomy.

Celebrations like the anniversary of the Pereiaslav agreement are often occasions for acts of clemency—political amnesties or pardons. This event, however, was an exception. On 19 May 1954 Vasyl Okhrymovych, a leader of the Ukrainian resistance movement, was shot, even though, as Radio Kiev announced, he had made a "detailed deposition on the conspiratorial activities of the Organization of Ukrainian Nationalists (OUN) abroad and named his fellow-spies in Ukraine." His execution during the tercentenary celebration cast an ominous shadow over the hymns of praise to eternal friendship and unity between the Russians and Ukrainians.

The Twentieth Party Congress: "Back to Leninism!"

The Nineteenth CPU Congress, held in Kiev from 17 to 21 January 1956, demonstrated how poorly the Ukrainian party organization was informed of the developments preceding the Twentieth Congress of the CPSU. Both the report delivered by First Secretary Kyrychenko and those of the congress delegates dealt mainly with local economic problems. Thus the Ukrainian leaders were evidently unprepared for the major development at the Twentieth CPSU Congress in February 1956: the exposure of Stalin's enormities.

The Twentieth CPSU Congress, held in Moscow (14–25 February 1956), appeared to herald changes in the party's nationality policy. Khrushchev's report entitled "Some Questions of Our Nationality Policy" was of particular importance for Ukraine:

Formerly, when there were few specialists, when the cadres in some republics were weak and when there were not so many industrial enterprises, the management of almost all enterprises was undertaken by the union ministries. Now the situation has changed: people grew along with industry in all union republics; national cadres were developed.... Under these new conditions the old methods of economic management must undergo serious revision.... The rights of the republican ministries are to be considerably expanded.

For example, an Economic Commission could be formed at the Nationalities Council of the Supreme Soviet to develop various projects in the economic field. Or take a question like the distribution of budgetary means among the union republics. Basically, these means are distributed correctly, but here too we should give serious consideration to increasing the republics' role and authority.

Socialism does not destroy national differences and characteristics; on the contrary, it secures the all-round development and flourishing of the economy and culture of all nations and peoples. Therefore we must not disdain these characteristics and differences but give them due and most attentive regard in all our practical work in the management of economic and cultural construction.[18]

Anastas Mikoyan addressed Ukrainian problems, especially in historiography:

A Moscow historian once had the presumption to assert that, if Comrade Antonov-Ovseenko or Comrade Kosior had never been in the Ukrainian party leadership, there might have been no Makhno or Grigoriev gangs, that Petliura would have failed, that there would also have been no enthusiasm for the creation of communes (a phenomenon which incidentally was at that time not only Ukrainian but also common to the party as a whole) and that Ukraine... would have immediately taken the course onto which the whole party and the entire country moved as a result of the NEP. Such historiographical scribbling has nothing in common with Marxist history. It is far closer to the idealist interpretation of historical events by the social-revolutionaries. I believe that there will be Ukrainian historians who will write a history of the emergence and development of the Ukrainian socialist state and do a better job than some Moscow historians who have tackled the task but who might have done better not to assume it.[19]

Mikoyan's candid speech was received sympathetically in Ukraine, particularly among historians. Ukrainians also reacted positively to the speech delivered by A. M. Pankratova, a leading Soviet historian who supported Stalin's thesis of the Russian master race and thus had contributed to its glorification.[20] At the congress, however, Pankratova regretted that the Moscow historians had not "unmasked" the shortcomings in Lykholat's work elucidated by Mikoyan. In fact the journal *Voprosy istorii*, of which she was chief editor, had praised it. She urged historians to review the party's nationality policy and related questions:

> All these questions cannot be solved correctly unless the errors made in presenting the situation of the nationalities in tsarist Russia are overcome. Hardly any attention is paid to the unmasking of national and colonial subjugation by the tsarist autocracy in our textbooks and books on the history of individual peoples. Some authors who, quite correctly, highlight the progressive significance of these peoples' union with Russia neglect the other side of the story. Tsarism subjugated peoples cruelly and impeded their political, economic and cultural development. As we know, Lenin described tsarist Russia as a "prison-house of peoples." Only the October Revolution destroyed this prison-house. The history of the national movements in Russia should be studied more thoroughly.[21]

The most dramatic event of the Twentieth CPSU Congress, however, was Khrushchev's secret speech against Stalin, the full text of which has never been published in the Soviet Union. The Soviet people learned of it only through foreign radio broadcasts. The congress delegates were instructed to brief the party rank and file confidentially on selected excerpts. The speech marked a turning-point in Soviet history, especially in its exposure of Stalin's deeds: the acts of terror against the old Bolshevik guard, the assassinations and tortures, and the violations of the "principle of collective responsibility." Khrushchev listed a number of party functionaries in Ukraine who had been liquidated, including Stanislav Kosior, Pavel Postyshev and Vlas Chubar. Of importance for future Soviet nationality policy was Khrushchev's condemnation of the mass deportation of entire ethnic groups, such as the Crimean Tatars, the Kalmyks, the Karachai, the Chechen-Ingush and the Balkars. Khrushchev concluded with the following remarks: "The Ukrainians avoided meeting this fate only because there were too many of them and there was no place to which to deport them. Otherwise he [Stalin] would have deported them also."[22]

Notes

1. *Geschichte der KPdSU* (Berlin, 1960), 312.
2. The names of the Communist Party of the Soviet Union (CPSU) and of the Communist Party of Ukraine (CPU) have changed several times. The CPSU was known as the Russian Social-Democratic Labour Party (Bolshevik)—RSDLP(B)—until 1918, when the name changed to the Russian

Communist Party (Bolshevik)–RCP(B). "Russian" here is *rossiiskaia*, not *russkaia*, and denotes the entire territory of the Russian state rather than ethnic Russia. In 1925 the party name was changed to the Communist Party of the Soviet Union (Bolshevik)–CPSU(B), and in 1952 the word "Bolshevik" was dropped. The Communist Party of Ukraine founded in 1918 was the Communist Party (Bolshevik) of Ukraine–CP(B)U; in 1952 "Bolshevik" was dropped.

Hereafter the abbreviations CPSU and CPU will be used except in direct quotations or when reference is made to the CPSU and the CPU in the prerevolutionary period.

3. *Narysy istorii Komunistychnoi partii Ukrainy* (Kiev, 1971), 555.
4. *Ibid.*, 556.
5. *Pravda*, 25 May 1945.
6. *Pravda*, 19 March 1953.
7. According to a western study, lectures were delivered in Russian at 77.7 per cent of the institutes of higher education and at 38.7 per cent of the technical institutes in Eastern Ukraine. See V. Felix [Vsevolod Holubnychy], "Chomu usuneno Mielnikova?," *Vpered*, no. 6 (1953).
8. Melnikov was Soviet ambassador to Romania from July 1953 and USSR Minister for the Construction of Coal Industry Enterprises from 1955. After the dissolution of this ministry in 1957, he held leading posts in Kazakhstan and the RSFSR. Since 1966 he has been Chairman of the State Committee for Industrial Safety and Mine Supervision attached to the USSR Council of Ministers. See *Radianska Ukraina*, 18 October 1956; *Pravda Ukrainy*, 24 June 1956.
9. V. Malanchuk, *Torzhestvo leninskoi natsionalnoi polityky* (Lviv, 1963).
10. Founded in Galicia (under Polish rule until 1939) in 1921, the Communist Party of Western Ukraine [Komunistychna partiia Zakhidnoi Ukrainy] was dissolved by Stalin in the summer of 1938 along with its parent organization, the Communist Party of Poland.
11. *Pravda*, 10 July 1953.
12. *Ocherki istorii Kommunisticheskoi partii Ukrainy* (Kiev, 1977), 628.
13. According to *Istoriia Ukrainskoi RSR*, "In the process of liquidating Beria's criminal gang, the party and the Soviet organs uncovered a series of previously unknown violations of socialist legality" (Kiev, 1958), 2: 657.
14. *Narysy istorii Komunistychnoi partii Ukrainy*, 577.
15. *Malaia sovetskaia entsiklopediia* (Moscow, 1931), 9: 115.
16. N. Podgorny, "Sovetskaia Ukraina v bratskoi seme narodov SSR," *Kommunist*, no. 8 (1954): 17.
17. *Ibid.*, 22.
18. *Pravda*, 15 February 1956.
19. *Ibid.*, 18 February 1956.
20. A. M. Pankratova, *Velikii russkii narod—vydaiushchaiasia natsiia i rukovodiashchaia sila Sovetskogo Soiuza* (Moscow, 1947), 4.
21. *Pravda*, 22 February 1956.
22. The text of Khrushchev's Secret Speech to the Twentieth CPSU Congress is contained in N. S. Khrushchev, *The Secret Speech* (Nottingham, 1976), 58.

Chapter Two

The Impact of the Twentieth CPSU Congress

Hesitation and Uncertainty

After the Twentieth Congress, the three main figures in Ukrainian politics were Oleksii Kyrychenko, first secretary of the CPU Central Committee; Demian Korotchenko, chairman of the Presidium of the Supreme Soviet and Nykyfor Kalchenko, chairman of the Council of Ministers. Neither the party chiefs nor the cadres, conditioned by their experience, dared initiate reforms, even though the Twentieth Congress of the CPSU had granted greater scope for such undertakings. Moreover, the Ukrainian party leaders doubted whether Nikita Khrushchev would get the backing of V. M. Molotov, G. M. Malenkov and L. M. Kaganovich, who had been Stalin's close associates for many years and could still affect the balance of power. Nonetheless, they supported Khrushchev's efforts unconditionally, particularly his ambitious programmes for improving Ukraine's economy. The Ukrainian party leadership, and the reform-eager party cadres and public knew that after the Twentieth CPSU Congress, much would depend on whether Khrushchev and his supporters could consolidate their positions. Another element adding to the uncertainty was that the decision to expose Stalin had been taken at the highest level: neither the people nor the party rank and file, nor even high-level party functionaries had been informed in advance. Khrushchev's denunciation therefore came as a complete surprise. Thus the Ukrainian party leadership now had to decide how to inform the public of the events at the congress.

The first commentaries in the Ukrainian press were cautious, and limited to ambiguous forays against the "harmful personality cult." *Komunist Ukrainy*, the theoretical organ of the CPU, stressed that the cult of Stalin's personality and the methods of leadership that caused such great harm to the party had emerged during the last stage of Stalin's life and career,[1] an assertion that did not quite correspond to the spirit of the party congress. Even after *Pravda*,[2] the Ukrainian central press and regional newspapers published the CC CPSU's statement "On Overcoming the Personality Cult and Its Consequences," at the first party meetings convened to discuss it, participants were reticent, limiting themselves to "praise for the CPSU Central Committee, which has taken courageous measures to eradicate mistakes connected with the personality cult."[3] There were still no firm guidelines on how to conduct propaganda, agitation and party discussions.

The debate took a new turn after 7 July, when *Pravda* published "The Communist Party: The Inspirer and Leader of the Soviet People." On 10 July, *Radianska Ukraina*, the central government and party organ in the republic, published "More Criticism and Self-Criticism," in which the article's Ukrainian author offered a more substantial analysis of the Twentieth Congress and emphasized the party's duty to support criticism from below: "An inherent task of the party is to heed the voice of the masses, the voice of the people and the ordinary party members." Nonetheless, mistrust and uncertainty persisted at party meetings. At one rally S. V. Chervonenko, a secretary of the CC CPU, lectured on the personality cult and the need to eradicate its consequences. Of the 1200 in attendance, only ten took part in the debate and these merely praised the Central Committee's decree.[4]

Many Western correspondents noted the different reactions to the Twentieth Congress: in Moscow, debate was immediate and lively, while in Kiev, discussion was hesitant, less forthright. But since civic groups throughout Ukraine pressed for more rapid de-Stalinization, party officials had to devise a strategy that would ensure that this process remained within their control. The first political meeting that confronted the party's role and its new policy was organized by the Kiev Pedagogical Institute, and adopted a resolution supporting the Soviet leaders' new policy:

> The whole activity of the Leninist Central Committee, directed toward the development of Soviet socialist democracy, toward enlarging the rights and competence of the Union republics, toward strict adherence to socialist legality, and toward a reconstruction of the planning system aimed at strengthening local initiative, activating the work of the local councils and

increasing criticism and self-criticism, receives the warm recognition of the entire Soviet people.[5]

Soon Stalin was attacked with vehemence. At a meeting of Ukrainian artists, the graphic artist V. Kasiian stated: "The hideous personality cult, which encumbered the work of many artists and forced them to colour reality and create pompous and 'beautiful' lies, is being condemned by our people today." The sculptor F. Kovalev declared: "The fictitious and untruthful works which glorified a single person will not find their way into our people's golden treasury of art. They are not true to life and do not reflect our people's spiritual wealth."[6]

The removal of traces of the cult of personality from the public realm first occurred in Lviv. On 17 July 1956 the Ukrainian press reported that "The Presidium of the Supreme Soviet of the Ukrainian SSR resolved to combine the Lenin and Stalin districts of the city of Lviv into a single Lenin District on 17 July of this year."[7] This began a tumultuous upheaval affecting all areas of public and social life in Ukraine.

More Rights for the Ukrainian Language

As the Russian people were elevated to a "master race," Russian had gradually replaced Ukrainian as the language of instruction in Ukraine's institutions of higher education. Stalin's polemic with the Soviet philologist Nikolai Marr provided the theoretical basis for the attack on the Ukrainian language. Stalin maintained that in the long historical process, during which some languages decayed and others became increasingly viable, the final goal was the emergence of a common language for all mankind. This common language would develop from the so-called national languages which "will merge into an international language that will not, of course, be German, Russian or English but will adopt the best elements of each national language."[8] Stalin considered the emergence of zonal languages as an intermediary stage in this development, and thought that a thorough blending of the Slavonic languages of the USSR, with Russian serving as the core, would be the most suitable basis for a Soviet zonal language. Such was the "ideological" justification for the enforced Russification of the Union republics.

In response to Stalin's dogma, a wide movement developed in defence of the Ukrainian language, which was supported even by a majority of party leaders in Ukraine. In October 1957, *Komunist Ukrainy* discussed not only the question of increasing the republics' rights but also language rights. The importance of the article was underscored by its appearance in the section "Lessons and Consultations," which was reserved for the propaganda apparat's instructions to the masses. The introductory passages proclaimed that school instruction in the native language, national literature and culture were thriving in all republics. In an admonitory tone, the article continued:

> Nevertheless, not all Soviet and party functionaries understand the nature of our party's language policy. Alas, we often encounter among them people, even from the national cadres, who, although they are working in their own nations, often do not know their people's language and history. It is the duty of the communist working in a national republic to support with every means the development of his people's national language and culture. Every functionary must, of course, speak this people's language and know its cultural history and national traditions, for otherwise there can be no real political and organizational work among the masses. In his "Draft Decree of the CPSU Central Committee on the Soviet Power in Ukraine," V. I. Lenin wrote that the party and Soviet organs should display great care for the national traditions and must grant the working masses the practical right to learn their mother tongue and speak it in all Soviet institutions, resist all Russification attempts aimed at pushing Ukrainian into second place, and make it a means for the communist education of the working masses.
>
> The development of national language, its introduction into all spheres of the republic's state, party and economic structure were questions of principle in Lenin's nationality policy. Together with this Lenin welcomed the process of the mutual enrichment of the Ukrainian and Russian cultures, the Ukrainian workers' access to the treasures of the great Russian people's democratic and socialist culture, and the learning of the great Russian people's language by broad circles of Ukrainians.[9]

Zmina, the central organ of the Ukrainian communist youth league (the Komsomol), also described resistance to Russification as one of the most important tasks facing Soviet Ukraine.

> Unfortunately, there are still people who disregard the Ukrainian language. There are people who believe that the Ukrainian language has little prospect for longevity. They believe that it will not be long before the Ukrainian language vanishes and is replaced by Russian.... The Russian language obtained a special significance through historical development. It unites all the Soviet peoples. It is of great importance. However, this does not mean that the Russian language should displace Ukrainian or other languages. No language may displace another. Herein lies the essence of equality. When a language disappears, a people disappears and dies with it.... The Ukrainian and Russian languages are sisters. The Ukrainian language is just as old as the Russian. And everything that Lenin said in his famous "Note on the Purity of the Russian Language" applies equally to the Ukrainian language; "We torture the Russian language, we use unnecessary loan words, and we use them incorrectly." Everything that Maxim Gorky once wrote and said about the purity of Russian also applies to Ukrainian: "You should love, cultivate and care for your language. It is your heritage, a heritage of

centuries and generations. Pass it on to your children and grandchildren enriched and still more developed, and they will hand it down to generations yet to come."[10]

The symptoms of change included, for example, appeals from Ukrainian officers in the Soviet armed forces to writers to organize Ukrainian literary evenings for military personnel. Major Hrebeniuk, who was stationed in Baku, complained that Ukrainian soldiers serving outside the republic could not get Ukrainian magazines and books at garrison libraries. In response, the library bought books and subscribed to newspapers. Major Hrebeniuk described the Ukrainian soldiers' reactions as follows:

This literature was a great success with the readers. The librarian at Unit X, Comrade Bidolakh, declared: "We had hardly finished announcing the arrival of Ukrainian books over the loudspeaker system when they were all taken out on loan!" The soldiers stand in line for the books. It's a pity that the Ukrainian authors write so little about military subjects. The soldiers are particularly fond of such books.[11]

These two articles published in 1956 and 1957 typify the mass movement in defence of the mother tongue whose slogans were: "Defend the Ukrainian language!" and "Speak Ukrainian!"

Against the Impoverishment of Ukrainian History

The most important issues of Ukrainian historiography had been discussed at the highest level in Moscow even before the Twentieth CPSU Congress, probably as a result of pressure from Ukraine. The greatest hindrances to Ukrainian culture and scholarship were the restrictive CC CPSU decrees dating from the *Zhdanovshchina*, which were still considered as guidelines for Soviet Ukrainian literature and historical research.[12] Only the decree on composers was later declared void.

An editorial of *Voprosy istorii* in July 1955 proved to be an invaluable aid for Ukrainian historians. Although the article was unsigned, the author was probably Pankratova, then chief editor of this journal. The article encouraged Ukrainian historians to pay attention to neglected aspects of the republic's past and to consider the special characteristics of its development:

The Ukrainian historians are right to treat the history of the Ukrainian SSR as part of the overall history of the USSR. The history of the Ukrainian people is indivisible from the history of all Soviet peoples. The Ukrainian SSR has marked up great achievements which are an indivisible component of the united Soviet Union. Nonetheless, the authors of the draft for the second volume of *Istoriia Ukrainskoi RSR* have abridged the material on the history of Ukraine itself to such an extent that the concrete nature of the Ukrainian people's development has almost completely vanished. Here it is necessary to consider the specific features in the historical development of the individual regions of the Soviet state.[13]

The article encouraged research on the history of Ukraine's western oblasts and criticized the level of historical research in Ukraine:

Creative discussions about the most important problems of historical scholarship are seldom held in Ukraine. Scholarly sessions and conferences are usually convoked in connection with some anniversary or other and are often show-case affairs. The papers read at these sessions are hardly ever discussed. Very rarely are scholarly problems submitted to the academic councils for examination. Thus, in 1954 only four meetings of the scientific council at the Institute of History of the Ukrainian Academy of Sciences heard scholarly reports. There was only one discussion of historical problems at the Lviv Institute of Social Sciences in 1954. Insufficient use is made of such powerful tools for the improvement of scholarly research as criticism and self-criticism, creative discussion and consultation. The development of historical scholarship in Ukraine is being retarded by the lack of a historical journal in the republic. Such a journal would help develop the history of the Ukrainian people more thoroughly.[14]

Two years later, in November 1957, the Ukrainian Academy of Sciences announced that it had decided to publish a journal devoted to Ukrainian history, *Ukrainskyi istorychnyi zhurnal*.

Central to efforts to end the impoverishment of historical scholarship in Ukraine was the development of research on the history of the CPU and on the rehabilitation of Stalin's victims: party leaders as well as Ukrainian cultural figures. Immediately after the Twentieth Congress, *Komunist Ukrainy* published an appeal to historians:

The Soviet people is entitled to expect our historians to represent in their works the true history of our people, especially the history of the Soviet epoch (the history of the Great Socialist October Revolution, the history of the Great Patriotic War, etc.), in its entirety and with total scholarly scrupulousness and to eradicate from their works the remaining influences of the personality cult condemned by the party. Our historians must develop a truly Marxist history of the party organization in Ukraine.[15]

As the discussion continued, historians demanded closer examination of the role of "Russian chauvinists" in the CPU during the revolution. Two events merited special attention: first, the party conference held in Taganrog on

20 April 1918, which endorsed Mykola Skrypnyk's proposal to make the CPU an independent party despite staunch opposition from Russophiles. Although Skrypnyk received strong support from the Kievan communists, the First Congress of the CPU, held in Moscow in July 1918, declared the party an autonomous organization of the CPSU. This marked the start of confrontation over the establishment of an independent CPU, and the Russophiles accused Skrypnyk of "national communism." The second event was the proclamation in the spring of 1918, after the first Bolshevik government of Ukraine had been established in Kharkiv, of the Donetsk-Kryvyi Rih Republic as an autonomous republic within the Russian republic. The Donetsk-Kryvyi Rih Bolsheviks, led by F. Artem [Sergeev], argued that their regions contained resources needed by Russia, and that Lenin had agreed to the creation of this republic. Their Ukrainian opponents, however, viewed their action as a violation of the communist nationality policy. The outcome of the dispute was of particular significance for Ukrainian communists.

Donetsk-Kryvyi Rih Bolsheviks even resisted Lenin's appeal to join Ukraine's struggle against the German occupation forces. On 15 March 1918 a session of the CC CPSU chaired by Lenin decreed that party members were duty-bound to form a common defence front: "The Donbas is considered part of Ukraine." At the Second All-Ukrainian Congress of Soviets in March 1918 party members from the Donbas declared that both oblasts, the Donetsk and Kryvyi Rih, belonged to Ukraine.[16]

The Ukrainian historian M. I. Suprunenko attacked the interpretaton of these events by Soviet historians during the Stalin era:

> Artem and his sympathizers did not understand the full import of the nationality question in Ukraine, and their position was clearly a concession to great-power nationalism. For the Donetsk-Kryvyi Rih Republic was that part of Ukrainian territory which, according to the instruction of the Provisional Government dated 14 August 1917, was separated from Ukraine. The separation of the most industrially developed region with the most qualified industrial workers weakened the proletarian basis of the Ukrainian Soviet state and impeded the development and consolidation of the alliance of the worker and peasant classes in Ukraine.[17]

In 1958, *Voprosy istorii* printed an article signed by A. V. Snegov, a former party leader from Kiev, and E. S. Oslikovskaia, also a Ukrainian Bolshevik.[18] The article was the first detailed analysis of the falsification of the early history of the CPU. It noted that "Lenin realized that the slightest symptom of that Great-Russian chauvinism which separated the Russian and Ukrainian comrades could inflict great damage on the cause of the Revolution." The article also dealt with Skrypnyk's role at the First Congress of the CPU:

As we see, there was nothing nationalistic or deviationist in Skrypnyk's statements. Isolated erroneous statements about the nationality question made by Skrypnyk several years after the First Congress of the CPU are no reason to slander this old leader of the Bolshevik Party and the Ukrainian Soviet government.[19]

For political reasons the events of the Stalin period were never elucidated in full, since that would have entailed rehabilitating the concept of the CPU as an independent party (albeit closely linked to the CPSU). "Vigilance" against manifestations of "national communism" in Yugoslavia and Ukraine also impeded a full explanation.

Historians and other groups demanded that the party not only end the "impoverishment of history" but also rehabilitate persons who had committed "mistakes," but never opposed the communist movement in Ukraine. These included Mykola Khvyliovy, Oleksandr Shumsky and above all, Skrypnyk, for even before the Twentieth Congress there were signs of his pending rehabilitation. Nevertheless, efforts to rehabilitate Shumsky and Khvyliovy failed. There was a strong backlash from orthodox Soviet historians. For example, H. Emelianenko dubbed their slogan—"Away from Moscow—For Unity with Europe"—an attempt "to nudge Ukraine onto the path of capitalist development and to turn it into a colony of international imperialism."[20] Emelianenko also accused Shumsky's supporters of distorting Leninist nationality policy: "They represented the programme of enforced Ukrainianization of Russians working in Ukrainian industry, tried to impose on the CP(B)U and the Soviet Ukrainian government a chauvinist policy with regard to the Ukrainian population and protested that the party and state administration in Ukraine was multinational in composition."[21]

Alongside Russophile and orthodox historians, Ukrainian party officials also tried to limit the rehabilitation process. S. V. Chervonenko, a secretary of the CC CPU, a former head of its science and culture department and a prominent ideologist, published an article denouncing "nationalist deviationists," citing not only Shumsky and Khvyliovy but also Skrypnyk as opponents of friendship between the Ukrainian and Russian peoples:

At the beginning of the 1930s the Communist Party of Ukraine unmasked and condemned the serious nationalistic errors made by Skrypnyk, who wanted to substitute the struggle against great-power chauvinism for the two-front struggle against great-power and local nationalism and thus supported the Ukrainian bourgeois nationalists. Skrypnyk's position was essentially directed toward alienating Ukrainian culture from the culture of the fraternal Russian people.[22]

A more objective treatment of CPU history was the second volume of *Istoriia Ukrainskoi RSR*, published in 1958 and edited by Suprunenko. Party ideologists criticized the work, however, as an attempt to rehabilitate the Borotbists.[23] The volume recalled the common struggle waged by communist organizations and the Borotbists against the White Guard, and the Borotbist Central Committee's proposal to co-operate with the CC CPU, which had been accepted "without making any concessions of principle to the Borotbists." (The two Central Committees signed this co-operation agreement on 17 December 1919.) It did note, however, that the Borotbists continued to disseminate nationalist propaganda. Party officials, alarmed by letters demanding the full rehabilitation of the Borotbists, also attacked L. Novychenko for underestimating the nationalism of the Borotbists in his 1956 study *Poeziia i revoliutsiia*. They questioned some assertions about the Borotbists in *Radianske budivnytstvo na Ukraini v roky hromadianskoi viiny, 1919–1920* and in the preface to S. Kryzhanivsky's *Vasyl Chumak* (1956), which had even referred to the Borotbists as an internationalist party. A series of articles in *Komunist Ukrainy* castigated such works for trying to rehabilitate the Borotbists.[24]

Discussion of the personality cult led to the publication of a new document in *Komunist Ukrainy* (June 1959),[25] drafted by a team of authors commissioned to prepare a history of the CPU. Unsigned, the document had the force of a directive and brought some advantages for Ukrainian historiography. It demanded the elimination of the results of the personality cult in this discipline, provided for increased rehabilitation of Ukrainian communist leaders and most important, made orthodox historians such as Lykholat more cautious.

Educators also joined the campaign against the impoverishment of Ukrainian history. Their demands for reform of history courses in Ukrainian schools appeared in *Radianska osvita*, the organ of the Ukrainian Ministry of Education and the Central Committee of the trade unions for workers in public and higher education and scientific institutions:

The historical roles of personalities such as the Tsars Ivan III, Ivan IV and Peter I have been idealized.... When we describe the foreign policy and wars of tsarist Russia we must stress that the aims of tsarism and the popular masses were different.... At the time when tsarism under Catherine II took on the role of Europe's gendarme, the role of the suppressor of the revolutionary and national-liberation movements, Russia's popular masses with the Russian revolutionary democrats at their head were struggling against tsarism and the exploiting class, thus aiding not only the country's progress but also the European liberation movement.... After the historically important directives of the Twentieth CPSU Congress and in the interest of historical truth it is necessary to describe correctly the national-liberation movements and the policies of Russian tsarism that oppressed Russia's numerous peoples and turned Russia into a "prison of peoples."... The teacher must emphasize that the Caucasian peoples' struggle under the leadership of Shamil against colonialist oppression by tsarism occurred at the time when Russia was the gendarme of Europe. The mountain peoples' struggle was progressive in character because it weakened the forces of tsarism. It corresponds fundamentally to the interests of the workers in Russia and the revolutionary forces in Europe that were fighting against tsarism. In stressing that the union of the peoples of Central Asia and the Caucasus with Russia was objectively progressive in character, we must at the same time demonstrate how Russian tsarism oppressed the Russian people and other peoples in our country.[26]

Two other interrelated factors played a part in this same matter: the rehabilitation of the Communist Party of Western Ukraine (CPWU), and the rehabilitation of partisans and communists who had been active in the underground movement in the German-occupied territories. The CPWU had been dissolved by a Comintern decree in 1938 together with the communist parties of Poland (CPP) and Western Belorussia (CPWB). The decree maintained that enemy agents had infiltrated these parties and were acting as *agents provocateurs* in the international communist movement. This statement was a fabrication made upon Stalin's instructions. In consequence, hundreds of revolutionaries were enticed from Western Ukraine into the USSR and liquidated. An entire chapter in the history of the communist movement in Poland, Western Belorussia and Western Ukraine from 1919–38 was wiped out. The brutality with which the Soviet security organs acted against members of these parties is illustrated by events during the Soviet occupation of Western Ukraine. The well-known CPWU leader Ludvik Rosenberg [Lvivsky, Chorny] was arrested and shot in Lviv, and Vasyl Pashnytsky [Bazio] was arrested in Stanislav (now Ivano-Frankivsk) and tortured to death.

After the Second World War, however, the party's attitude toward the West Ukrainian communists became more lenient. There were several reasons for this. First, many of the communists had participated in the resistance movement against the Germans, and although numerically small, were of great political importance to the Soviet leaders. Second, and more important, many former members of the CPWU not only had enjoyed political asylum in the People's Republic of Poland, but some, like the deputy foreign minister M. Naszkowski, had even held high political office there.

After Stalin's death the most courageous move toward the rehabilitation of the CPWU came from Poland. A meeting of former West Ukrainian communists, held on 30 May 1958 at the Institute of Party History attached to the Central Committee of the Polish United Workers' Party (PUWP) in Warsaw, decided to establish a commission for the history of the CPWU.[27] Meetings of former West Ukrainian communists were held in Poland even before this conference, while the Ukrainian-language journal *Nashe slovo* and its supplement *Nasha kultura* published considerable information about the CPWU and the members who had been liquidated.

In the USSR also attempts were made to rehabilitate former CPWU members. A joint decree of the central committees of the CPSU and the CPU adopted in August 1956 rehabilitated all former members of the CPP, CPWU and CPWB, some of whom had been accepted into the Soviet party since 1945. The prime motivation behind this measure was to alleviate the shortage of cadres. The decree did not completely exonerate the CPWU, however, and discussion about the limits of rehabilitation continued in the all-Union and Ukrainian party apparatuses.[28] According to V. Malanchuk, the joint decree eventually led to recognition of length of party membership for former West Ukrainian communists and to a revival of the study of the history of the CPWU:

Many members of the these parties who had been groundlessly accused and liquidated during the personality cult were rehabilitated. This act was of positive significance for the education of communists and workers of the western oblasts of the Ukrainian SSR in the spirit of revolutionary traditions. In keeping with the decree of the CPU Central Committee, anthologies of the reminiscences of former members of the CPWU and biographical profiles of well-known functionaries were prepared and published. Preparations for the publication of a collection of documents about the history of the CPWU began at the Institute of Party History attached to the Central Committee of the CPU.[29]

The final rehabilitation of the CPWU took place in July 1963 when the CPSU's theoretical journal *Kommunist* published an unsigned article "For the Correct Elucidation of the History of the Communist Party of Western Ukraine." The same text appeared in the August issue of the Ukrainian party journal, *Komunist Ukrainy*. Only after the publication of this document did major studies on the CPWU appear in Ukraine, the most important of which was Ievhen Halushka's *Narys istorii ideolohichnoi ta orhanizatsiinoi diialnosti KPZU v 1919–1928 rr.* (Lviv, 1965).[30]

The problem of rehabilitating members of the anti-Nazi resistance was, in some respects, related. During the German occupation the Soviets tried to organize partisan movements in Ukraine. These were officially controlled by the CC CPSU, the State Committee for the Defence of the USSR and, after 1942, by the central staff of the partisan movement. Headquarters were also established in the republics and oblasts. In October 1942 the Politburo established an underground Central Committee and tried to build up a clandestine party apparatus. According to Soviet reports, between 1941 and 1944 Ukraine had twenty-two illegal oblast committees, thirteen large party groups and 200 city and district [raion] committees. During the same period the Komsomol is said to have had more than fifty underground city, district and oblast committees. The same source states that these organizations included over 100,000 communists, Komsomol members and non-party "Soviet patriots."[31]

A number of people who subsequently played an important role in the Ukrainian party organization operated behind enemy lines. Among them were: D. S. Korotchenko, then secretary of the CC CPU and later Presidium chairman of the Supreme Soviet of the Ukrainian SSR; Army General A. A. Epishev, then first secretary of the Odessa oblast committee, now head of the Main Political Directorate of the Soviet army and navy; A. P. Kirilenko, then secretary of the Zaporizhzhia oblast committee, now a Politburo member and secretary of the CC CPSU; L. R. Korniiets, then deputy chairman of the republic's Council of People's Commissars, later chairman of the USSR State Procurement Committee; and Z. T. Serdiuk, then first secretary of the Kiev oblast committee, now deputy chairman of the Committee for Party Control attached to the CC CPSU. Ukrainian cultural figures were also active in the partisan movement; the writers Iurii Zbanatsky and Platon Voronko, for example, commanded partisan units.[32]

After the war many partisans rose to positions of importance in the republic's political life, because of their war experience and their connections with Khrushchev. The clandestine oblast committees were in a similar position. After the Soviet army had re-entered Ukraine, its cadres were given preferential treatment in high-level appointments to party organizations. Some also played key roles in the apparatus of the CPU in the postwar years. Other partisans and underground leaders, however, were considered suspect and persecuted after the war. In December 1954, *Partiinaia zhizn* published a report which reflected the atmosphere of mistrust that had developed:

> Recently the Central Committee of the CPU adopted a decree on the rehabilitation of a number of active participants in the partisan movement and their reinstatement in the party. Instead of examining facts, some officials of the Vinnytsia oblast and city committees have treated the activities of the underground organizations behind enemy lines during the war in an irresponsible and subjective manner. An unhealthy atmosphere was created around certain former underground fighters and partisans. They were accused of anti-patriotic behaviour while they were on the territory temporarily occupied by Hitler's conquerors. The investigations were conducted tendentiously and by false methods. The CPU Central Committee annulled this decree and reinstated in the party those comrades who had been accused groundlessly. Officials who had been guilty of an subjective approach to the examination of the Soviet patriots' partisan activities were reprimanded by the party.
>
> The constant heightening of the revolutionary vigilance of all communists and workers is an important task of the party organizations'

political-educational work. A strict understanding of political vigilance, however, has nothing to do with suspicion and global mistrust of communists in general. Such mistrust and suspicion would serve only the enemies of the people.[33]

The Creative Intelligentsia Demand Rehabilitation

In addition to the historians, the creative intelligentsia also demanded the rehabilitation of key figures: forgotten, forbidden and, above all, liquidated writers and artists. The first reports about the rehabilitation of writers killed under Stalin appeared in the Ukrainian daily press in 1956:

> Today, following the CPSU Central Committee's energetic measures, the violations of socialist legality have been eliminated and the good name of well-known Ukrainian Soviet cultural personalities who had been calumniated and falsely accused of bourgeois nationalism, of people like V. Ellan [Blakytny], V. Chumak and I. Mykytenko, has been restored. Now that the personality cult has been overcome there is nothing that can impede the creative activity of the cultural intelligentsia and this will ensure a new blossoming.[34]

All the charges against the writer Volodymyr Sosiura—the chief of which were directed against his poem "Love Ukraine!"—were retracted. A campaign began to rehabilitate the leading Ukrainian playwright Mykola Kulish. Arrested in 1934, Kulish had died in a labour camp in 1942. He was considered a supporter of Khvyliovy, who had not been rehabilitated, and of Les Kurbas, a director, who is considered the founder of modern Ukrainian theatre. Like Kulish, Khvyliovy perished in a labour camp in 1942. The liquidated Ukrainian Canadian writer Myroslav Irchan was also rehabilitated.[35]

The question of the rehabilitation of Les Kurbas was finally clarified in 1958. In February the literary journal *Vitchyzna* published an unsigned article, "On a Lacuna in the History of Our Theatre."[36] The article was a bold plea to eliminate, finally, the consequences of the personality cult in the Ukrainian theatre and to rehabilitate Kurbas. In April the writer Vadym Sobko responded in *Literaturna hazeta*: he recalled Kurbas' many "errors"—ranging from nationalism to formalism—but at the same time stated bluntly that the Ukrainian intelligentsia was no longer willing to withhold Kurbas' name from its cultural history: "It must be acknowledged that the confusion and complexity of Les Kurbas' creative efforts can lead to rejection and condemnation. They can be an object of dispute, but they can never constitute grounds for eradicating Kurbas' name from the history of Ukrainian theatre...."[37] Since Kurbas' rehabilitation, Soviet reference works have published summaries of his life and works. His pupils, some of whom suffered reprisals, have also been rehabilitated.

The rehabilitation of Oleksandr Dovzhenko, the internationally acclaimed film director and co-founder of Ukrainian cinematic art, was also an important political event. Forced to leave Ukraine in the late 1930s, he was persecuted by the Stalinists even after 1945 and died in Moscow on 25 November 1956. He was awarded a Lenin Prize posthumously in 1959. On 10 November 1962, *Literaturna hazeta* published some of the notes written by Dovzhenko during his years of persecution:

> My comrade Stalin, even if you were a god, I would never believe you [when you say] that I am a nationalist whom one should calumniate. . . . If there is no hatred, no scorn, no ill-will toward people in this world . . . is then love for one's own people nationalism? Why have you transmuted my life into agony? Why have you robbed me of joy, trampled on my name? And yet I forgive you all. Because I am part of the people. Therefore I am more than you.

The campaign for the rehabilitation of the Ukrainian liberal, political figure, scholar and publicist Mykhailo Drahomanov began soon after the Twentieth Congress. Pressure to end the ban on the works of this important representative of nineteenth-century Ukrainian culture and scholarship increased in 1958 when the press demanded that he be restored to his rightful place in history. *Vitchyzna* played a major role in this campaign. Drahomanov was partially rehabilitated: his works were discussed in journals and scholarly essays, but not without critical comments. Although a two-volume edition of his works was published in 1970, some are still proscribed.[38]

An impressive event in Ukrainian cultural life during this period was the Kiev writers' meeting of 21 September 1956, at which Chervonenko, secretary of the CC CPU, read a paper "On Overcoming the Personality Cult and Its Consequences." In addition to writers, journalists and representatives of Ukrainian cultural groups attended. During the debate, speakers not only attacked Stalin but also made proposals for the enrichment of the republic's culture: the publication of Ukrainian scientific dictionaries, a Ukrainian encyclopedia and the expansion of publishing activities in general. They complained that not enough copies of Ukrainian-language books were printed and, moreover, that those issued were often unobtainable in rural areas. Several authors criticized the standing of Ukrainian-language instruction at higher and secondary schools.[39]

The Kiev meeting typified the tactics employed by the Ukrainian intelligentsia: on the one hand, it professed total loyalty to Khrushchev and the party's new course and, on the other, it tried to obtain maximum benefits for Ukrainian culture in the more relaxed political atmosphere. Two factors influenced this behaviour. First, in the second half of 1956 the intellectuals felt confident enough to demand a more thorough commitment to eliminating the consequences of the personality cult. Although the Ukrainian press does not provide a complete chronicle of this process, articles by party officials reveal their fears that the process might escape their control.[40] Second, the leaks of information about the power struggle involving Khrushchev, Malenkov, Molotov, Kaganovich and other leaders spread uncertainty in Ukraine.

In May 1957, Khrushchev changed his tactics. This became evident from his speech at a writers' meeting and at a reception for cultural figures a week later. Dissociating himself from some of his earlier reproaches of Stalin, he affirmed the former leader's service to the Soviet state: "We were sincere in our respect for Stalin when we wept at his coffin. We are sincere now in our evaluation of his positive role in the history of our party and the Soviet state."[41] At the same time he denounced unorthodox writers such as Vladimir Dudintsev and the staff of the journal *Novyi mir*, which was under the editorship of Aleksandr Tvardovsky.[42] Although Khrushchev reneged on his earlier, more liberal policies, the Ukrainian intelligentsia still supported him as the "lesser evil."

In May 1958 the CC CPSU published a decree, "On the Correction of Errors in the Evaluation of the Operas 'The Great Friendship,' 'Bohdan Khmelnytsky' and 'From My Whole Heart,'" which rehabilitated composers and authors who had been condemned in an earlier CPSU decree.[43] But the party leadership still considered all decrees passed during the *Zhdanovshchina* to be "correct in principle." This attitude is reflected in the remedial decree "On the Correction of Errors in the Evaluation of Certain Composers in the Ukrainian SSR," issued in June 1958 by the CC CPU:

> On the whole, these decrees [of *Zhdanovshchina*] have played a positive role in the development of Ukrainian music. They condemned the formalist tendencies in the works of some Ukrainian composers, underscored the necessity of the struggle for greater ideological-artistic skill and of exploiting the best achievements of the Motherland's classical and folk music, and heightened [our] awareness of the necessity of creating large-scale musical works [*muzyka krupnykh form*] on contemporary themes.
>
> These principles retain their basic significance in our day, too, when we are faced with the full acuity of the problem of protecting Soviet musical art from the infiltration of bourgeois ideology and revisionism, and of strengthening and deepening by every means the ties between art and the life of the people.[44]

The decree noted that although a number of Ukrainian composers had committed "errors," they could not be accused of being "representatives of an anti-popular, formalist trend pernicious for Soviet music."[45]

Society in Turmoil

Between 1956 and the early 1960s there were two notable trends in
Ukraine. One was a marked apolitical attitude especially among the
younger generation in the cities, which formed social groups and clubs in
defiance of the authorities. The young people decried the *ennui* and
monotony of Soviet life, the primitive and superficial political education,
outmoded moral concepts, dress regulations and official rulings on social
activity. Youth protest, which spread throughout the Soviet Union,
acquired forms in Ukraine that caused the party's guardians of morality
many headaches. The efforts of the Komsomol to channel this unexpected
development elicited a second trend: the emergence of the *stiliagi*; young
people who displayed unorthodox fashions in dress and manner.

Komsomol publications printed articles about love, and the official
Komsomol organ *Molod Ukrainy* expressed amazement at the number of
letters it received from young readers. The daily press was shocked that
Western "pop" songs were being sung in Kiev, and the latest imported
Western "pop" records were in great demand. Journalists reported that
over a thousand were sold in a single store within two hours after word of
their arrival got out, while only three records by Mozart, Mendelssohn and
Schumann crossed the counter.[46] One newspaper, while defending
traditional values, tried to show tolerance in musical taste: "How about
light music? It is necessary too. Youth is always youth. We are not against
jazz either, but jazz needs melody and rhythm, not screaming, clamouring
and caterwauling."[47]

Many young people discussed and became involved in sensitive political
problems, which elicited the following comment from *Radianska Ukraina*:
"During a party conference at Shevchenko University, it was ascertained
that there were numerous cases of lack of discipline and amoral behaviour
among the students and that unhealthy moods are making themselves
felt."[48] In its description of a student meeting in Kiev, *Stalinskoe plemia*
characterized a large percentage of the participants as "destructive student
types," "demagogues" and "loudmouths."[49]

The independent clubs and groups organized also by schoolchildren
alarmed authorities. *Komsomolskaia pravda* noted the creation of "illegal
associations" at schools in Kharkiv. At School 131, it stated, the pupil
Anatolii Bosenko had been elected *otaman* [Cossack leader] of a
conspiratorial and criminal group, all of whose members were Ukrainian.
A similar group at another Russian school in Kharkiv was led by Nikolai
Klimov, whom *Komsomolskaia pravda* described as "a well-read youth, a
dreamer and a good organizer."[50] These illegal or semi-legal school
associations were largely apolitical, but their existence as early as 1954
reflected the rapidly changing atmosphere in the Soviet Union.

This period saw strong student involvement in the movement for the
defence of the Ukrainian language and the enrichment of Ukrainian
literature. *Radianska kultura* published an open letter from students in

Dnipropetrovsk requesting more Ukrainian films: "The film studios in Kiev and Odessa should make their films in Ukrainian. We need not fear that this would prevent the films being screened throughout the Soviet Union. After all, Bulgarian and Korean films are shown all over the Soviet Union." The newspaper also published a letter from a group of students in Lviv to the writer Maksym Rylsky. The students praised the trend toward greater use of the mother tongue since the Twentieth CPSU Congress: "The Ukrainian language now prevails everywhere, proudly and openly. No one may now forbid us to sing our beloved Ukrainian songs, to hold readings of Ukrainian literature, to hear lectures in the Ukrainian language, to write poems about our homeland."[51]

There was a notable increase in industrial conflict after the Twentieth Congress. Protests against low wages and bad working conditions mounted; workers, especially in the industrial centres, displayed a lack of trust in the regime. In *Pravda*, V. N. Titov, first secretary of the Kharkiv oblast committee, reported that some local communists wanted to abolish one-man management [*edinonachalie*] in industry and to subject managers to workers' control, a system already introduced in Yugoslavia. The article described a party meeting at a leather factory:

> The factory director, Comrade Ashaulov, was rightly criticized for his attitude to the workers' needs and for ignoring the proposals of the trade-union organization. In their justifiable criticism ... comrades Kalynychenko and Omelianenko rejected, as communists, the one-man management principle adhered to by the director. They demanded that each of the director's orders and instructions be discussed collectively before implementation.[52]

Titov spoke of other "politically immature elements" who "had not understood" the party's struggle against the consequences of the personality cult and were trying to use party meetings to propagandize ideas alien to Leninism. The Ukrainian press complained of anarchic trends among workers, carrying numerous reports about low-quality work, poor discipline and negligence. There were also reports of workers' protests and demonstrations.[53]

Released labour-camp inmates posed a special problem for the Soviet authorities because they informed their relatives and friends about their experiences. Although former Bolsheviks constituted the smallest group of released prisoners, they played a major role in revealing the extent of the great purges of 1936–8. The press gave extensive coverage to the ex-inmates, stressing that many had returned to their former jobs in the party apparatus and the civil service. From *samvydav* publications, however, it is known that some became politically active again and that many were rearrested and sentenced to long terms. Among these were former members of the OUN, who were accused of engaging in "nationalist agitation."[54]

Although a revolutionary situation did not develop in Ukraine after the Twentieth Congress, there was rapid social change. The public was better informed politically and prepared to defend its convictions more openly, a situation that provided the seeds for future political opposition to the Soviet regime. Initially, however, the public was concerned less with large-scale political programmes than with the promotion of national interests (especially in the cultural realm) during this period of relative tolerance. The party, fearing turmoil, tried to ensure strict observance of its "rules" in the campaign against the personality cult. Broad interpretations of these rules were immediately decried as anti-party activity. Nevertheless political life had become more dynamic. Ukrainian communists strove first and foremost to expand their republic's rights and competence. Various groups from the intelligentsia campaigned for the "enrichment" of history, literature, arts, films and other areas. Other groups (the churches and sects, for example) tried to broaden their scope of activity.

Malanchuk describes the movement in Western Ukraine, which typified the republic;

> The struggle against the consequences of the personality cult and against the violation of Leninist norms in intra-party life in the western oblasts of the Ukrainian SSR was not easy. Nationalistically inclined people who had nothing to do with the party tried to use the party's slogans for activities inimical to the party cause and to distort their true content. They tried to replace criticism of the personality cult with criticism of Marxism-Leninism. They questioned the basic principles of party activity in the western oblasts of the Ukrainian SSR, especially the policy of industrialization and collectivization of agriculture, and the workers' struggle against the nationalists in the first postwar years. While most of those who were released under the amnesties proclaimed at the time acknowledged their guilt before the people and the state and returned to honest work in the factories or collective farms, some of those who had not renounced their original convictions tried to resume their anti-Soviet activity and recruit new supporters. This applied above all to former nationalist leaders, to Uniate priests and also to sect members, some of whom were direct agents of American imperialism and its intelligence services.[55]

Unrest in Eastern Europe

After the Twentieth Congress there was intense popular pressure for political and social reform in Eastern Europe, which encouraged similar demands in Ukraine. Workers' protests in Poland in 1956, such as the

Poznan uprising, helped Władysław Gomułka, the former party leader who had fallen into disfavour, to return to power. The Polish authorities limited the power of the security organs, decentralized economic management and provided for more amicable relations with the Roman Catholic Church. These moves provided for open ideological debate throughout Poland—a debate that questioned the very nature of the Soviet system.

The discussion affected Ukrainians, many of whom were deeply concerned about freedom in literature, art and sciences. After 1953 cultural relations between Ukraine and Poland developed rapidly. During Polish–Ukrainian Friendship Month, in October 1956, party officials were disturbed by a Polish delegation that included leaders of the reform movement who did not hesitate to promote their views and to urge the Ukrainian intelligentsia to join their struggle for artistic freedom. Further encouragement was given in an article published in *Ukrainska kultura*, the official organ of the Ukrainian Ministry of Culture, written by Scibor-Rylski, editor-in-chief of the Polish journal *Nowa kultura*:

> As you know, Polish scholars and writers are in the midst of an extensive discussion about ways of developing art. The controversy centres on the problem of the methods applied to contemporary realism. Different people express different ideas.... We in Poland favour a variety of trends, a variety of artistic viewpoints; we are for variety in art. Our discussion has found an echo among the Czechs, Yugoslavs and Hungarians. It would be a good thing if the Ukrainian artists were to state their opinions on this matter.[56]

Whereas in the Soviet Union the settling of accounts with Stalin was limited to condemnation of the personality cult, in Poland there emerged the *wściekłych* [angry young man] movement, which opposed Stalinism not only as a doctrine but also as a system of government. One of Stalinism's most prominent critics was Leszek Kolakowski, whose brilliant essays had circulated in Ukraine before *samvydav* [*samizdat*] developed. The central problem in Kolakowski's writings—the interrelationship between politics and morality—sparked a particularly lively discussion and encouraged those Ukrainian intellectuals critical of the state.

The Hungarian Revolution in 1956 also had an enormous impact in Ukraine, especially in the Transcarpathian region, where there was a relatively large Hungarian ethnic group (47,989 in 1959).[57] As Soviet propagandists declared, the revolt contributed greatly to the "activation of the remnants of nationalist elements" in Western Ukraine.[58] The propagandists maintained that Ukrainian emigres in Stepan Bandera's OUN had helped to organize the Hungarian uprising and asserted that "about ten groups of Bandera's men infiltrated Hungary on the eve of the uprising."[59] The purpose of such "reports" was to alert Ukrainians to the dangerous influence of emigres, "revisionists," and "national communists."

In July 1957 *Komunist Ukrainy* published an article by I. Kravtsev, head of the instructors' group in the CC CPU Department of Agitation and Propaganda. He excoriated national communism as "an imperialist diversion against the Soviet Union" and a pseudo-contradiction between the national peculiarities of individual countries on the one hand and the "universal laws of the development of society and socialism" on the other.[60] In an attack on Polish and other "revisionists," Kravtsev asserted:

> In reality there is no "Stalinism" as a separate doctrine or social system.... Stalin was an important Marxist who was guided by Marxism-Leninism in his activities. He made a significant contribution to this theory but did not leave a doctrine of his own. Stalin made a number of serious mistakes, both theoretical and practical. Nevertheless, these mistakes changed nothing in the socialist character of the revolutionary transformations that occurred in our country: the workers of the USSR built and are continuing to build a new life, a task in which they are guided by the immortal teachings of Marxism-Leninism.[61]

Kravtsev denounced several authors in the socialist countries, including the Pole, Edda Werfel: "Werfel declares that 'a spectre is haunting Eastern Europe—the spectre of humane socialism,' and that it is frightening not only the capitalists but also the Stalinists." Werfel, he claimed, was thus trying to replace communism with the obscurantist slogan—"Humane socialism."[62] The Ukrainian press also condemned the Polish revisionists J. Szacki and J. Wiatr, the sociologist Z. Bauman, the Hungarian philosopher Georg Lukács and revisionists in non-socialist countries.[63] Party ideologists were particularly suspicious of national communism after Yugoslavia had asserted its independence from Moscow. In the past, the Soviet regime had persecuted Ukrainians who adhered to this concept. Now, the ideologists claimed that proponents of international imperialism wanted to revive the notion:

> In reality, the speculations about "special" paths to socialism and about "national communism" merely camouflaged the chauvinistic and narrowly nationalist attitudes of a few inconstant communists. Such postures are not new. In their time "national communists" in our country, above all the Ukrainian bourgeois nationalists, propagated similar views. The ideas of "national communism" were advanced by the Borotbists, the Ukapists and other bankrupt petty-bourgeois nationalist parties in Ukraine.[64]

Soviet ideologists and the Central Committee Department for International Affairs, headed by Boris Ponomarev (a man with little enthusiasm for reform), scrutinized the effects of events in Eastern Europe on Ukraine. At an ideological conference in Kiev on 29–31 May 1958,

Ponomarev read the main paper, "Major Problems of the International Communist Movement," before an audience of journalists, cultural figures and Ukrainian government, party and Komsomol officials.[65] On 2–10 June a similar seminar for oblast and city committee instructors of the CPU was organized.[66] Both the topics and the speakers invited to the conference and the seminar demonstrated Moscow's mistrust of the ideological work of CPU organizations. Not a single Ukrainian scholar or party official with responsibility for ideology was asked to speak.

The Twentieth Congress had done much to destroy the Stalin myth and to engender reform. Nevertheless, de-Stalinization in the Soviet Union lagged far behind that achieved in Poland and Hungary through the uprisings in those countries. The turmoil in these two countries belied the unity of the socialist countries in the Soviet sphere. In response, the Soviet regime strengthened the role of the party, returned to a more rigid ideology and restored the power of the security organs. Particularly harsh measures were applied in Ukraine. But the impact was reduced by an event that took place in Moscow in June 1957.

The Defeat of the Anti-Party Group

Khrushchev emerged victorious over the Stalinist conservatives. At the June 1957 CC CPSU plenary session he accused Malenkov, Kaganovich, Molotov and D. T. Shepilov of constituting an "anti-party group" and removed them from office. To justify their actions, Khrushchev and his supporters asserted that the anti-party group had opposed de-Stalinization, the restoration of socialist legality, a just nationality policy and the normalization of relations with Yugoslavia.

Ukrainians celebrated Khrushchev's triumph as a victory over the initiators of the hard-line course. Spontaneous demonstrations of support denounced the "opponents of equality in Ukraine." The main target of hostility was Lazar Kaganovich. In the media and at meetings he was attacked particularly for his term of office as first secretary of the CC CPU. These denunciations were clearly manipulated and exaggerated, because he had held this position only from March 1947 to January 1948, during which he was a slavish executor of Stalin's policies. The tenor of the meetings held in Ukraine to discuss the activities of the anti-party group is reflected in the following report:

> Various participants at assemblies and meetings in our republic show partic-
> ular indignation about Kaganovich, who, in the course of his brief term as
> secretary of the CPU Central Committee, calumniated and humiliated sever-
> al honourable and loyal people in all sorts of ways. He made serious and
> unfounded accusations against executives and representatives of the
> progressive Ukrainian intelligentsia, including talented and popular authors.
> It is difficult to imagine how much damage Kaganovich would have inflicted

on the Communist Party and the entire Ukrainian people had he not been recalled to Moscow.[67]

At a meeting of Kiev writers on 9 July 1957, the author Andrii Malyshko declared:

> [Kaganovich] called the poet Maksym Rylsky, one of our literature's most famous, a "Petliura supporter." [He did this] by distorting Rylsky's poem *I, son of the Land of Soviets* and asserting that Rylsky had glorified Petliura's Central Rada.... In particular, he tried to force the young writers Oles Honchar, Leonid Novychenko, Vasyl Kozachenko and others to make depositions against the older writers and to accuse them of nationalism.[68]

Maksym Rylsky himself took part in the discussion. His condemnations were directed not so much against Kaganovich as against the entire anti-party group: "The conspirators supported the decadent tendencies of individual writers, who, under the guise of 'objectivity,' distort wonderful Soviet reality and inflate individual shortcomings." During the period of restrictive policies the Ukrainian intelligentsia felt that demonstrations of sympathy for Khrushchev's campaign against the anti-party group would improve relations with Moscow and generate a better understanding of their position. The intelligentsia's attitude was well expressed at the Kiev meeting by Andrii Malyshko's lyrical appeal for solidarity among Ukrainian intellectuals: "Perhaps you have seen cranes in flight. If one crane cannot follow, all the other cranes help him to fly on. Thus we shall in our position leave nary a colleague to fall victim to the enemy—not as cranes in migratory flight but as steeled communists."[69]

When the campaign against the anti-party group began to ebb late in 1957, Ukraine obtained a new party chief. In December O. I. Kyrychenko, first secretary of the CC CPU, was made secretary of the CC CPSU. He was succeeded in Ukraine by M. V. Pidhorny, who had been secretary of the CC CPSU.[70]

In Defence of Ukrainian Literature

Conflict and tension marked the Fifth Plenum held by the board of the Ukrainian Writers' Union on 28 February 1958. The union's deputy chairman, Iu. Smolych, echoed Khrushchev's statements on literature:

> Various anti-Soviet works have been praised to the heavens by all kinds of pseudo-writers, snobs and *stiliagi*, with the catchword of an alleged struggle for "creative freedom." This was followed by foreign and transatlantic reactions exploiting these ugly works as a new kind of weapon in the imperialists' ideological Cold War.[71]

Smolych criticized the backwardness of Ukrainian literature and spoke of the "errors" of many writers: "In our Ukrainian literature, especially in recently published works, we find incorrect descriptions, false images of people or all those things that lead directly to a distortion of reality, and also to the mental confusion of the reader instead of helping him to visualize the events of present-day life."[72]

Although the party sought greater control over literature, writers were not intimidated. At the plenum, I. Bash complained that publishing houses printed only small editions of Ukrainian books; the management of Ukraine's book publishing authority [Ukrknyhotorh], he reported, had decided to publish only 3,000 copies of the *Anthology of Ukrainian Poetry*. After readers protested, the edition was enlarged to 8,000 copies. Further public pressure had forced the publisher to print another 20,000 copies. V. Sobko noted that the decision of the Union publishing house in Moscow to print Russian translations of twenty-seven Ukrainian books in 1958 was a great success.[73]

The contradictions became clearer during the Sixth Plenum of the board of the Ukrainian Writers Union held in March 1959. Because of the Russification of secondary schools, a primary problem concerned usage of the Ukrainian language. Mykola Bazhan addressed the issue:

> The Ukrainian writers demanded categorically: purity of language, respect for and love of its laws, its lexigraphic [sic] wealth. . . . We cannot, for example, fail to concern ourselves with the style of our newspapers, the degree and character of the use of the mother tongue in public and private life, and the standard of scholarly work on philological problems.[74]

Bazhan also attacked Molotov, a departure from the Ukrainians' usual practice of blaming everything on Kaganovich. But despite his comments he paid lip-service to the new hard-line ideological course and deplored "the bourgeoisie's frenzied attacks," the incursion of bourgeois ideology and how "our country's foes are placing their hopes on the rejuvenation of relics [of the past]." Bazhan's attacks were not confined to political leaders; he considered the "errors" and "deviations" of Les Kurbas unpardonable and his full rehabilitation impossible. Bazhan also criticized the Lviv poet Dmytro Pavlychko with particular vehemence pointing out that some of his poems contained motifs "that have nothing in common with the great truth of our reality." In these works, Pavlychko "had turned away from the friendship of the peoples."

Another speaker, Pavlo Tychyna, cited poems by Pavlychko in which he detected "ambiguities, obscurities and pessimism." Novychenko claimed that "None of us want to accuse the said comrade [Pavlychko] of a criminal offence." He protested that Soviet critics, instead of analyzing Ukrainian literature, "constantly express suspicions" about it. "There are rules for seeking out the kind of recriminations in criticism that sound more like bills of indictment under Paragraph 55 of the old Criminal Code. This only damages the cause of achieving clarity in various questions, which is in the party's interests."[75]

For the first time Ukrainian writers dealt in detail with the question of their compatriots in the emigration. Bazhan admonished a young poetess who had expressed her sympathies in a poem entitled *To Ukrainians Abroad*: "As you know, our compatriots abroad are of a different hue, and it is not worthwhile addressing them so soon and in such a friendly tone as in this poem." The writer A. Khyzhniak predicted that the surviving nationalists were doomed to extinction. L. Novychenko discussed the works of several emigre authors, notably D. I. Tschizhewskij, a specialist in Ukrainian and Russian literature at the University of Heidelberg. L. Dmyterko warned that the danger from exiled nationalists should not be overrated because, "influenced by the rapid development of a free and independent socialist Ukraine, a process of dissolution and final spiritual decay is growing steadily within the circle of Ukrainian nationalists."[76]

During the congress it was evident that the Ukrainian intelligentsia were determined to defend the Ukrainian language and the rights of the republic despite the hard-line course. Several speakers, such as Dudintsev and Tvardovsky, declared their faith in Khrushchev, describing him as a friend of Ukrainian culture and literature.

Resistance to Russification in the Educational System

Hopes that the defeat of the anti-party group, which removed the more conservative and anti-reform party leaders, would hasten the promised expansion of the republics' rights soon proved illusory. On 16 November 1958 the CC CPSU enunciated a set of theses on how the educational system could fulfill society's needs. In keeping with the Khrushchev style, the public was expected to "discuss" the theses and decide whether they were a basis for reform. Khrushchev argued that during the era of the personality cult, the educational system had been so perverted that it had lost any real relationship to life and society. The training of highly qualified personnel had been conducted in this atmosphere, and cadre development had not been oriented toward the needs and tasks of industry and agriculture. The theses also proposed basic changes in the study of national languages. The question whether the language of instruction should be Russian or the national language sparked protests. Up to 1958 both languages had been compulsory in all republics, both union and autonomous. In schools where the language of instruction was Russian, the national language was a compulsory subject and vice-versa. The theses stipulated that parents should decide what kind of school their children should attend and the schools that taught Russian should offer the national language as an optional subject and vice-versa:

To grant parents the right to decide what language a child should study as a compulsory subject would be a most democratic procedure. It would eliminate arbitrary decisions in this important matter and would make possible the termination of the practice of overburdening children with language study.[77]

The democratic choice, however, was offset by a massive propaganda campaign in favour of the Russian language, so that most parents would be likely to choose it as the language of instruction for their children.

In Ukraine the theses were regarded as a means of Russifying the educational system. Even high-ranking CPU officials requested the retention of both languages as compulsory subjects. According to a report in *Literaturna hazeta*, "The teachers, parents and young people are in favour of Russian as a compulsory subject at all schools in the union and autonomous republics, but at the same time they consider that the national language should be obligatory at schools where the language of instruction is Russian."[78] The report also referred to a resolution adopted by the Board of the Poltava Pedagogical Institute: "The Institute board believes that on no account should the learning of the mother tongue be displaced in the national and autonomous republics. On the contrary, the role of native language and literature should be expanded throughout the entire educational system."[79] P. Tronko, then secretary of the Kiev oblast committee, commented that "the school reform should promote the general and cultural development of youth. Under the conditions of our republic ... the learning of Russian, Ukrainian and a foreign language should be compulsory in all schools."[80] Even Kravtsev, a firm supporter of the Russification of Ukraine, took the same view.[81]

The unrest evidently affected the CPU party *apparat*. Mykhailo Hrechukha, a Presidium member of the CC CPU and deputy chairman of the Council of Ministers of the Ukrainian SSR, declared himself in favour of retaining both languages as compulsory subjects.[82] Maksym Rylsky and Mykola Bazhan wrote to *Pravda* in the same vein, trying to convince readers that the children would not be overly taxed by language instruction:

Both Ukrainian and Russian must remain compulsory subjects at all eight-grade schools in Soviet Ukraine, from the first through the eighth grade; four additional hours are devoted to these two subjects each week (i.e., four hours more than for Russian or Ukrainian alone). Our schools' long practice shows that the fear that instruction in two languages—Ukrainian and Russian—could overburden pupils is unfounded.[83]

Iryna Vilde, also a writer, thought that since Khrushchev's proposal to curtail language instruction in the union republic threatened not only the

Ukrainian language but also the Russian, she should make a plea for Russian by demanding that in Ukraine, Russian and a foreign language be learned in addition to the mother tongue. She also dismissed the notion that language lessons overburdened children, and called instead for improved teaching methods.[84] Despite the protests, the USSR Supreme Soviet approved the new school law on 25 December 1958 and the republics were required to sanction similar bills. The Supreme Soviets of two republics, Lithuania and Azerbaidzhan, rejected Khrushchev's proposals and adopted laws making Russian and the national language compulsory subjects. Subsequently, the officials responsible for these laws were removed from office and the legislation was amended.

Ukraine's Supreme Soviet met on 15–16 April 1959 to adopt the school law. The minister of education, I. K. Bilodid, read the main report, "On the Restructuring of Secondary Education in the Republic." Referring to the language of instruction, he said: "The Communist Party's Leninist nationality policy guarantees all our homeland's peoples the opportunity to instruct their children in their native language. In the Ukrainian SSR parents are entitled to determine which language their children should learn. In the republic there are schools with Ukrainian, Russian, Moldavian, Hungarian and Polish as the language of instruction."[85] Granting parents a choice meant further "democratization" of the school system, and Bilodid held the Ukrainian government responsible for improving the instruction of the national language, whether or not it was the primary language of instruction. The Ukrainian intelligentsia, however, saw this as a blow to national culture and expected catastrophic consequences.[86] Although party and government officials tried to soften the impact of the law by making it compulsory (de facto, if not de jure) to learn Ukrainian at schools where Russian was the language of instruction, the law did, in fact, contribute greatly to the Russification of the Ukrainian school system. Khrushchev's attitude to the role of the national languages in the school system was expressed at a meeting between a French Socialist Party delegation and members of the Presidium of the CC CPSU:

As for the nationality question, I will quote the example of Moldavia. The intelligentsia of this republic does not like to send its children to the Moldavian schools. It prefers the Russian schools. Russian schools are preferred in Ukraine, too. This can be explained by practical considerations and the interests of the population itself. People would much rather send their children to the Russian schools because, after graduation from a Moldavian school, it is much more difficult to get accepted at a college (except in Moldavia itself), whereas a diploma from a Russian school opens the door to colleges throughout the Soviet Union.[87]

In October 1959 an important personnel change in the CC CPU boded ill for Ukraine. S. V. Chervonenko was appointed ambassador to the People's Republic of China. His successor was A. D. Skaba, a former secretary of the Kharkiv oblast committee and later Ukraine's minister for higher and secondary education. Skaba, a historian and Kharkiv University graduate, had revealed his ideological mettle as oblast secretary. In this position he had pressed for increasing party control over literature and art in Kharkiv oblast and believed that the directives of the Twentieth CPSU Congress augured the party's total control of society. An article by Skaba in *Komunist Ukrainy* in April 1957 reads like a catechism for the die-hard conservatives among the party ideologists. Describing the situation of writers and others among the cultural intelligentsia, he wrote:

Our country's entire artistic public understands very well that the Communist Party's ideological and political direction is one of the basic principles of socialist ideology and guarantees the unremitting development of Soviet literature and art. For this reason our creative intelligentsia unanimously rebuffs all inimical attacks on the party's leading role in the development of art and literature and decisively rejects all tendencies aimed at "liberating" art from the "party's custody" and propagating that so-called creative freedom which bourgeois ideologists and their henchmen discuss so loudly nowadays. Upheld by the historic directives of the Twentieth CPSU Congress and true to the ideas of Marxism-Leninism, to the ideology of proletarian internationalism and peoples' friendship, the cultural intelligentsia are fighting enthusiastically for the further ideological and artistic development of the literature and art of socialist realism.[88]

Skaba's commission was to tighten the party's control over ideological work in Ukraine. This was a difficult task at a time of social upheaval.

Notes

1. *Komunist Ukrainy*, no. 4 (1956): 7.
2. *Pravda*, 3 July 1956.
3. *Radianska Ukraina*, 5 July 1956.
4. *Ibid.*, 12 July 1956.
5. *Radianska osvita*, 14 July 1956.
6. *Radianska kultura*, 11 July 1956.
7. *Radianska Ukraina*, 18 July 1956.
8. *Pravda*, 2 August 1950.
9. H. Emelianenko, "Leninski pryntsypy natsionalnoi polityky KPRS," *Komunist Ukrainy*, no. 10, (1956): 58ff.
10. *Zmina*, 7 July 1956.
11. *Literaturna hazeta*, 16 July 1957.

12. The decrees are given in *Narysy istorii Komunistychoi partii Ukrainy*, 555.
13. "Za glubokoe nauchnoe izuchenie istorii ukrainskogo naroda," *Voprosy istorii*, no. 7 (1955).
14. *Ibid.*
15. *Komunist Ukrainy*, no. 3 (1956): 12.
16. Cf. *Pytannia istorii SSSR* (Kharkiv, 1974), 26ff.
17. M. Suprunenko, "Do pytannia pro vyvchennia istorii hromadianskoi viiny na Ukraini," *Komunist Ukrainy*, no. 10 (1956): 29ff.
18. E. S. Oslikovskaia and A. V. Snegov, "Za pravdivoe osveshchenie istorii proletarskoi revoliutsii," *Voprosy istorii*, no. 3 (1956): 138ff.
19. *Ibid.*, 140.
20. H. Emelianenko, "Torzhestvo Leninskoi natsionalnoi polityky," *Komunist Ukrainy*, no. 6 (1958): 47.
21. *Ibid.*
22. S. Chervonenko, "Pod znamenem marksizma-leninizma," *Partiinaia zhizn*, no. 12 (1958): 26ff.
23. The Borotbist Party developed from the left wing of the Ukrainian Social-Revolutionary Party and derived its name from the newspaper *Borotba* [Struggle], which appeared in Kiev from 1917 to 1920. In 1919 the Borotbists proclaimed a communist political platform and called themselves the Ukrainian Party of Social-Revolutionaries (Communists). Members were also referred to as Communist-Borotbists. After unification with the left Ukrainian social democrats they renamed the party as the Ukrainian Communist Party-Borotbists (UCPB). Their goal was an independent communist Ukraine.
24. O. Ovcharov, "Z pryvodu vysvitlennia pytannia pro borotbyzm," *Komunist Ukrainy*, no. 2 (1958): 36ff.
25. "Do vysvitlennia deiakykh pytan istorii Komunistychnoi partii Ukrainy," *Komunist Ukrainy*, no. 6 (1959): 37ff; *Ocherki istorii Kommunisticheskoi partii Ukrainy* (Kiev, 1964), 466.
26. *Radianska osvita*, 14 August 1956.
27. *Nashe slovo*, 8 June 1958.
28. The rehabilitation of the CPP and CPWB took a similar course. This was, however, much more complicated because it was linked with attempts to rehabilitate part of the Belorussian communist resistance movement. In the course of the Second World War the largest Belorussian resistance group (in Minsk) had been declared "provocatory."
29. V. Malanchuk, *Torzhestvo Leninskoi natsionalnoi polityky* (Lviv, 1963), 557.
30. The most important study of the CPWU was published in Poland. See J. Radziejowski, *Komunistyczna partia Zachodniej Ukrainy, 1919–1929*, (Cracow, 1976). An English version of this book was published recently: *The Communist Party of Western Ukraine, 1919-1929* (Edmonton, 1983).
31. *Ukrainskaia SSR v Velikoi Otechestvennoi voine Sovetskogo Soiuza*, (Kiev, 1975), 414.
32. I. L. Demianchuk, *Partyzanska presa Ukrainy* (Kiev, 1956), 95ff.
33. P. Komarov, "O trebovatelnosti i chutkosti," *Partiinaia zhizn*, no. 17 (1954): 23.

34. *Pravda Ukrainy*, 28 July 1956. Vasyl Blakytny (1894–1925), writer and trade-union official; Borotbist leader; joined the CPU in 1920; 1920–5, member of CPU Central Committee. Vasyl Chumak (1901–19), poet; active member of CPU; captured and shot by Denikin's men. Ivan Mykytenko (1897–1937), writer; joined the CPU in 1925; a leader of the Proletarian Literary Organization in Ukraine.
35. *Literaturna hazeta*, 20 September 1956. Myroslav Irchan (1897–1937) [Andrii Babiuk], writer; joined the CPU in 1920; emigrated to Canada, where he edited the journal *Robitnytsia* (1923–9); led the literary organization *Zakhidna Ukraina* after his return to Ukraine; perished in 1937.
36. *Vitchyzna*, February 1958.
37. *Literaturna hazeta*, 25 April 1958.
38. M. Drahomanov, *Literaturno-publitsystychni pratsi*, 2 vols. (Kiev, 1970).
39. *Literaturna hazeta*, 22 September 1956.
40. Several oblast committees met to discuss the problem. On 4 December 1956, for example, the Bureau of the Lviv oblast committee condemned the efforts of certain literary specialists "to rehabilitate West Ukrainian nationalist writers."
41. N. S. Khrushchev, *Vysokoe prizvanie literatury i iskusstva* (Moscow, 1963), 30.
42. *Ibid*.
43. *Komunist Ukrainy*, no. 7 (1958).
44. *Ibid*., 24ff.
45. The maligned Ukrainian composers were Borys Liatoshynsky, Mykola Kolessa, Mykhailo Verylivsky, Roman Symovych and Gleb Taranov.
46. *Pravda Ukrainy*, 10 February 1957.
47. *Ibid*., 6 June 1957.
48. *Radianska Ukraina*, 7 December 1957.
49. *Stalinskoe plemia*, 13 September 1956.
50. *Komsomolskaia pravda*, 6 May 1954.
51. *Radianska kultura*, 9 December 1956.
52. *Pravda*, 3 September 1956.
53. For example, on 21 July 1955, Radio Sumy broadcast reports of "public disturbances in the town."
54. The *samvydav* publication *Ukrainskyi visnyk*, no. 4 (January 1971) (Paris, 1971), 180, reports that Ivan Shevchenko and Mykhailo Lutsyk were rearrested and sentenced to fifteen years in labour camps in 1959. Other sentences were: V. Kobrinchuk, 1957 in Rovno, ten years; Andrii Turyk, in Dnipropetrovsk, death by firing squad, subsequently commuted to fifteen years; Oleksii Tykhy, 1958 in Donetsk, five years; Borys Kyian, in Luhansk, ten years; Ihor Kychak, in Dnipropetrovsk, ten years. *Ukrainska intelihentsia pid sudom KGB* (Munich, 1970), 230ff. Information on many other such trials has reached the West.
55. Malanchuk, *Torzhestvo Leninskoi natsionalnoi polityky*, 564ff.
56. *Radianska kultura*, 7 October 1956.
57. In 1946–7 the Soviet security organs suppressed a "reactionary" Hungarian resistance movement in the region that was allegedly supported by Britain

and the United States and collaborated with the resistance movement in Hungary.
58. Malanchuk, *Torzhestvo Leninskoi natsionalnoi polityky*, 490ff, 564.
59. *Ibid.*, 565.
60. I. Kravtsev, "Natsionalnyi komunizm-ideolohichna dyversiia imperializmu," *Komunist Ukrainy*, no. 7 (1957): 25ff.
61. *Ibid.*, 30.
62. *Ibid.*, 31.
63. Cf. I. Holovakha and F. Horovsky, "Revizionizm na sluzhbi mizhnarodnoi reaktsii," *Komunist Ukrainy*, no. 4 (1958): 32ff.
64. *Ibid.*, 40. The Ukapists is the name given to members of the Ukrainian Communist Party, founded in 1920 by left-wing Social-Democrats and Ukrainian Social Revolutionaries. Although the party merged with the CPU, a group existed in Vienna from 1921 to 1922 under the leadership of V. Vynnychenko.
65. *Radianska Ukraina*, 1 June 1958.
66. *Ibid.*, 11 June 1958.
67. *Literaturna hazeta*, 9 July 1957.
68. *Radianska Ukraina*, 12 July 1957.
69. *Ibid.*, 12 July 1957.
70. *Ibid.*
71. *Literaturna hazeta*, 4 March 1958.
72. *Ibid.*
73. *Ibid.*
74. *Ibid.*, 11 March 1959.
75. *Ibid.*
76. *Ibid.*
77. *Radianska Ukraina*, 16 November 1958.
78. *Literaturna hazeta*, 9 December 1958.
79. *Ibid.*
80. P. Tronko, "Tsioho vymahaie zhyttia," *Komunist Ukrainy*, no. 12 (1958): 23.
81. *Robitnycha hazeta*, 17 December 1958.
82. Cf. his speech at the session of the USSR Supreme Soviet, in *Zasedaniia Verkhovnogo Soveta SSSR, Piatogo sozyva, vtoraia sessiia (22–25 dekabria 1958 g.): Stenograficheskii otchet* (Moscow, 1958).
83. *Pravda*, 22 December 1958.
84. *Pravda Ukrainy*, 3 January 1959.
85. *Radianska Ukraina*, 16 April 1959.
86. Cf. J. Kolasky, *Education in Soviet Ukraine* (Toronto, 1968).
87. See shorthand report on this meeting in the French journal *Réalité* (May 1956).
88. A. Skaba, "Polipshuvaty kerivnytstvo tvorchymy orhanizatsiiami," *Komunist Ukrainy*, no. 4 (1957): 39.

Chapter Three

Cultural Unrest and Economic Reform

A Return to Intimidation

After the Twentieth Congress the CPSU's efforts to restore total party control of society were, up to the 1960s, largely ineffective in the face of pressures for reform. Accordingly, the party resorted to the methods of the Stalin era but tried to avoid its extremes. The prime targets were once more "bourgeois nationalists" and "Zionists," although the campaign, which continued through 1958–9, was directed at a broad cross-section of the population.

In January 1960 almost all cinemas in Ukraine showed the documentary film *The People Accuse!*, which focused on the collaboration of Ukrainian nationalists in Rivne oblast with the Nazi occupiers. The film also depicted the activities of the OUN leaders Stepan Bandera and Andrii Melnyk and the partisan leader Taras Bulba-Borovets. Propaganda brochures attacking the OUN were published in large editions. In his report to the Twenty-first CPU Congress in February 1960, First Secretary Pidhorny said:

> Among the forces of international reaction engaged in anti-Soviet propaganda we also find old traitors—the Ukrainian bourgeois nationalists who are vegetating abroad. They are very disturbed, especially now that the Cold War is slackening. For all these malicious forces, including the

Ukrainian nationalists, a life of peace and friendship between the peoples is worse than death.[1]

The press reported the trials of former Vlasov Army members, Ukrainian "collaborators" and OUN members or supporters.[2] Most trials of OUN members were held between 1954 and 1956. The purpose of these belated reports was to heighten vigilance against the nationalists. The Moscow journal *Iunost* cited the illegal operations of a pro-Bandera organization whose members included a priest, thereby implying that there were close contacts between the clergy and the OUN. Moreover, it reported that OUN had been active among the Ukrainian minority in Kazakhstan and had occasionally received assistance from the local population.[3] Such propaganda was parallelled by a defamation campaign against the dissolved Greek Catholic Church in Western Ukraine and increased reprisals against Orthodox clergymen.[4]

In mid-October 1960 the Soviet Union and other socialist countries, notably the German Democratic Republic, began a propaganda campaign against Professor Theodor Oberländer, formerly chief political officer of the Ukrainian "Nachtigall" unit that was posted on the Eastern Front together with German units, but did not see action.[5] The campaign blamed the "Nachtigall" unit not only for the murder of thousands of Lviv citizens in Brygidky Prison shortly before the Germans occupied Lviv (an atrocity carried out by the Soviet security organs),[6] but also for the murder of Polish professors (an atrocity carried out by the SS).[7] The campaign was particularly intense in Ukraine, where its protagonists tried to mobilize public opinion against "collaborators" and the "Nazis in Bonn." In the same month the Ukrainian press published its first reports on Stepan Bandera's murder in Munich: "Bandera...was eliminated by Professor Oberländer's agents. He was pushed out of a fourth-floor window."[8]

In 1959 the Society for the Propagation of Political and Scientific Knowledge published a 43,000-copy second edition of T. K. Kychko's booklet *The Jewish Religion, Its Origins and Nature*, first printed in 1957. In contrast, the print-run for the society's booklets on Lenin and the Seven-Year Plan was only 22,000 copies in that year. In 1964 Kychko, who still enjoys the reputation of being Ukraine's "leading expert" on chauvinism and Judaism, published *Judaism Without Embellishment*. The booklet proports to construct an indissoluble link between Judaism and Zionism. According to Kychko, the Jews and Zionists were working hand-in-hand with American imperialism and reactionary forces throughout the world. Kychko reiterated the assertion, made in Stalin's time, that the Zionists had collaborated with the Gestapo and anti-Semitic parties in Hungary. The booklet, however, omitted completely the extermination of East European Jewry by the German forces.

The booklet reveals that the Soviet leadership had begun to persecute Jewish believers, with trials of rabbis and prosecution for "illegal assembly" and economic crimes. Kychko shows how Jewish believers, forced underground, formed clandestine religious communities known as *miniani*, to which they tried to recruit young people. The anti-Jewish campaign was less an attack on Jewish believers than an attempt to revive the anti-Jewish course pursued before Stalin's death, when many prominent party members and intellectuals in Ukraine discriminated against Jews under the pretext of fighting Zionism.[9]

The press published examples of co-operation between Ukrainians and Western politicians. The strongest reaction was elicited by the "Ukraine Declaration" of the Canadian prime minister John Diefenbaker. The Soviet press condemned his statement on Ukrainian aspirations to independence, which he delivered to a session of the UN General Assembly, as a slanderous pronouncement "that has also been severely condemned by emigre Ukrainian workers in the United States and Canada." At the same time his declaration was cited as proof that "bourgeois nationalists have influential friends abroad."[10]

The Ukrainian media displayed a special antipathy toward North American scholars, including those of Ukrainian extraction, who dealt with Ukrainian questions. Professor Tschizhewskij, it was claimed, was "not a master-spy, nor a trained diversionary or hired killer, but certainly occupies a bourgeois-nationalist position. He is a bourgeois nationalist who spreads the lie that the communist regime consciously and systematically resists the development of the non-Russian peoples' national literature."[11] Western scholars who disproved the claim that bourgeois nationalists had co-operated with the Nazis were favourite targets. These included John Armstrong, the American author of *Ukrainian Nationalism*; I. Kamenetsky, an emigre Ukrainian and author of *Hitler's Occupation of Ukraine (1941–1944)*; and V. Markus, author of *L'incorporation de l'Ukraine Subcarpathique à l'Ukraine Soviétique (1944–1945)*, and especially the Munich-based journalist Ivan Majstrenko, author of *Borotbism*.[12]

Thus the propaganda apparatus had returned to the slander and intimidation of the *Zhdanovshchina* period. After the Twentieth CPSU Congress the glorification of the Russian people had initially ceased to be a *sine qua non* of political life. The emphasis shifted to the restoration of the republics' rights and the return to "Leninist internationalism." To a certain extent even the party encouraged discussion of the rights of Ukrainian and other national languages. Then, however, it reversed policy. An increasing number of articles and brochures invoked the Russian people's "selfless" aid to the other peoples of the Soviet Union. Russian authors emphasized that "voluntary" union with Russia meant progress for the non-Russian peoples. They proclaimed the thesis that the Russian language was not just a means of communication in a multinational state but the second mother tongue of all Soviet people and a new achievement that would determine the non-Russian republics' future cultural development.

Whereas in the past, Soviet propaganda referred to the flourishing cultures of the Soviet peoples, the new catchword was "wholehearted rapprochement."

Khrushchev, who initiated the theory that Russian alone ensured access to the treasures of world literature, science and technology, tried to justify that theory with his economic reforms. The path to scientific and technical progress, he declared, should be consistent and the means of travelling it "rationalized" to a maximum. He thus denied the national languages the right to develop their own scientific and technical terminology, and increased the efforts to Russify the republics.

Kravtsev, a leading theorist of Russification, tried to equate the new course in nationality policy with the requirements of Khrushchev's economic reforms. He belittled the defence of local economic interests at the city, district, oblast or republic level as parochialism (*mestnichestvo*) and as a form of nationalism.[13] Only in the first years after the Twentieth CPSU Congress was any attempt made in Ukraine to implement the recommendations—originally advanced by Lenin—that Russians who reside permanently in the national republics should learn the local language. By the end of the fifties, it was no longer even mentioned. Kravtsev formulated the official viewpoint:

> Nationalist survivals also reveal themselves in the practice of juxtaposing the cadres of the basic nation to the cadres of the other nations living in a given republic in an attempt to *select cadres solely under the national aspect or in accordance with knowledge of the national language.* The rights of persons who do not belong to the basic nation are often infringed in the [process of] cadre rotation. In this respect the Leninist principle of the selection and promotion of cadres primarily according to their political and professional qualities is ignored and violated.[14]

In Ukraine, the maxim was that "The guarantee for a new flourishing of our multinational culture lies in the enrichment and development of all the national languages. The linguistic education of the workers will continue to remain an integral element of communist education." Both intellectuals and many Ukrainian communists saw this viewpoint as part of proletarian internationalism and the principle of the equality of all nations and peoples. This did not signify a sense of enmity toward the Russian language, since the latter had developed into a *lingua franca*. In the words of Vitalii Rusanivsky: "In our country the Russian language has long since become the language of communication between the nations, a powerful instrument for the Russian people's further cultural development and simultaneously an indispensable instrument of communication between the nations." However, "the development of the cultures of the socialist nations (above all that most important element of nationhood—the national language) is one of the most important tasks for officials on the cultural front in the period of all-round construction of communism in our land."[15]

The Soviet leaders curbed efforts to increase the rights of the national languages and enrich the national cultures and began an ambitious campaign to Russify the national republics, which the Ukrainian intelligentsia resisted with unprecedented ferocity.

Agriculture: Khrushchev vs. Ukraine

Economic developments in Ukraine after Stalin's death had a decisive influence on political events. In 1961 relations between Khrushchev and the Ukrainian party leadership deteriorated because of the latter's failure to fulfill agricultural plans. Although after 1953 the CPSU passed many measures to improve agriculture, plans for the production and procurement of grain and other agricultural produce were frequently underfulfilled.

In January 1961 the CC CPSU held an enlarged plenary session which was attended by leading officials and agricultural experts from all the union republics. Khrushchev devoted part of his keynote speech to grain production in Ukraine. Noting that state purchases in the republic had declined steadily from 9.8 million metric tons in 1948 to a mere 5.7 million in 1960, Khrushchev warned the Ukrainian comrades against "blaming everything on the inclement weather conditions." He cited inadequate work as the main reason for the declining figures.[16] After Khrushchev's fall, party leaders disputed his often harsh criticism and the accuracy of his arguments.

Pidhorny, then first secretary of the CC CPU, spoke for the Ukrainian SSR at the plenary session. Although he criticized Ukraine's agricultural performance, he tried to avoid the impression that it was catastrophic. When he tried to blame bad weather for the 1960 harvest failure, he was repeatedly interrupted by Khrushchev. The following exchange published in *Pravda* is typical of the atmosphere that prevailed at the plenum:

Khrushchev: Comrade Podgorny, I'm convinced that the corn harvest figures you just mentioned account for only half of the harvest. The other half of the ripened crop was carried off, stolen from the fields.
Pidhorny: That's right, Nikita Sergeevich.
Khrushchev: Then what has the weather got to do with it? The harvest was carried off, stolen, and you say the weather didn't permit you to achieve a high harvest. Is that so?
Pidhorny: Yes, that's so.
Khrushchev: Then why don't you talk about it?[17]

Khrushchev blamed careless management of agriculture for the republic's poor corn harvest. After Pidhorny had capitulated and admitted that serious mistakes had been made, Khrushchev commented: "Don't cheat yourself and don't deceive the collective farm peasants and the state farm workers, because you must take the responsibility for bad management yourself. It's important to take this into account in the future, too.... That is, [this] 'theory' of self-deceit and deceit of the state."[18] Although Pidhorny acknowledged the correctness of Khrushchev's reproofs and exhortations, he criticized the USSR Council of Ministers and other central organs for the shortcomings in the supply of agricultural machinery, seed and fertilizers to the Ukrainian SSR:

> Getting high corn harvests is a large and complicated business which is decided not only by people but also by technical equipment. Every effort is made in the republic to obtain high corn yields, but we also need a certain amount of support from the union organs. Specifically, we need corn-sowers and other technical equipment.

In his speech, Pidhorny criticized the policies of the USSR Council of Ministers and Gosplan, the central planning organ. He revealed that excessive centralization had caused problems in many areas of the republic's economy. Pidhorny denounced the centralized system of supplying industrial goods to agriculture. As he noted, even "nails, spades and other small items are distributed centrally by the USSR State Planning Committee" (Gosplan). He also maintained that the republics should have more rights in the economic sphere and criticized the 1960 decision which had abolished republics' entitlement to over 50 per cent of all agricultural machinery and equipment produced in excess of their quarterly and supplementary plans.[19] Pidhorny's comments received belated support from the Soviet authorities after Khrushchev's fall, when the latter's speech was described as a subjective attempt to insult and discredit Ukraine's leading cadres:

> After discussing the reports of the union republics' party organizations about the development of agriculture and animal husbandry, the January [1961] plenum of the CC CPSU pointed to the backwardness of these important branches of the economy and stressed the urgent necessity of a rapid increase in agricultural production. The plenum decided on a number of measures to this end. At the plenum, however, N. S. Khrushchev—instead of clarifying the reasons for this backwardness in agriculture in a business-like fashion—accused the local party, Soviet and agricultural organs of failing to fulfill the state plans for the production and sale of agricultural produce. The plans proposed by the plenum for increasing the production and state purchases of grain, meat and milk were not supported by the necessary financing and material supplies.[20]

The CC CPSU plenum was followed on 26 January 1961 by an enlarged plenary session of the CC CPU. Besides numerous party and state officials (including some from the Moldavian SSR), scientists and agricultural experts, Khrushchev himself came to Kiev for the meeting. Pidhorny's speech exemplified the Ukrainian party bureaucracy's subservient attitude toward Khrushchev. Although Khrushchev continued to insult and criticize the republic's cadres, Pidhorny and the party officials attending the plenum glorified the party chief and thanked him profusely for his advice. Pidhorny devoted a long section of his speech to the "moral decay" of party officials in the countryside and the agricultural cadres. False reports on plan fulfillment (the famous *pripiski*), theft and other violations were common in Ukraine, he said. This time Pidhorny even refrained from the self-confident statements that he had used to defend the republic at the Moscow plenum.

Khrushchev once again blamed the Ukrainian party and agricultural cadres for the failures in agriculture: "The production and sale of grain in the republic decreased even though the collective and state farms are technically better equipped today than in the past.... So why did the republic lower grain production? The main culprit is the management."[21] Khrushchev's Kiev speech was once more a mixture of demagoguery, sarcasm and—especially with regard to the Soviet Union's ability to overtake the United States in all spheres of the economy—fantasy:

> In the past some foreign politicians asked me: "Mr. Khrushchev, do you really believe you can catch up with America economically?" No one puts the question like that any more; instead they say: "Mr. Khrushchev, in what year do you think the Soviet Union will catch up with America?" Now that's a different question, a different conversation. They've stopped doubting that the Soviet Union will catch up with the United States. Only one question troubles them now: When? I answered: "You can put it down in your notebook that we will catch up, overtake and forge ahead of them in the volume of per capita industrial production in 1970." This very day, when the party is criticizing the shortcomings revealed in the development of agriculture, we say with conviction: If people there work properly, Ukraine could catch up with America in the per capita production of meat in three or, at the most, four years.[22]

The events of early 1961 deepened the rift between Khrushchev and the Soviet Ukrainian cadres. In the eyes of the Ukrainian intelligentsia, Khrushchev had already lost his prestige with the 1958 school reform and now their hopes that the Ukrainian SSR had a protector at the head of the CPSU faded still further. This was an important factor in the political radicalization of Ukraine.

The Beginnings of Organized Opposition in Ukraine

Arrests and political trials for "anti-state activity" remained commonplace in Ukraine even after Stalin's death. In 1958, for example, there was a trial of a group of young workers and students who had founded the United Party for the Liberation of Ukraine. The names of eight members of this party, who were sentenced to terms ranging from two to ten years in March 1959 by a court in Ivano-Frankivsk, reached the West in an open letter to Petro Shelest from Ivan O. Kandyba, a Mordovian labour camp inmate.[23]

The same source reports that in Lviv, from 23 to 26 December 1961, a trial was held of the Ukrainian National Committee, an organization whose goal was to separate Ukraine from the Soviet Union. The number of workers among the accused was relatively high. Two of them, Ivan Koval and Bohdan Hrytsyna, were sentenced to death and shot. Death sentences against two others, Volodymyr Hnat and Roman Hurny, were commuted to fifteen years' imprisonment. The other sixteen accused received sentences ranging from ten to thirteen years in labour camps.

In December 1961 the trial of seven founding members of the Ukrainian Workers' and Peasants' League took place. One of the organization's best known members was Lev Lukianenko. He was born in 1927 in the village of Khrypivka, Chernihiv oblast, graduated from the Faculty of Law at Moscow University in 1957 and was an active party member. Before his arrest he was a lawyer and full-time party propagandist in the Radekhiv and Hlyniany districts of Lviv oblast. Another prominent member of the group was Ivan Kandyba, a lawyer born in 1930. At the trial, known as the "Ukrainian Lawyers' Trial," the state maintained that Lukianenko had arranged his transfer to party work in Western Ukraine because he believed it would be easier to find supporters there. From the court record, a copy of which reached the West, we learn that the prosecution classified the party programme drafted by Lukianenko as an anti-Soviet platform aimed at separating Ukraine from the USSR. The death sentence passed on Lukianenko was later commuted to fifteen years in labour camps with confiscation of his property. Four co-defendants received ten-to-fifteen-year terms with confiscation of their property. The treason charges against two others were changed to "anti-Soviet propaganda" and their sentences reduced from ten to seven years. From documents (mostly written by Lukianenko or Kandyba) it is evident that the Ukrainian Workers' and Peasants' League had merely formed a debating circle to discuss the problems of Ukraine's future. The basis of discussion was Lukianenko's programme, which the security organs attacked as "nationalist." In the programme we read:

As an independent and socialist state, Ukraine should remain in the community of socialist states; we are struggling for an independent Ukraine which guarantees the material and spiritual needs of its citizens on the basis of a nationalized economy and develops toward communism, whereby all citizens may truly enjoy political liberties and determine the course of economic and political development.

In the letter to Shelest mentioned earlier, Kandyba reported that the court had claimed falsely that the draft programme was the programme of an actual Ukrainian Workers' and Peasants' League. In fact, said Kandyba, no organization of this name had ever existed, nor had the members of the group ever attempted to realize the draft programme's aims. He described the formation of one group as follows: "We were a handful of people who saw all kinds of abuses going on around us—constant violations of socialist legality and of the citizens' political rights, national oppression, the arbitrary rule of Russian great-state chauvinism, contempt for the peasants and many, many other anomalies."[24]

The group was arrested on the testimony of a KGB informer. The documentary material about the trial that reached the West shows that, despite the proclaimed return to "socialist legality," the KGB was persisting in its illegal practices, manufacturing the evidence needed for a conviction. It was also evident that numerous Russifiers and fully Russified Ukrainians—i.e., people who did not speak Ukrainian and took every opportunity to vilify it—were still at work in the security organs. Prosecutor Ie. B. Starikov, for example, informed the defendant I. Iu. Borovnytsky that the Ukrainian language was unworthy of being a state language and the Ukrainian nation was incapable of statehood. "That is why," he said, "Bohdan Khmelnytsky handed Ukraine over to the Russian state, and that is why Ukraine was incorporated into the Soviet Union in 1922."[25]

The Twenty-Second CPSU Congress: New Hopes?

In February 1961 N. T. Kalchenko was removed from the post of chairman of the Council of Ministers and replaced by a man from the younger generation, V. V. Shcherbytsky, until then secretary of the CC CPU. Kalchenko was demoted to deputy chairman and appointed minister of procurement. Kyrychenko had left the republic in 1957 for a career in the CPSU, while Korotchenko retained the figurehead post of chairman of the Supreme Soviet. The middle generation of party officials came increasingly to the fore, rejuvenating the CPU leadership.

In the middle of 1961 it was revealed that a new party programme was to be adopted at the Twenty-second Congress. Khrushchev was trying to reduce the tensions between himself and the Ukrainian leadership and intelligentsia, who had no alternative but to support him. The latter's hopes in Kyrychenko, who was for a while considered Khrushchev's potential successor, had been disappointed. After his demotion to the position of first secretary of the Rostov oblast committee, he lost even this post six months later and became an "unperson."[26]

Khrushchev made demonstrative gestures to improve the political mood in Ukraine. On 28 May 1961 he interrupted a journey to Vienna to stop over in Kiev with his wife, Nina Petrovna, who enjoyed great popularity in Ukraine. At a mass meeting he averred that he had interrupted his journey to kneel at the grave of Taras Shevchenko in Kaniv. The crowd broke into a storm of applause. On Shevchenko's grave he laid a wreath with the dedication: "To the great Ukrainian poet, revolutionary and democrat, Taras Hryhorovych Shevchenko, from N. S. Khrushchev." Near the grave he planted a young oak tree and then, although he had often visited it before, he viewed the Shevchenko Museum. This achieved the desired effect, and *Radianska Ukraina* rejoiced that, despite his many commitments, "our Nikita Sergeevich" had found time "to visit the hallowed grave of that brilliant son of the Ukrainian people, Taras Shevchenko."[27]

A new note was injected into the prolonged campaign to increase the "vigilance" of the masses, namely "militarism and revanchism in the Federal Republic of Germany." Every opportunity was used to create fear and alarm. In June 1961 West Germany was the target of verbal attacks at a mass demonstration on the twentieth anniversary of the outbreak of the German-Soviet war. At a meeting in Kiev on 22 June, CPU First Secretary Pidhorny lashed out at the Western powers' refusal to sign a peace treaty with the German Democratic Republic. "But," he continued, "this treaty will be signed regardless of the United States and its allies. All peace-loving peoples will conclude this treaty with the German Democratic Republic." The Federal Republic of Germany, asserted Pidhorny, represented "the greatest threat of war in Europe."[28]

The Twenty-second CPU Congress was held on 27–30 September 1961. It was preceded by a "public discussion" of the draft for the new party programme. The draft was a disappointment for many people: the collective farm peasants were disconcerted by the announcement that the cultivation of private plots would soon be abolished, a point on which Khrushchev had been able to sell his earlier idea that the swift development of collective farming would soon make the collective farms self-sufficient. On nationality policy, the text was ambiguous, but a reading between the lines indicated an end to the de-Stalinization, which had seen expansion of the republic's rights after the Twentieth CPSU Congress.

The CPSU draft programme topped the agenda at the Twenty-second CPU Congress and I. P. Kazanets, second secretary of the CPU Central Committee delivered a report on the subject. Another topic was the amendment of the party statutes. Pidhorny's report to the Ukrainian congress revealed that the Ukrainian party bureaucracy was trying to keep its involvement in all-Union problems to a minimum while stressing the republic's economic development. Pidhorny declared that Ukrainian industry had achieved a very high development rate and could fulfil the seven-year plan (1959–65) proclaimed at the Twenty-first CPSU Congress in five to six years. Yet he left himself room for retreat by pointing out that Ukraine had to make a major contribution to the defence industry. International tensions, he said, required all party, state and economic organs to increase their involvement in the arms industry.

Ukraine achieved a record grain harvest in 1961 and exceeded the planned figure of 32 million metric tons. The crop of winter grains was over 16 million tons, as opposed to the planned 14.4 million. Other crops brought higher yields than originally planned and Kiev expected Khrushchev to give the republic due credit for its achievements.

In his report to the congress, Pidhorny made the obligatory attacks on "nationalists" and their "lying propaganda," but cautioned against equating them with the majority of Ukrainian emigres. He also called for vigilance against "imperialist circles who abused the friendship of Soviet Ukrainians and sometimes exploit tourism and other visits to the Soviet Union for anti-Soviet propaganda and often even for espionage." He also encouraged anti-religious propaganda because some of the population was still under the influence of the churches.[29]

That economic success had given the Soviet Ukrainian leaders self-confidence was clear from the "Resolution" and "Declaration" adopted by the CPU Congress. On the one hand, these offered unswerving loyalty to the CC CPSU, but on the other they were replete with pride that the Ukrainian delegation would not come empty-handed to the Twenty-second CPSU Congress. Official reports on the CPU Congress picture Pidhorny as a highly competent statesman. His appearances were marked by increasing *savoir-faire* and self-confidence. His speeches and articles of the early 1960s were far superior to those of the second half of the 1950s.

The Twenty-second Congress of the CPSU was held on 17–31 October 1961. Its political significance is comparable to that of the Twentieth CPSU Congress and would have surpassed the latter if the resolutions concerning the changes in the party statutes, the rotation and rejuvenation of party cadres and the avowed determination to complete de-Stalinization had actually been implemented.

The Ukrainian delegation to the congress consisted of "prominent speakers" (First Secretary Pidhorny and the writer Oleksander Korniichuk) and "representatives of the people" ("heroes of socialist labour" collective-farm chairman Vasyl Kavun and tractor-brigade leader Oleksandr Hitalov). Only Pidhorny's speech, however, had any political significance. Predictably, he first delivered a glowing report about the republic's achievements in industry and agriculture. He announced an enlargement of the area for the cultivation of corn and a planned yield of forty to fifty centners per hectare in 1962, when the irrigated area was to be increased to 27.2 million hectares. He complained loudly about the shortage of means to complete this project, but added: "Time has confirmed the correctness of the course taken by the party on Khrushchev's initiative to consolidate and encourage the all-round development of grain farming."[30]

Pidhorny stressed that not only was Ukraine a rich republic with a high standard of living but also that the Ukrainian people's culture was developing rapidly: "Thousands of foreign tourists visit Soviet Ukraine every year. Hundreds of Ukrainian emigres have come, too. After their return many of them reported truly how rich and happy the Ukrainian people were. They reject with indignation the mouthings of imperialist and nationalist propaganda that the Ukrainian people are 'still in great need.'" Pidhorny also spoke of the ever closer "organizational links between Ukrainian culture and the culture of the great Russian people and all the peoples of our country." He pointed out that Ukraine's successes were due not only to the party but also to Khrushchev personally: "The Ukrainian people thanks the dear Communist Party, its Leninist Central Committee, and you, Nikita Sergeevich, from its whole heart! It gives thanks for the constant attention, for the concern for the welfare and happiness of the workers in Ukraine, for the welfare and happiness of all Soviet people!"

Pidhorny lambasted the "anti-party group" around Molotov, Kaganovich and Malenkov, concentrating on Kaganovich's "provocations" in Ukraine: "Like a true sadist Kaganovich found gratification in mocking the activists and intelligentsia, humiliating them, threatening them with arrest and imprisonment. It is not by mere chance that, up to this very day, many party and Soviet officials, many cultural workers call Kaganovich's tenure the black days of the Soviet Ukraine."[31] Not satisfied with persecuting Ukrainian communists, Pidhorny noted, Kaganovich even tried to convene a plenary session of the CC CPSU to discuss "nationalism as the greatest danger for the CPU," although no such danger had existed. To loud applause, Pidhorny continued:

> It could not have existed at all because, luckily for us, that constant Leninist Nikita Sergeevich Khrushchev was for many years the head of the CC CPU, [a man] who educated the communists and the Ukrainian people in the spirit of internationalism, peoples' friendship and selfless loyalty to the great ideas of Leninism. Comrade N. S. Khrushchev enjoyed great authority among the communists and all workers in Ukraine and, relying on their support, thwarted Kaganovich's provocations by all means. And if we find that the outstanding communist poet and Lenin Prize winner Maksym Rylsky is here today among us delegates to the Twenty-second Party Congress, and if many other Ukrainian literary workers continue to struggle actively for the party cause, then we must above all thank the courage and unbending will of Nikita Sergeevich Khrushchev for this.[32]

The settling of accounts with Stalin reached its apogee at the Twenty-second CPSU Congress with the decision "On the Removal of

Stalin's Body from the Lenin Mausoleum and its Burial in the Kremlin Wall." The delegates extended their massive attacks on the "anti-party group" from Molotov, Kaganovich, Malenkov and Shepilov to K. E. Voroshilov, N. A. Bulganin, M. G. Pervukhin and M. Z. Saburov, who were considered to be fellow-travellers of the former group. The charges against the "anti-party group" were formulated in such a way that—apart from crimes attributed to individual members—each of them was depicted as an inspirer of Stalin's crimes and, in particular, an opponent of the party's new course under Khrushchev. The proposal to remove Stalin's corpse from the mausoleum was made by representatives of party organizations that had been particularly damaged by Stalin's terror. I. V. Spiridonov, first secretary of the Leningrad oblast committee, gave a detailed account of the terror in 1935–7 (after Kirov's murder) and 1949–50 (the Leningrad affair) and added: "One cannot become reconciled to the fact that, next to Vladimir Ilich Lenin, to whom not only the workers but also honest people from all over the world come in a constant stream, there lies a man who stained his name with great injustice."[33] The delegates who addressed this subject included P. N. Demichev, first secretary of the Moscow City Committee, and G. D. Dzhavakhishvili, chairman of the Georgian Council of Ministers. Pidhorny closed the debate on the mausoleum:

> As early as 1956, after they had familiarized themselves with the materials of the Twentieth CPSU Congress, the communists and workers in Soviet Ukraine and the other republics expressed the opinion that Stalin's body should not lie in the shrine of the Soviet peoples and the workers of the world—V. I. Lenin's Mausoleum.[34]

In the name of the Leningrad, Moscow, Ukrainian and Georgian delegations, Pidhorny was commissioned to present a draft resolution "On V. I. Lenin's Mausoleum," which was adopted and approved by the party congress.

Reaction in Ukraine: "Back to Truth!"

The campaign against the crimes and excesses of the personality cult set off a chain reaction among the Soviet population. In Ukraine, the cultural intelligentsia pressed for complete exposure of all the crimes committed under Stalin and a radical settling of accounts with Stalin himself. At a party meeting of Kievan writers held on 21 November 1961, members who had attended the event as official delegates presented a report on the Twenty-second CPSU Congress. The first speaker was Pavlo Tychyna:

We writers, myself in particular, believed Stalin. We wrote about him in our articles, songs and, especially, collective poems composed in the name of all writers for festive occasions. Similar glorification was noted not only among the artists of the word but also among other professions. Accordingly, all delegates to the Twenty-second CPSU Congress felt joy when, in his report to the Twenty-second Party Congress, Nikita Serhiiovych said: "During the Twentieth Party Congress the party unmasked the personality cult. By implementing the resolutions of the party congress, it eliminated distortions and errors and established measures that were intended to prevent the repetition of such errors in the future...." I repeat once more: Only the party had the strength to resolve something like this. Its authority now rises to an immense height.[35]

The speech delivered by Korniichuk was of greater political significance. He tried to reassure the Ukrainian intelligentsia about several ambiguous passages in chapter 4 of the new party programme on "The Tasks of the Party in the Field of National Relations." (Incidentally, this document, which is replete with the frivolous concepts, theses and prognoses that were so typical of Khrushchev, is still valid today.) One passage in question maintained that between 1971 and 1980 the Soviet Union would create the economic and socio-political preconditions for the construction of a communist society: "By virtue of this a communist society will be basically constructed in the Soviet Union." The creation of such a society would change the relations between the nations of the USSR:

With the victory of communism in the USSR the nations will come even closer to one another, their economic and ideological unity will grow still further, and the common communist traits of their spiritual character will develop. Nevertheless, the disappearance of national differences, especially in language, is a process that will take a considerably longer time than the disappearance of class differences.[36]

Korniichuk noted that such changes could not be brought about by decrees, but his reassurances did not go beyond the official interpretation, and left considerable scope for manoeuvre and manipulation without decrees, such as the enforced Russification of the school system and scholarly publications. Korniichuk vehemently condemned the argument dating from Stalinist times that the peasant backgrounds of a part of the Ukrainian intelligentsia had been primarily responsible for their attitudes and actions. Quoting Lenin, he urged his Ukrainian colleagues to remember the life and works of writers like Blakytny, Kulish and Kurbas and never again to permit the impoverishment of Ukrainian literature. He suggested the publication of a "Library of the Great Twenties" to popularize the works of forgotten writers who had perished under Stalin. Other speakers discussed Kaganovich's activities in Ukraine in 1947, especially the persecution of young writers and literary scholars. The wave of anti-Stalinism gained momentum in Ukraine, and reformers demanded the fullest possible analysis of the events of the Stalin era. Initially, the Ukrainian party leadership supported these hopes.

On 9 November 1961 First Secretary Pidhorny gave the principal speech at a meeting of the Kiev city oblast party organizations. Referring to the developments after the Twenty-second CPSU Congress as "a fresh wind ... in the party," he asked: "Why was there so much more talk about the anti-party group at the Twenty-second Party Congress?" The answer was that these hypocrites had not given up their old tactics. They had made no effort to help the party to eliminate the consequences of the personality cult, had persisted in their erroneous views and had used "the party's humane attitude toward them to develop activities directed against the party." Many of the speakers recalled the crimes of Stalin's time. I. D. Nazarenko, director of the Institute of Party History attached to the CC CPU, provided a new insight: "Kaganovich tried to destroy a number of important party documents, and it is only thanks to Nikita Sergeevich Khrushchev that these documents were saved."[37]

The third plenum of the Ukrainian Writers' Union was held in Kiev in 1962. The main report, delivered by Oles Honchar, began by stressing the positive effects that de-Stalinization had had on Soviet Ukrainian literature:

> Regrettably, the phase of the cult of Stalin's personality is known to us not only by virtue of the fact that it put shackles on creativity, oriented art toward false pomp, a ceremonial style, ode-writing, and fanned intrigues and bickering in literary circles. Another reason why the memories of these days weigh heavily on us is that, at the time, some deep wounds were inflicted on us and our culture by the physical annihilation of a number of gifted artists who have now been completely and justly rehabilitated.[38]

Months of impassioned discussion had divided Ukrainian writers. One group, loyal to the party, was still very much tied to the past. Another group was made up of the cautious writers who, after long hesitation and consideration, supported the new course for fear of conflict with the party. At the same time there was a strong group of young writers who wanted total de-Stalinization and defended the rights of the republic and Ukrainian culture uncompromisingly. The first signs of a conflict between the generations emerged. The young writers blamed many well-known and respected older colleagues for having supported or even participated in the illegal practices of the past out of sheer opportunism and careerism. After the Twenty-second CPSU Congress, these young men and women proclaimed: "Back to Truth!" According to *Literaturna hazeta*, among those who issued this call were the poet Dmytro Pavlychko, Ivan Dziuba (then little known) and, among the representatives of the older generation,

Borys Antonenko-Davydovych, who had been persecuted in the 1930s and had spent several years in labour camps.[39]

At the writers' plenum, Pavlychko formulated his viewpoint: "Only one thing can help us best to solve a variety of important literary problems—the truth. This is not only a matter of the mind but—what is most important—a matter of our hearts." Because of the falsehoods in Stalin's time, he said, a large number of people in the Soviet Union had been "lost to us." The return to truth was also a dominant theme in the speech of Dziuba, who noted the progress made since the Twenty-second CPSU Congress in revealing the social and national life of the Ukrainian people "in a truer light and with greater concern for its essence."[40]

At this time Mykhailo Stelmakh was a popular writer in Ukraine. His novel *Pravda i kryvda*, for which he was awarded a Lenin Prize, was the first to deal with the problems faced by Ukrainian peasants during Stalin's collectivization. Dziuba praised this novel, remarking that it should mark the beginning of a new stage in Ukrainian literature. Pointing to the dangerous consequences of the Stalin cult for the education of youth, he said: "We just have to picture the complex ideological and psychological atmosphere in which our youth took shape during the personality cult and we will see how great is the scope of activity for the present-day writer." He reminded the plenum that there were still pro-Stalinist circles in Ukraine which believed that the past should be left uncovered. But, he declared, "How can we understand the present if we do not know the past!"[41]

Reporting on the plenum, *Literaturna hazeta* noted: "At the present time a natural creative trend toward originality, colourfulness, artistic serendipity and a unique world outlook is beginning to show itself among our young poets and prose writers." The literary critic L. Novychenko felt that this trend harboured dangers of formalism, to which Dziuba retorted that this was a way of playing down the problem of new literature and that the works of the younger poets contained "new ideational motifs [that] do not appear in the works of their older colleagues."

Speakers at the plenum urged a renewal of literary style. The younger generation's position at the plenum was so strong that even the main speaker, Honchar, decided to support them: "Realism can never be viewed as something stable and immutable.... Even if it is mainly our young people who are critical of the 'traditionalist artists,' this can never be attributed to 'ill winds from the West.'... Dogmatism is a false god that you cannot cast into the Dnieper with a single motion."[42]

The Writers' Rebellion

By the end of 1962 a sense of unease pervaded cultural life in Ukraine, especially in the universities, writers' organizations and clubs. The dominant question was: Why is the party concealing the truth about Stalinism? The intelligentsia wanted an end to the regulation and administration of art and literature. It also demanded the recognition of progressive styles as co-equal with socialist realism providing that they maintained "communist principles." Some representatives of the intelligentsia upheld the inviolability of the Ukrainian language and its function as an integral part of communist education. Others called for a consistent policy of rehabilitation.

Writers discussed these questions at a high emotional level. The party wanted to preserve its influence in all fields, but it was aware that a hard-line course would only build up greater tension. Even party conservatives like Skaba, CC CPU secretary for ideological work, Iu. Iu. Kondufor, head of the Central Committee Department for Science and Culture, and H. H. Shevel, head of the Central Commitee Department for Propaganda and Agitation, tried to steer a cautious course. Kondufor led the movement to eliminate the consequences of the personality cult in scholarship, including the social sciences. At the All-Union Conference of the Heads of Social Science Faculties held in Moscow from 30 January to 2 February 1962:

> Iu. Iu. Kondufor raised the question of establishing conditions for creative activity on the part of teachers. No university discipline, he said, is subject to such formal regulation as the social sciences. This encourages the levelling of the individual characteristics in the sector and makes it impossible to react swiftly to current events.[43]

An example of the uncertainty that infected the party bureaucracy at this time is an article by Skaba that appeared in *Komunist Ukrainy*. In a conciliatory tone, Skaba made an effort to allay the generational conflict among the intelligentsia without denigrating its younger representatives:

> A typical feature of literature and art in our days is the arrival of creative young people, whose success will depend on talent and work, on the degree to which they are involved in the life of the people and the depth of their understanding of the Communist party's policies. It is only necessary to warn the young artists against pseudo-innovation and a nihilistic attitude toward the works of the older generation. We must give young people our help at the right time; stern, but well-meant help. We must correct them tactfully and warn them against deviations from the overall path along which the art and literature of socialist realism are developing. One feature of the personality cult in art and literature was the attempt to administer these subjects. Today no one will try to impose his subjective tastes and personal preferences on artists, because this leads to a levelling of the authors' individual characteristics, to an impoverishment of genre, style and forms. The party leadership is primarily an ideological leadership. The communist, be he an artist or a party official, cannot stand on the sidelines in the struggle for the ideological purity of our *Weltanschauung* in the field of artistic creativity. All we need to do is to conduct the discussion of the phenomena in art and literature with convincing arguments, with the noble wish to help the cause.[44]

The rebellious young writers were led by poets: Lina Kostenko, Ivan Drach, Mykola Vinhranovsky, Vitalii Korotych, Ievhen Hutsalo and Hryhorii Kyrychenko. Lina Kostenko, whose poems often criticized the party, was very popular. Ivan Drach's verse was appreciated even by official literary critics. In his courageous symbolic poem *The Knife in the Sun*, he describes how he roamed Ukraine in the company of an "eternal devil." The most moving passage in the poem is the description of a visit with an old widow who had lost three sons: one near Berlin, one near Warsaw and the third in the purges of 1937. It was clear that the bereaved mother was a symbol for the Ukrainian people.

The Lviv literary critic M. Rudnytsky reported that throughout its entire history, the city of Lviv had never experienced such all-embracing criticism as at one particular students' meeting. The Ukrainian Writers' Union now organized regular literary evenings for young poets to present their latest works. Russian and Belorussian authors took part in one such event held in Kiev in May 1962. In a speech delivered at the meeting, S. Kryzhanivsky, a literary critic who sympathized with the young poets' desire to experiment, said: "I think that, after a phase of inactivity and stagnation like the one caused in our literature by certain social factors, we now need renewal through experimentation, perhaps even failure on the part of one poet or another, for this can make an important contribution to the further development of our poetry." In his closing speech at the same meeting, Tychyna declared: "I fully agree that our literary youth is gifted and strong. May it climb the creative heights as soon as possible."[45]

The development of literature surprised many of the older generation of writers and party officials. As a result of their attitude rather than their ambition, the *shestydesiatnyky* (the Sixties Group), as the young writers were called, found themselves increasingly in conflict with the older generation. They denounced Rylsky, Tychyna, Sosiura and others as opportunists for having supported Stalin, and declared their refusal to act as cynosures of political leadership for youth. Their position was enunciated during a meeting of the Kiev writers' union. As reported in *Literaturna Ukraina* (2 November 1962), Iu. Zbanatsky, the main speaker, declared:

> It is unfortunate that a part of our young literary talent is in such artificial opposition to the older generation. Some young people are shackled by foreign literary fashions. They are trying to transplant the modernist exercises of individual foreign authors onto Soviet soil and forget the great tradition of our literature's classical writers.

Oles Honchar's contribution to the discussion struck a different tone: "There is no doubt that our young people have brought a lot of freshness and individuality to literature. We view them as our successors." He made a plea to try to defuse the conflict: "Older generations of writers began under somewhat different conditions, and we should not forget that, even under the personality cult, works appeared that were worthy of the Soviet people and its cause.... We must not erase the achievements of the older generation and we must not isolate ourselves from them."[46] This was a voice from the middle generation of authors, who tried to act as mediators, although they made no secret of their sympathy for the younger talents. The speeches delivered by representatives of the *shestydesiatnyky* were not published, and their conflict with the party apparatus deepened. The following brief poem by Vinhranovsky is an example of the kind of criticism the young writers directed at officialdom, although, let it be said, such criticism was not the only reason for the deteriorating relations: "Enough, enough! I am weary from shame for the apes who learned to speak, slowly, dully, dumbly, presumptuously, who speculated with our age's name!"

While such literary critics as Mykola Sheremeta and Mykola Ushakov became increasingly hostile toward the younger writers, other critics—Stepan Kryzhanivsky, Ivan Dziuba, Ievhen Sverstiuk, Iosyf Kyselev, Mykola Sydoriak and Kuzma Hryb—defended them.

One reason for the deterioration in the position of the younger literary generation in Ukraine was that the Moscow leadership was caught unawares by similar processes in the Russian cultural centres, especially Moscow, and in all the non-Russian republics. The central apparatus was concerned that public opinion favoured the younger writers, many of whom (for example, the Russian, Evgenii Evtushenko) enjoyed great popularity. The bold demands of young Belorussian writers for a renaissance of their national culture also surprised Moscow. One of the "rebellious" writers' central concerns was to raise the standard of Soviet literature and, at the same time, to promote the development of contemporary cultural forms of the national republics; young authors wrote demonstratively only in their native tongues. Eventually, Khrushchev decided to take personal charge of the campaign against the young rebels.

The Hard Line Restored

A plenary session of the CC CPU, convened from 9 to 11 August 1962, discussed two problems: the development of the economy of the Ukrainian SSR and problems of ideological work. In his report to the plenum, Skaba, the CC secretary responsible for ideology, declared: "The most important task of ideological work in the light of the directives of the Twenty-second CPSU Congress is to educate Soviet people in the spirit of patriotism, peoples' friendship, socialist internationalism, and the struggle against symptoms of hostile ideologies, especially Ukrainian bourgeois nationalism." Historians, economists and literary scholars, said Skaba, should stand at the forefront of this battle. Reviewing the latest cultural developments among younger writers and artists in Ukraine, he said:

> Among the creative intelligentsia we also find people who, under the pretence of combatting administration [of the arts], are trying to compromise the very idea of party leadership in literature and art. They demand a brand of creative "freedom" that would be completely free of communist ideology. We must explain to these comrades that, in our society, barriers that prevent the artist from developing his creative individuality do not and cannot exist, provided that his activity serves the people's interests. Unfortunately, such demagogic attacks, such attempts to impose alien views on our ideology do not always receive the rebuff they deserve from the heads of the creative unions and some leading artists.[47]

During the discussion there were no calls for a tougher ideological course, not even in the form of the main theses in Skaba's report. Only V. V. Kulyk, a secretary of the Ukrainian Komsomol's Central Committee, spoke of shortcomings and abuses in the education of creative youth and the work of the Komsomol organizations. The plenum was also addressed by Shelest, then first secretary of the Kiev oblast committee, who discussed economic problems and praised the intelligentsia's participation in ideological work. He did, however, criticize the poor artistic quality of films produced at the Dovzhenko Studios in Kiev and shortcomings in publishing activity, especially in the work of the *Radianskyi pysmennyk* publishing house.[48]

Meanwhile, under Khrushchev's supervision, the CPSU leadership prepared an all-out offensive against writers who refused to support the party line. On 17 December 1962, leading party and government officials met with representatives of the cultural intelligentsia in Moscow and stated bluntly that the dissent that had spread throughout the Soviet Union must be stopped. The main speech at the meeting was delivered by Moscow's chief ideologist, F. Ilichev. Taking up the party's attack against "formalism" and "modernism," he criticized several Russian writers and artists and reiterated that "the development of art and literature is determined by our party's programme."[49] Ilichev also implied that Khrushchev's visit to a Moscow art exhibition and critical remarks about modern and abstract art had motivated the party's new offensive.

The critical remarks about the modernists and formalists applied ipso facto to the *shestydesiatnyky*. That the party as yet had not begun to persecute young artists and writers is borne out by an article by Rylsky that first appeared in the Kiev evening newspaper *Vechirnii Kyiv* and was later reprinted by *Literaturna Ukraina* on 29 January 1963. In this article Rylsky recalled how Lenin had defended writers and artists when they "sought the best means of expression": "Every artist, including the man of letters, seeks the best means to express his own ego and to describe the world around him. If the search is called off, art ends. Young artists seek, too. A cohort of young poets in Russia and Ukraine are on a quest." Rylsky supported the view that there was no need to flatter Ukraine's literary youth, but, he said, "Under no circumstances should we place them under a cold shower."

The Moscow apparatus then began a massive campaign against Ilya Ehrenburg—probably on Khrushchev's initiative. Ehrenburg was accused of influencing literary youth "in the wrong direction." At the same time a similar action was instituted against Viktor Nekrasov, a Russian author who lived in Ukraine. *Novyi mir* ceased publication of Nekrasov's impressions of a trip to the United States after two installments. The article had criticized the supervision of Soviet tourists and warned against painting an over-simplified picture of life in America. Nekrasov also wrote a satire about a tourist from Kiev who was prevented from taking a close look at anything during his visit to America but was considered competent to lecture on that country when he returned to Kiev. When the tourist was unable to answer questions from the public, his excuse was that he had not taken an interest in the subjects concerned. His decrial of alcoholism in the United States elicited derision from his questioners.

Nekrasov and Ehrenburg were the prime targets of Khrushchev's biting attacks at a second meeting between officials and the intelligentsia, which was held in Moscow on 7–8 March, 1963. The Ukrainian party apparatus received advance notice of the meeting with instructions to make the appropriate "preparations." At the beginning of March 1963 an enlarged session of the Commission for Literary Criticism of the Ukrainian Writers' Union was convened to hear the first open attack on those who had supported the *shestydesiatnyky*, mainly Dziuba, Sverstiuk and Svitlychny. Their most vehement critic was V. Kozachenko.[50] Ilichev and Khrushchev addressed the Moscow meeting. The subtitle (and leitmotif) of Khrushchev's speech was: "Unity with the Party and People—The Most Important Principle of Our Art." The speech was a typically Khrushchevian concoction of reminiscences and fiery tirades against certain writers.

> In the last years of his life Stalin was a very sick man who suffered from suspicion and a persecution mania.... If the Ukrainian Bolsheviks had yielded to Stalin's whims at that time, the Ukrainian intelligentsia would certainly have suffered great losses, and a "Ukrainian nationalist affair" (*delo*) would probably have been created.[51]

Khrushchev blamed "imperialist espionage services" for taking advantage of Stalin's disease and supplying him with such 'affairs' and 'documents'. He castigated "Comrade Ehrenburg" for subverting the morals of young writers like Evtushenko. Of others he said: "The trip made to France by the writers Viktor Nekrasov, Konstantin Paustovsky and Andrei Voznesensky left an unpleasant impression. Valentin Kataev was careless in statements he made during his trip to America." Khrushchev also criticized aspects of Evtushenko's visit to France and West Germany. He ended his speech with an appeal to the intelligentsia: "We call on all Soviet literary and artistic workers, the party's true helpers, to close their ranks even further and to strive under the leadership of the Leninist Central Committee to achieve new successes in the construction of communism."[52]

The main speech on behalf of the Ukrainian writers attending the meeting was delivered by Andrii Malyshko, who had been criticized by the party on several occasions, despite his adherence to "socialist realism." He was one of the writers who championed the rights of the Ukrainian language, and this alone was sufficient to draw charges of "nationalist deviations." Although no friend of the *shestydesiatnyky*, Malyshko adamantly opposed persecuting them. In his Moscow speech he eschewed attacks against young writers and instead condemned formalism and abstractionism, noting that certain Stalinist dogmas now "covered by the stagnant water of untruth and wretched opportunism" were partly responsible for such reactions. He stressed the defence of national literatures and regretted that in a country like Yugoslavia (which he had recently visited), he was unable to find books by Ukrainian, Belorussian, Uzbek, Turkmenian, Azerbaidzhani, Armenian, Georgian, Latvian, Estonian and other non-Russian writers.

Shortly after this meeting *Radianska Ukraina* published declarations of solidarity with Khrushchev. Volodymyr Sosiura wrote of "Nikita Sergeevich Khrushchev's precise and stirring speech" and of how the people "oppose abstractionism and formalism in art." He endorsed Khrushchev's demand that writers should create new patriotic works but warned against indifference to "negative phenomena in our life" and "embellishing reality." The Lviv writer Volodymyr Gzhytsky, a victim of the personality cult, also agreed with Khrushchev that "only those people who are in a position to do good with their works can write about this period of history, not those who seek sensations and find gratification in new themes."[53] Ukrainian writers attacked Ehrenburg and Evtushenko, but Nekrasov escaped with relatively mild criticism. The purpose was apparently to divert attention from the problems of the Ukrainian literary establishment.

A republican conference of members of the Ukrainian creative intelligentsia and ideological officials was held in Kiev on 8–9 April 1963. In the principal speech Skaba declared that "Ukraine's writers, artists and composers stood and stand by the party's Marxist-Leninist positions, have consistently defended and continue to defend the ideological purity of literature and art, the principles of socialist realism." Skaba cited many new books and musical compositions to prove that Ukraine's cultural development was following the guidelines set by the party. "Only a few artists," he said, "damage themselves with themes like reprisals, despotic actions and illegality under Stalin." He assured the party that the activities of these writers did not endanger the republic's cultural development, but that the campaign against them should not be relaxed. Skaba praised V. Kolomiiets, V. Korotych, V. Symonenko, R. Tretiakov and M. Som, whose works, he said, were "imbued with lively and joyful chords, with love for the party and people." For M. Vinhranovsky, I. Drach and L. Kostenko, however, Skaba had nothing but criticism.[54]

Pidhorny's speech at the conference was much harsher in tone. He warned against "imperialist propaganda" and the hundreds of foreign "institutes" and "scholarly centres" that were studying social and political life in Ukraine in order to propagate ideas inimical to socialism. Basically, Pidhorny reiterated the theses propounded by Khrushchev at the Moscow meeting. He attacked Drach, Vinhranovsky, the playwright S. Holovanivsky and Professor Fainerman of the Kiev Polytechnic Institute, all of whom had expressed open support for abstractionism. Pidhorny also reproached Ukrainian critics for their permissive attitude toward Nekrasov and accused them of lacking principles.[55] Since Pidhorny delivered his speech shortly before his recall to Moscow, it may be assumed that he was propounding the official viewpoint of the central apparatus, which diverged considerably from the views of the Ukrainian party bureaucracy. His tirade against *Literaturna Ukraina*, which he accused of contributing to the popularization of literary works of a low ideological and artistic quality, boded ill for that newspaper.

The conference reached a climax with the statement made by Vinhranovsky:

> After the Kremlin meeting and after the republican ideological conference I thought things over. I saw many things in a new light and changed my attitude. I am very grateful to the comrades who criticized some of my poems in the spirit of comradeship. I accept this criticism. I never wanted to set the writers of the younger generation against the older. I myself am a sergeant. I remember Oleksandr Dovzhenko and I want to learn from him love for my people, modesty and a sense of artistic principle.... To the pitiable pygmies from Europe's nationalist refuse-dumps I would like to declare loudly: I will never hand bread to the enemy from my own house. I would like to reiterate that I was never Ehrenburg's disciple and that I will do everything to be a son and servant of the people. I am most deeply aware that I must prove all this with deeds, as I was advised to do at the republican ideological conference. What does this mean in concrete terms? It means that I must go to my heroes. They are everywhere in my fatherland's wide fields.[56]

Drach and Korotych endorsed this self-criticism, although the latter made an effort to soften the condemnation of those authors who had committed "errors."

The brunt of the party's criticism was borne by Dziuba, who, according to *Literaturna Ukraina*, gave a speech that "boiled down to a general insult and was, in parts, absurd and tactless." Dziuba spoke so frankly and uncompromisingly that representatives of the older generation, such as Holovanivsky, who had expressed solidarity with the young writers, dissociated themselves from some of his theses. Incidentally, none of the literary critics who attended the conference asked for permission to speak, a fact that was noted with regret.[57]

The representatives of the large group of Russian and Russian-writing authors who lived in Ukraine, excepting Nekrasov, supported the party line unreservedly. They followed the discussion in the Ukrainian literary world with anxiety, especially when it concerned the rights of the republics and their languages. The Russian-writing author Ivan Riadchenko stated in *Literaturna Ukraina* that: "There is a large cohort of Russian poets in Ukraine. I am glad that there is not a single adherent of this new-fangled modernism among them."[58]

In 1963 the CPU began to stress the necessity of intensifying ideological work. An editorial on this subject in *Komunist Ukrainy* attacked "literary critics who have adopted a liberal attitude toward I. Drach, M. Vinhranovsky and I. Dziuba"—who, on account of their "political immaturity," had succumbed to the influence of enemy propaganda by imitating the worst features in the works of Ehrenburg, Nekrasov, Evtushenko and Voznesensky. Thus they had begun to produce ideologically false works and were addicted to formalistic gimmicks:

> Only a weakening of political vigilance can explain why our literary and artistic criticism did not provide a timely evaluation of these false and ideologically immature works ... and even praised these works as in the case of the well-known critic L. Novychenko, who advertised the formalistic exercises of the aforementioned I. Drach. Some of our newspapers and magazines, especially *Literaturna hazeta, Dnipro* and *Prapor*, as well as publishing houses and theatres neglected the principles and demands of the party. This also contributed to the propagation in art of works that were of no use to the people.[59]

The same line was taken by Malanchuk, then secretary of the Lviv industrial oblast committee. In an article in *Komunist Ukrainy*, he described the progress of the "abstractionists" and "formalists" in Western Ukraine:

> A group of formalist "theoreticians" even surfaced at the Lviv Institute of Applied and Decorative Art. The subject was discussed at a meeting of the

CPU oblast committee bureau. Measures were taken to remedy the situation at the institute and reinforce the teaching body. We cannot entrust the education of our creative youth to people who try to lead them onto the false path.[60]

Malanchuk gave a detailed account of the debates about culture in Western Ukraine and the demands of the intelligentsia, who wanted "the rehabilitation not only of certain persons but also of their ideas." Malanchuk decried the "erroneous ... efforts of some literary scholars to show the literature of the past as a uniform literary stream, to popularize the works of former proponents of bourgeois nationalism or, at least, to achieve their partial rehabilitation." Some young and inexperienced writers and artists, said Malanchuk, who wanted to slip into the "role of the foremost fighters against the personality cult, paid excessive attention to the negative phenomena of this period and, furthermore, praised the works of Western authors like Erich Maria Remarque."[61]

On 4 May 1963 in *Pravda*, Malanchuk called for an intensification of the struggle against nationalist tendencies in Lviv oblast. The newspapers, he stated, should carry regular reports about the "servile role of the Ukrainian bourgeois nationalists [who] are in the service of American imperialism." Malanchuk reported that the oblast's campaign against religion had had several successes. The number of church weddings, he said, had decreased and the party was encouraging the celebration of such Soviet "holidays" as the "Day of Winter," and the "Day of Songs" in spring, instead of the religious feast days. Many districts, he added, also marked holidays such as the "Hammer and Sickle" and "Evenings of Workers' Glory."

At the plenary session of the CC CPSU held in June 1963, the ideological crackdown was stepped up. Central Committee Secretary Ilichev delivered the main report, entitled "The Current Tasks of the Party's Ideological Work." Many Ukrainians were surprised by the tactics used by Skaba. The latter included in his report on developments in Ukraine harsh criticism of Drach, Vinhranovsky and L. Kostenko, whose works the "Ukrainian nationalist ragtags abroad are so fond of quoting," but assured the Central Committee that many writers had already acknowledged and regretted their errors. He then made an unsubtle attempt to shift all the blame to Nekrasov, who, Skaba said, had written a letter to the CC CPU admitting that the criticism of his stories was justified, but at the same time had tried "to play down the political significance of his errors." Nevertheless, Skaba expressed the hope that some day Nekrasov and the few other writers from Moscow that supported him would recognize fully the error of their ways and "take their place in the ranks of the fighters for a New World."

Surprisingly, Skaba criticized the still valid decrees on historiography dating from the *Zhdanovshchina*:

We cannot accept that the biographies of the tsars, princes and generals take up so much of the history curriculum in secondary schools. We may take the textbook *History of the USSR* used in the ninth grade at secondary schools as an example. Frankly speaking, some chapters of this textbook have "tsarist" titles: "Tsar Fedor Alekseevich," "Sophia's Regency," "Tsarina Sophia," "Tsar Peter's Youth," "The Beginning of Catherine II's Regency," "Paul I." At the same time the textbook does not give enough space to the class struggle and other socio-economic problems. Of the thirty-four pages in chapter one, only one is devoted to describing the peasant uprising under K. Bulavin. Equally little space is devoted to the Pugachev and other popular rebellions against slavery.

"In the name of the Ukrainians," Skaba profusely thanked the party and the government for the decision to celebrate the upcoming 150th anniversary of the death of the Ukrainian poetess Lesia Ukrainka and the 150th anniversary of the birth of Taras Shevchenko: "The nationwide commemoration of important representatives of scholarship and culture among the various peoples is of substantial importance for the inculcation of Soviet national pride and socialist internationalism."[62]

The death of the gifted Ukrainian poet Vasyl Symonenko on 13 December 1963 touched off unexpected political reactions in Ukraine. Symonenko, who was born in 1935 and joined the party in 1960, left several collections of poetry that earned him broad recognition during his short life. Symonenko kept a journal that began only on 18 September 1962 and ended 20 September 1963. This brief document bears witness to the difficulties he experienced; how he was persecuted by the authorities. For example, the entry for 6 July 1963 states: "Last Sunday we were in Odessa, where the narrow-minded local officials amused us greatly with their idiotic fear that 'something might go wrong!' We were forbidden *de facto* to speak at a memorial evening in honour of Shevchenko. So quite a few people are still afraid of Taras today. Philistines of the Revolution!" In another entry he wrote: "*Literaturna hazeta* castrates my articles."[63]

Symonenko's death inspired a series of lectures on his life and works, which were held mainly in the high schools and institutions of higher learning. A collection of his poems was circulated in *samvydav*. The texts of lectures delivered by the literary critics Ivan Svitlychny and Ievhen Sverstiuk at a Symonenko memorial evening held at the Kiev Medical Institute in December 1963 have been preserved in *samvydav*, as have the texts of speeches given by Dziuba on 13 December 1964 (the thirtieth anniversary of the poet's birth) at the Republican House of Writers.[64]

Symonenko was not only an unusual literary personality but also a symbol of moral rectitude. Initially, the party tolerated Symonenko's popularity in Ukraine and even published some of his works posthumously. His journal and some of his poems, however, were anathema to party leaders. Their publication in the West—when Symonenko's popularity was ebbing in Ukraine—was greeted enthusiastically by Ukrainians abroad, especially in the United States and Canada. Memorial evenings were held to read his poems, and Western newspapers and magazines showed great interest in the life and works of this unusual poet. In Ukraine a dispute about Symonenko broke out between the party and writers who followed the party line, and members of the cultural intelligentsia. The former ran into trouble with their assertion that Symonenko's journal was a forgery. Although they did not dare to expunge his name from Ukrainian literature, they made every effort to minimize his importance. Many reference works gave him an incomplete biography and an edition of his collected works omitted several of his poems.

A constant in Ukraine's political development after 1953 was the courageous struggle for the rights of the Ukrainian language. In December 1962 seven pupils at a secondary school in Uman sent an open letter to the Institute of Linguistics at the Ukrainian Academy of Sciences in which they called for love, knowledge and cultivation of the mother tongue. The letter declared that although the Ukrainian language was a compulsory subject at secondary schools, the pupils had been unable for a variety of reasons to learn it perfectly. The letter evoked a positive reaction in teaching circles and was even published in *Radianska osvita*.[65]

At the All-Ukrainian Scientific Conference on the Cultivation of the Ukrainian Language, held on 11–15 February 1962, there were impressive demonstrations on behalf of the mother tongue. Several speakers condemned Russification, among them Lida Orel of Kiev University, M. Shestopal of the Faculty of Journalism at Kiev University, and V. F. Lobko, a veteran of the Second World War who worked at the Ukrainian Academy of Sciences. Interrupted repeatedly by applause, Lobko said:

> The people of the Soviet Union, among them the Ukrainians, supporting the decisions of the party congresses regarding the liquidation of the band of criminals, waged a decisive struggle against the evil that arose from the personality cult; and how strange, if not painful, that the consequences of this cult are with us today. Apparently the Stalin–Kaganovich disciples have power, since it is because of their opposition that the Ukrainian people have not been able to reclaim that which was forbidden by these criminals, have not been able to achieve that which is ordinary and natural, but which is most basic, most important and most sacred, that which all people possess—the privilege of education in the Ukrainian language...and the wide use of this language in all spheres of the life of our people.... The Ukrainian community has already more than once placed this question before responsible organizations of the republic, but to this day no results have been forthcoming. Moreover, they do not even reply to our proposals to introduce instruction in the native Ukrainian language in secondary and higher

educational institutions and to re-establish Ukrainian cultural institutions in
those districts where millions of Ukrainians live—Siberia, Kazakhstan, the
Far East and the Kuban.[66]

No Soviet Ukrainian newspapers reported this speech, but it appeared in
Nasha kultura, the supplement of the Ukrainian-language weekly *Nashe
slovo*, which is published in Warsaw. The growing influence of writers and
artists on public opinion prevented the CPSU from taking harsh measures
against the cultural intelligentsia. Also, although the security organs were
very active, the dissident question, with a few rare exceptions, had not yet
become a "police" concern.

At this time historical studies were of special significance for nationality
policy. From 18 to 21 December 1962 Moscow hosted an all-union
conference to discuss ways of improving the training of history teachers.
The conference was attended by some two thousand historians from all
republics, including history teachers and archive directors. In open debate
progressive historians defended their views in a manner that was no longer
possible by the 1970s. O. K. Kasimenko of Kiev criticized the
consequences of the Stalin cult for the history of the Ukrainian people and
the Ukrainian SSR: "During the Great Patriotic War Stalin was incapable
of understanding or assessing the magnificent contribution made by the
Ukrainian and other peoples of the Soviet Union in routing the German
conqueror." Touching on still unresolved questions, he said: "This
underestimation cost the partisan movement in Ukraine a very high price."
Kasimenko described the situation of Ukrainian historians under Stalin,
complained about the limitations imposed upon them for visits to socialist
and non-socialist countries, and demanded a fairer allocation of travel
permits.[67]

Suprunenko joined the progressive historians on this occasion and
criticized historical works published in Ukraine that still adhered to
Stalinist dogma. As an example he cited Strelsky's *The Basic Principles of
the Scientific Critique of Historical Research in the USSR* (Kiev, 1961),
in which the author had stated that Stalin's January 1930 speech was
essential for an understanding and interpretation of historical events.
Another example given by Suprunenko was *The History of the Ukrainian
State and Law* (1961), which glorified the period 1937–41 as "a flowering
of Soviet democracy, including the court system." According to the
authors, during these years the state had democratized the legal system,
perfected its structure and improved its operation. As Suprunenko saw it:
"Every reader was expected to draw the conclusion that the massive and
groundless reprisals were in keeping with the tasks of strengthening and
developing socialist society. And this sort of thing was being written in
1961!"[68] Suprunenko then demanded more substantial research on the
national-liberation movements in Russia's outlying regions and condemned

biased analyses that dealt only with "the struggle against bourgeois nationalism."

Another meeting devoted to nationality problems took place in a similarly tolerant atmosphere. This was the Moscow session of the Scientific Council of the USSR Academy of Sciences held under the title "The History of the Great Socialist October Revolution." The main theme was the nationalities problem before and during the revolution. The chairman of the council, academician I. I. Mints, criticized Stalin's thesis that in February 1917 the national movement in the outlying regions of the Russian empire was essentially a bourgeois liberation movement. Moreover, M. S. Dzhunusov accused Stalin of having ignored Lenin's thesis on the dual and contradictory character of the socialist movement in oppressed nations.[69]

The Ukrainian historian S. M. Korolivsky of Kharkiv delivered a paper on "The Ukrainian National Liberation during the Preparation and Implementation of the Great Socialist October Revolution." He argued that, for most Ukrainians, as opposed to the Ukrainian bourgeoisie, "national" motives had been relatively unimportant. He maintained that the workers' and peasants' goals (e.g., the overthrow of the monarchy, an end to the war and the expropriation of the big estates) were largely identical with those of the Ukrainian National Council. (*Ukrainska Natsionalna Rada*) founded in Lviv on 18 October 1918. According to Korolivsky, "despite its moderation, inconsistency and opportunism, the council's nationality policy during the period of coalition rule bore traces of belligerent democratism insofar as it coincided objectively with the demands of the masses and was, therefore, positive in character."[70]

The second half of 1963 and, to an even greater extent, 1964 saw a deterioration in the domestic political situation in Ukraine. Backed by the security organs, party ideologists identified reformists with the "bourgeois nationalists" aiding the Soviet state's enemies abroad. Newspapers published a growing number of denunciations of the activities of religious believers, in particular, members of the Greek Catholic Church in Western Ukraine. In 1963 the authorities tried, through deception or outright force, to abort meetings organized in honour of famous Ukrainian writers. In a memorandum to the Ukrainian Writers' Union, Ivan Dziuba described incidents connected with the legal celebration of the fiftieth anniversary of the death of Lesia Ukrainka. A *samvydav* document describes how the ceremony, scheduled to be held in Kiev's Central Culture and Recreation Park on the evening of 17 August 1963, was disrupted by the authorities. Following some scuffles, the organizers moved the ceremony to a park near the Dynamo Stadium. While Dziuba made a speech and a number of writers, including Ivan Drach and Mykola Vinhranovsky, read poetry, groups of thugs tried to break up the meeting.[71] The disturbers, notably, did not include Komsomol members, several of whom took part in the ceremony.

In another effort to regain influence among the Ukrainian population, "certain" party circles encouraged anti-Semitism. In this context, Kychko became the central figure of a major scandal in Ukraine. The publication of his book *Judaism Without Embellishment* by the Ukrainian Academy of Sciences (which had not accepted his earlier books) sparked protests both in Ukraine and abroad. American Jewish organizations, Western communist parties and prominent fellow-travellers demanded an explanation. Thus the Kremlin instructed the party's ideological committee to dissociate itself from the most obnoxious passages of Kychko's opus.[72] Although critical reviews were published in Ukraine, only *samvydav* articles condemned Kychko's book outright. A review in *Radianska kultura*, the official organ of the Ministry of Culture, recalled the Holocaust and criticized the book's illustrations as "pretentious, carelessly executed and of a low artistic standard that could only insult believers"; it failed to mention, however, that these "illustrations" were caricatures in the style of the Nazi party newspaper *Der Stürmer*. The responsibility for the Kychko affair lay with Moscow's ideological apparatus, which was then headed by Ilichev and the same group of inveterate anti-Semites in Ukraine that had inspired the campaign against "Jews, cosmopolitans and bourgeois nationalists" shortly before Stalin's death.

One member of this group was the chief editor of *Literaturna Ukraina*, L. Dmyterko. On 15 October 1963 this newspaper published a newly discovered poem by the national bard, Ivan Franko. Describing the social conditions in Ukrainian villages at the turn of the century, the poem implied that the inn-keeper—a Jew—was to blame for the widespread alcoholism and indebtedness among the peasants. Ivan Franko, the author of the famous poem "Moses," which glorified the people of Israel, was a democrat and a socialist—certainly not an anti-Semite. Dmyterko, however, juxtaposed the poem with a report about the Kievan militia, which claimed that the police's most regular customers were the city's Jews. The report contained a photograph of a Jewish couple who had been arrested for black-marketeering.

These examples illustrate the tensions in Ukrainian society and the methods by which opponents of reform attempted to regain influence over the intelligentsia and youth. Such an atmosphere encouraged radicals to take extreme measures. On 24 May 1964, in what one *samvydav* document calls "a felony without parallel in the history of world culture," a psychotic Russophile, Pohruzhalsky, set fire to the public library of the Ukrainian Academy of Sciences in Kiev. The devastation was almost complete: invaluable books and documents, irreplaceable monuments of Ukrainian history and culture, were burnt. According to unconfirmed reports, the arsonist, who boasted of his "patriotic motives" during his trial, was sentenced to ten years' imprisonment. However, the security organs and the party made every effort to obscure the motivation behind the crime, and depicted Pohruzhalsky as a loner, even though he had asserted in court that he represented a political current. During the trial he recited Russophile poems, such as "Culture's Foes in Freedom Roam."[73] Despite protests from the West, Soviet authorities still conceal the titles of the books and documents that survived the fire or of which photocopies exist.

Important personnel changes were made in the Ukrainian leadership in June and July 1963. At the June plenum of the CC CPSU, Pidhorny moved to Moscow to take up a secretaryship in the CPSU. At the plenary session of the CC CPU held in the following month, Petro Shelest, a secretary in the CC CPU, was elected to succeed Pidhorny.[74] On 29 June a decree of the Presidium of the Ukrainian Supreme Soviet transferred Shcherbytsky "to other work" and replaced him as chairman of the Ukrainian Council of Ministers by I. P. Kazanets. The Ukrainian party leaders believed that they now had another advocate in the Soviet leadership in the person of Pidhorny. Despite tensions, the Ukrainian leadership continued to support Khrushchev as a matter of principle. They feared that his successor would move to the right in domestic and foreign policy, particularly in view of the split between the CPSU and the Communist Party of China. These fears were not entirely unfounded.

The Moscow–Peking Conflict as a New Factor in Foreign Policy

Much of the Soviet population was unable to understand the Moscow–Peking conflict for lack of information. Initially, the Soviet leaders had no desire to exacerbate differences with Red China. Ukraine harboured strong sympathies for China, with which it had a lively cultural exchange. The Ukrainian press gave extensive coverage to the month-long China tour undertaken by the Ukrainian Song and Dance Ensemble in August 1956. The ensemble gave twenty-two concerts to a total audience of two hundred thousand people. The press reports noted that the welcome signs at Peking's main station had been written in Chinese and Ukrainian.[75] The new course adopted by the Chinese Writers' Union ("Let a hundred flowers blossom, let a hundred schools of thought contend"), which was exactly what pro-reform communists in other socialist countries wanted, was widely discussed in Ukraine as soon as it was reported by the Soviet press.[76] Ukrainian writers felt that Peking's new course lent them additional support in their struggle against the remnants of the Stalin cult.

In October 1957 Ukraine made a special effort to mark the eighth anniversary of the Chinese People's Republic. A *Radianska Ukraina* editorial declared that:

> The friendly economic and cultural ties between Soviet Ukraine and the Chinese People's Republic are being strengthened and expanded on the basis of the fraternal relations between the Soviet and Chinese peoples. The number of translations from Chinese classical and modern literature increases in

Ukraine every year. On the other hand, the Chinese people display great interest in Ukrainian culture. The works of T. Shevchenko, I. Franko and other Ukrainian writers have been translated into Chinese. Several representatives of the Ukrainian people have visited China in the last three years. During the same time about seventy Chinese delegations came to Ukraine.[77]

The works of M. Kotsiubynsky, D. Korniichuk, W. Wasilewska, V. Sobko and several other Ukrainian writers were also translated into Chinese.[78] According to Ukrainian sources, between 1950 and 1957, thirty Ukrainian translations of Chinese literary works were published in a total edition of one million copies. Cultural co-operation between the two countries was led by the Ukrainian branch of the Soviet-Chinese Friendship Society, which was established in 1958 and had local chapters in a number of Ukrainian towns.[79]

When relations between Moscow and Peking deteriorated, reports about China vanished from the Ukrainian press. The presses of all Soviet republics limited themselves to statements and articles reprinted from the central press. Articles on Sino-Soviet relations by Ukrainian authors did not reappear until the second half of 1963. In September the CC CPU's department of propaganda and agitation organized protests against the Chinese leadership and forced scientists to participate. Henceforth, Moscow increased its efforts to mobilize the Ukrainian public against the Chinese. The first major article in this campaign was published by *Komunist Ukrainy* in September 1963. Its author, H. Starushenko, a specialist on the international communist and workers' movement, criticized China's strategy in the Third World.[80]

By 1964 anti-Chinese propaganda in Ukraine was approaching a peak. In April the CC CPU discussed the conflict at a plenary session attended by Pidhorny. However, the anti-Chinese campaign was limited by the Soviet leadership's inability to agree on a strategy. Documents published in later years show that some party leaders did not exclude the possibility of a reconciliation with Peking. The Soviet leaders' efforts to depict the Chinese leaders as representatives of conservative communism created unease in Ukraine, where Mao's popular slogan "Let a hundred flowers blossom" had nourished the hopes of the liberals.

Economic Reforms

Between 1953 and 1964 the Soviet leadership announced economic "reforms" and reorganization, most of which, however, were never implemented fully. The aim was to modernize and increase the efficiency of economic structures and operations. The reforms were inspired by Khrushchev, whose abundance of ideas and theories turned Ukraine into a vast field of experiment—frequently with unpredictable consequences.

According to a decree of the USSR Supreme Soviet of 17 June 1950, the USSR Council of Ministers consisted of thirty union and twenty-one union-republican ministries.[81] Most of Ukraine's major industries such as coal and metallurgy, machines and equipment, building and power, were directed from Moscow. After Stalin's death, the Presidium of the USSR Supreme Soviet decided to merge several ministries. On 26 April 1953 the number of union ministries was reduced from thirty to twelve and the number of union-republican ministries from twenty-one to thirteen.[82] These measures brought no benefits for the union republics, however. Exactly one year later, the USSR Supreme Soviet approved another change that increased the number of union ministries to twenty-four and that of the union-republican ministries to twenty-two.[83] This decree brought the first major changes for the republics, as a number of union ministries (coal, ferrous and non-ferrous metallurgy) were now given union-republican status. This led to a new phase in the union-wide development of the economy under the slogan: "More Rights for the Republics in the Economic Field!" In Ukraine between 1953 and 1956, over 10,000 enterprises and industrial organizations were put under Ukrainian control. This increased local responsibility for the industries in the republic from 36 per cent in 1953 to 76 per cent in 1956,[84] a development that was welcomed by both the CPU and those responsible for economic and industrial development. The press and specialist publications spoke of a new historical stage in the development of the Soviet Union, especially after Khrushchev declared a return to Leninist norms in the relations between the central government and the republics.

A heated debate about the changes took place within the CPSU leadership itself. It resolved finally that the central economic administration should be closer to the actual production process. This foresaw the elimination of bureaucratic excesses, rationalization of the forms and methods of management and better use of available resources. This question was discussed at a plenary session of the CC CPSU in February 1957, and on 10 May legislation for the improvement of organization and management in industry and construction was passed. The Presidium of the USSR Supreme Soviet decided to abolish ten union and fifteen union-republican ministries. Economic councils [*Sovety narodnogo khoziaistva* or *sovnarkhozy*] were made the supreme organs of economic management in the economic administrative regions. On the basis of lists approved by the USSR Council of Ministers, they were given responsibility for enterprises and organizations which had formerly been the domain of the union and union-republican ministries.[85]

The CC CPU met in a plenary session on 25–26 April 1957 to discuss the Presidium's decision and decided to establish eleven administrative economic regions in Ukraine, each with its own economic council.[86] At the end of May the Ukrainian Supreme Soviet abolished eleven union-republican and four republican ministries in accordance with the decree of the USSR Supreme Soviet. Two union-republican ministries, the Ministry of Construction and the Ministry of the Building Materials Industry, were given republican status.[87]

The Central Committee's decisions were preceded by a lively public debate about the theses on the improvement of industrial management. In Ukraine, two schools of thought emerged: the centralists, who were mostly former high-level ministerial bureaucrats and Gosplan (State Planning Commission) officials, tried to keep the number of economic regions and councils as low as possible. Their opponents, supported by the district and oblast party organizations, wanted to increase them. Political considerations—such as efforts to increase or retain influence—also played an important role in this controversy. At the April plenum of the CC CPU, the advocates of fewer economic regions prevailed.

Interesting nuances developed during the debate. Khrushchev thought that the economic councils should be guided primarily by Gosplan. Others favoured subordinating the councils to the Council of Ministers. The CC CPU wanted the Ukrainian Gosplan to be recognized as the most important state planning organ in the republic: "It should control the management of the economic planning carried out by the economic councils, the ministries and the oblast administration with regard to the fulfilment of the current and long-term plans and co-ordinate the economic work of the districts, oblasts, ministries and organizations."[88]

As we have seen, after Stalin's death the Ukrainian intelligentsia became more confident; their demands grew bolder, and they succeeded in advancing the republic's national interests. High-level Ukrainian party officials realized that the interests of the republic and social groups had to be considered in the decision-making process. Consequently, there was a corresponding growth of self-confidence among managers, economists and technical specialists. The economic reform of 1957 lent considerable impetus to this development.

One of the great ills of the Stalinist era—bureaucratic excess—was discussed during the third session of the Ukrainian Supreme Soviet in March 1957. It was pointed out that twenty-nine different ministries and authorities were involved in the procurement and export of wood in the republic, assisted by over 700 specialized organizations. The manufacture of furniture was handled by enterprises under the jurisdiction of thirty-five ministries and authorities, of which two-thirds had union or union-republican status. Thirty-two authorities were involved in the manufacture of tiles, fifty-nine in metal goods and thirty-eight in ready-made clothing (half of them with union status). Eleven ministries and authorities were responsible for the production of footwear. This excess jurisdiction resulted in a multiplication of command. In 1957, for example, seven billion kilometre-tons of cross-transports were registered in Ukraine, a figure that represented 20 per cent of the republic's total freight traffic. This particular idiocy cost 250 million rubles and half a million metric tons of coal. A typical example of the bureaucratic chaos was that the enterprises in Ivano-Frankivsk oblast, which is one of the country's chief timber sources, were supplied with wood from the north and east of the USSR, notably the Karelian ASSR and Arkhangelsk oblast.[89]

Although the reform decree was adopted only on 10 May, Khrushchev and his supporters demanded that it take effect as early as 1 June 1957. The haste with which this wide-ranging and complex plan was pushed through, however, had disastrous consequences for the subsequent development of the economy. Economic officials in Ukraine also pressed for early implementation of reform, which they saw as a means of eliminating current shortcomings and obstacles. That their approach was not devoid of "republican patriotism" is evident from a *Komunist Ukrainy* editorial that appeared shortly after the law was passed:

> As we all know, the Soviet Ukrainian economy occupies an important place in the country's overall economic balance. The republic supplies almost one-fifth of the entire industrial production of the USSR. In the past year alone our republic produced (in terms of the all-union plan) 48 per cent of the crude iron, almost 58 per cent of the steel, 39 per cent of the metal-sheeting, 56 per cent of the iron ore and 32 per cent of the coal. Ukraine now supplies 2.3 times more coal than France and produces more crude iron than England, France and other capitalist countries in Europe. In 1956, 35.5 billion kilowatt-hours of electricity were produced in the Ukrainian SSR, that is, 18 times more than in the whole of tsarist Russia or 65 times more than in the territory of Ukraine in 1912.[90]

A month later *Komunist Ukrainy* described the change in the republic's economy:

> From the following data we can see how the rights of the union republics, especially the Ukrainian SSR, have been expanded. In 1950, 65 per cent of the enterprises in Ukraine (measured by total production) were subordinated to union ministries, while 35 per cent were controlled by republican, oblast and district organizations. In 1956 the corresponding figures were 24 per cent and 76 per cent. Today, after the seventh session of the USSR Supreme Soviet, there are two lines of subordination for industry: first, the union-republican, which has been transferred to the competence of the economic councils, whose entire activity is subordinate to the Ukrainian Council of Ministers; second, the local, which is directly subordinate to the local soviets of workers' deputies. Such important questions as deciding the number of economic regions, the structure of each economic council, and the need for the continuing existence of certain republican ministries were also transferred to the republics' sphere of competence. This expansion of the union republics' rights is a clear demonstration of the Communist Party's wise Leninist nationality policy.[91]

In the West the Soviet reform of industrial management was interpreted as decentralization. In the Soviet Union, however, there was some doubt whether the reform constituted a decentralization or a perfected form of centralism. Khrushchev himself never spoke of decentralization. As the party press stressed at the time: "The party believes that centralism in economic management must never be weakened." *Partiinaia zhizn* commented on this thesis:

> We should consolidate and improve centralized planning; we should improve centralized statistics and financing, as well as control, to preserve state interests and state discipline. Any weakening of the principles of centralism would contradict the vital interests of the people and could stimulate parochial trends and the tendency to turn each economic region into a closed shop.... Experience shows that centralized leadership is the most basic element of a socialist economy.[92]

A number of people both in the West and in the Soviet Union believed that further development of the economic reform would bring it closer to the "Yugoslav model," a theory that the CPSU rejected as speculative. In the words of the party's theoretical journal, *Kommunist*:

> The Leninist principle of democratic centralism was forged in the struggle against the anarcho-syndicalist "theory" of the decentralization of economic management. In the first years of Soviet power, when small businesses had the lion's share in the country's economy and we lacked the experience of economic construction, there were people who opposed the principle of democratic centralism, centralized planning and state control of the economy. The so-called Workers' Opposition, for example, in 1920–1922 ... called for renunciation of centralized state control of the economy and the transfer of economic management to a proposed "producers' collective," which should be united in unionized production organizations. This was an anarcho-syndicalist position reflecting petty bourgeois attitudes.... It is surprising that there are now people abroad who repeat the principles of the Workers' Opposition. They are seriously trying to convince all and sundry that a decentralization of economic management and the creation of a local self-management mechanism as a basis for a society of free producers would be the best way to secure the victory and development of socialism in this country....[93]

Soon after the establishment of the economic councils, many people in Ukraine and the Soviet Union acclaimed the reforms as an important step toward recognition of the self-management system.[94] Khrushchev, however, maintained that a communist production system could only be organized and centralized on an all-union basis. He repeatedly declared that there could be no decentralization of economic management, especially in the period of the all-round construction of communism. Instead, the reform was an experiment aimed at greater harmony between the principles of centralized planning and a strengthening of democratic centralism.

The economic councils were regional organs charged with the administration of industry and construction within the borders of the administrative economic regions. They were managed by boards consisting of a chairman, a deputy chairman and the board members. The executive consisted of administrations or departments responsible for specific areas or branches of industry and construction. In Ukraine the reform increased the responsibility of the republic's main planning bodies.

The foremost problem at the beginning of the reform was the staffing of the economic councils. The council management tried to employ local cadres but at the same time leading executives and specialists from the dissolved union-republican ministries made a bid for the best jobs. The ranks of the latter were augmented by numerous prominent officials from the defunct union ministries. Thus, despite claims made by the Ukrainian press in June 1957 that the economic councils were "in principle" recruiting their staff "from the local cadres," by this time the leading managerial posts in such important industrial centres as Donetsk and Zaporizhzhia were already in the hands of men from Moscow.[95] This is illustrated by the following report on the staffing of the Zaporizhzhia Economic Council, whose chairman was the Ukrainian, Ivanovsky:

> Moscow has provided a considerable number of staff for the Economic Council. These include First Deputy Chairman Bakuna, who headed a department in the USSR Ministry for the Construction of Enterprises in the Metallurgical and Chemical Industry, and Deputy Chairman Korolev, formerly head of this ministry's Main Administration for Procurement.[96]

In 1957 personnel cuts were made throughout the Soviet Union. The number of officials employed by the state and economic administrations was reduced by 56,000, which meant a saving of approximately 600 million rubles but did not achieve any noticeable degree of rationalization. By 1958 it was obvious that administrative reorganization required "further improvement."

The first reports about the success of the reforms came from Ukraine. In one report we read:

> The advantages of the new system of managing industry and construction were proven convincingly in the very first months. The restructuring of management had an immeasurable moral-political and organizational effect: the role of the public organizations and the people employed in production management was strengthened; the management of the auxiliary organizations,

enterprises and institutions has improved significantly, becoming more concrete and efficient; the conditions created have been beneficial in eliminating clerical-bureaucratic methods (reducing correspondence, etc.); the enterprises and construction sites have been strengthened by qualified personnel. The great political significance of the reform is that it represents an important step forward in the implementation of Leninist nationality policy.[97]

In 1957 Ukrainian industry fulfilled the overall production plan by 104 per cent, a 10-per-cent improvement over the previous year. The ninth session of the USSR Supreme Soviet in December 1957 announced that various enterprises had requested higher planning figures for 1958 because they had found new reserves in their production capacity.[98] An increasing number of attacks on *mestnichestvo* or localism appeared in the press. The term was applied to economic council executives who gave priority to local rather than all-union obligations. Khrushchev viewed this as a form of bourgeois nationalism. But in Ukraine, the attacks were accompanied by glowing reports about the fulfilment and overfulfilment of the planning targets set by Ukraine's economic councils. The impetus for the massive campaign against localism came from Moscow, after both the economic councils and the republic had made their own adjustments to their all-union commitments. Khrushchev, for example, reported that while the Ukrainian SSR had fulfilled the meat-procurement plan for the first half of 1959 by 95 per cent, and had covered 92.1 per cent of its own needs, it had only delivered 47 per cent of the required amount to the all-union fund.[99]

In 1958 the Dnipropetrovsk economic council was held up as an example of localism, in spite of the region's considerable increase in industrial production. The council had permitted local enterprises to deliver their products primarily to other enterprises in the region, thus ensuring an adequate local supply of raw materials and semi-finished products at the expense of deliveries to other economic regions. Moreover, the council was guilty of localism in capital investment; appropriations were diverted to undertakings such as the construction of housing, for example—that benefited the local population rather than the central planners.[100]

CPU Secretary Shcherbytsky committed himself to the campaign against localism. In one article he reported that the Stalino (Donetsk) and Luhansk (Voroshylovhrad) economic councils' deliveries of coal to other republics had fallen short by 44,000 metric tons in the first four months of 1958, while two million metric tons of fuel had been supplied for local needs. Ten of the thirty-three machine manufacturers in Kharkiv economic region that were working on commissions for other republics had failed to fulfil their plans. The Luhansk economic council had diverted 76.6 million rubles earmarked for capital investments in the coal industry to local construction projects—5.5 million of them for the building of the council's own offices. Shcherbytsky spoke of a blatant disregard for the interests of the state as a whole: projects that satisfied local needs were built, while those that had all-union importance were neglected. He complained of "violations of state discipline": "The engineering and technical personnel spent most of their time in their offices. . . . The old flood of sicknesses, letter-writing and telegrams swells under the new conditions; the bureaucratic style is spreading."[101]

To remedy the situation, the Ukrainian Council of Ministers replaced the chairmen of several economic councils. The campaign against localism became more vehement, and was encouraged by Khrushchev personally. In 1960 three new economic regions, the Crimea, Poltava and Cherkasy, were created in Ukraine to improve the organic structure of other regions.

The Soviet leadership also considered the creation of co-ordinating centres in republics, composed of several economic regions. Such centres would be responsible for the activities of the economic councils and would supervise plan fulfilment. Thus, on 6 July 1960, the Ukrainian Council of the National Economy [*Ukrainska rada narodnoho hospodarstva*] was created,[102] and soon turned into a cumbersome, slow-moving and inflexible bureaucratic machine. It consisted of special administrations for the various branches of the economy, specialized main administrations and a large number of divisions and departments. It also included numerous planning and research institutes that had hitherto been subordinated to Gosplan. This became a source of serious tension between the two organizations, necessitating a reorganization of Gosplan and large staff reductions. A year after the establishment of the Ukrainian Council of the National Economy, Ukraine was divided, on the basis of decisions taken by the CC CPSU and the USSR Council of Ministers, into three major economic regions with their own co-ordinating and planning councils. These were the Donetsk-Dnipro Region, the Southwestern Region and the Southern Region.[103] The problem of localism was not unique to Ukraine; it infected other republics and led to pressures for a reduction in economic regions through merger and consolidation. In December 1962 a plenary session of the CC CPU, acting on a decree approved in the previous month by the CC CPSU, decided to reduce the number of economic regions from fourteen to seven.[104]

These measures heralded a return to centralism, a trend crowned on 13 March 1963 with the creation of a new body—the USSR Supreme Council of the National Economy [*Vysshii sovet narodnogo khoziaistva SSSR*].[105] At the same time, the rights of the Ukrainian Council were greatly increased. Besides the so-called operational management of the economic council and the control of plan fulfilment, it became responsible for planning at all levels, from the local to the union-republican. The press declared that these measures were an improvement in the management of industry and construction, as the climax of the drive begun in 1953 for a more efficient and flexible system of economic management. In truth, however, instead of freeing industry from slow-moving centralism and a rigid bureacracy, these measures reinstated most of the methods of economic management practiced before the reform.

Agriculture

One of the most important aims of Soviet economic strategy after 1953 was to overcome the crisis that had beset agriculture since the 1940s. In the first months after Stalin's death his successors were either ignorant of or ill-informed about the problems in agriculture. Malenkov, then chairman of the USSR Council of Ministers, asserted that the grain problem had been solved and that the needs of the Soviet population could be met. Khrushchev capitalized on this misconception. At a plenary session of the CC CPSU in September 1953, he delivered a shocking report about the failures in agriculture and proposed plans for boosting production.

A month later the CC CPU met to discuss the decisions taken at the Moscow plenum. In 1953 a major problem concerned the agricultural cadres. Of the 74,000 agricultural specialists with specialized secondary or post-secondary education who were employed by the Ukrainian ministries of agriculture and procurement, only slightly more than 5,000 were working on the collective farms and only about 10,000 on the Machine-Tractor Stations (MTS). Of the 15,770 collective farm chairmen, only 455 had post-secondary education and only 3,070 had specialized secondary training. The party organizations in the countryside were numerically weak, and 2,401 collective farms lacked party organizations.[106]

From the outset Khrushchev realized that only palpable successes in agriculture could secure his position in the party and his authority among the people. One of his most spectacular ventures was the cultivation of virgin and fallow land in Kazakhstan, Siberia, the Urals, the Volga region and part of the North Caucasian regions. The decision to introduce this project was taken at a plenary session of the CC CPSU in February 1954. This plenum also decided to increase the area sown with grain (mainly wheat, millet and corn) in these regions to 13 million hectares. This huge project had considerable significance for Ukraine, too. Khrushchev was convinced that the yield from the cultivation of virgin and fallow lands would not only cover the population's requirements but also provide enough grain for the development of animal farming, export and stockpiling. In this context Ukraine's role as the main supplier of grain was to be changed. Greater emphasis was to be put on the cultivation of sugar beets and the development of animal husbandry.

Khrushchev's scheme required Ukraine to provide considerable material and technical means, and a large number of agricultural specialists to help realize the virgin-lands project, all of which the republic sorely needed for its own agriculture. Between 1954 and 1956 over 80,000 Komsomol members were sent from Ukraine to the virgin lands in Siberia and Kazakhstan. In the first year of the project alone, thousands of agricultural machines and trucks were sent to Kazakhstan. Large numbers of Ukrainian drivers transported the grain. As late as 1958 there were still 75,000 young Ukrainians working in the virgin and fallow land regions. Numerous agronomists, livestock experts and veterinarians were dispatched from Ukraine to work in these regions.[107]

The Ukrainian leaders tried to increase the efficiency of agricultural management in the republic. First, they placed the more backward collective farms under the patronage of urban industrial enterprises. These enterprises were expected to supply the farms with the technical equipment produced in excess of the plan. The collective farms were expected to pay for such equipment, and, according to press reports, this led to considerable friction. Second, from 1953–5 the leaders sent about 40,000 specialists and technicians from the cities to work in agriculture, which noticeably improved the management of the collective farms and the MTS. During this period the number of MTS directors with a post-secondary education increased from 29 to 62 per cent. The corresponding growth rates for chief engineers at the MTS and repair shop managers were 17 to 83 per cent and 3 to 43 per cent, respectively. At the end of 1954 every collective farm in Ukraine had at least one agricultural specialist. By 1 December 1959, the republic boasted 86,128 agricultural specialists with either a post-secondary or specialized secondary education. In 1960 the figure was 114,600.[108]

In March 1953 the union and union-republican ministries of agriculture and procurement were merged in order to centralize agricultural management, including forestry, in a single organization both nationally and in the republics. At oblast and district levels the local agricultural administrations were also made responsible for procurement. This proved unsuccessful, however, and was abolished after the September plenum of the CC CPSU. The district (raion) departments for agriculture and procurement were dissolved and management of collective farm production transferred to the MTS.[109] Specialists working in industry and official organizations were constantly pressured to accept jobs on the MTS and collective farms. Meanwhile party organizations on the MTS in Ukraine had been strengthened, and party leaders were convinced that they were capable of handling their new duties. Reports in the press about the agricultural reforms were generally positive. Some did note, nevertheless, serious conflicts between the collective farm peasants and those specialists from the city who lacked agricultural training. A new social group, the "agricultural technocracy," developed on the MTS and collective farms during this period. The professional and critical attitude of its members contrasted with that of previous agricultural managers.

At this time, a movement for the abolition of the MTS developed in Ukraine. Its proponents argued that the MTS could not cope with the problems facing agricultural development. Addressing a conference of MTS party secretaries in May 1954, CPU First Secretary Kyrychenko declared that the MTS was impeding the development of farming in the republic. The opposition to the MTS is perhaps best typified by an incident at the "Ukraina" collective farm in Kiev oblast that received considerable publicity in the Soviet Union. The collective farm chairman, Marchenko, formerly an engineer with the Kiev Railroad Administration, said at a meeting of collective farm peasants: "Where there are two masters on the same piece of land—the collective farm and the MTS—there can never be order."[110]

Khrushchev himself used the same words to justify his subsequent reform of the MTS system at the plenary session of the CC CPSU in February 1958. He announced that since the collective farms were now economically viable and had enough qualified personnel, the agricultural equipment controlled by the MTS should be sold to the collective farms, and the MTS should be converted into Repair and Service Stations [*Remontno-tekhnicheskie stantsii* (RTS)]. All agricultural equipment was now in the hands of the collective farms. The task of the RTS was merely to provide a repair and maintenance service, and to deliver new machines, spare parts and fuel to the collective farms. The RTS were also required to lend the collective farms equipment that they had not yet been able to purchase and to train agricultural machine-operators.

The MTS had been responsible for collective farm management since 1953. They had supervised plan fulfilment not only of increased production but also of the state purchase of agricultural produce. The new system provided for the creation of production and technical councils attached to the executive committees of the raion (district) Soviets of Workers' Deputies. These councils were made up of executives and specialists from the raion agricultural inspectorates, the raion collective farms, state farms, MTS and other local agricultural organizations, representatives of the scientific research and training institutes, and reliable farmworkers. Here we have another example of the kind of mammoth organization that the authorities, encouraged by Khrushchev, created in the belief that it would boost efficiency. The agricultural inspectorates, which were responsible for collective farm operations, were subordinated to the new council. They were organs of the raion Soviet executive committees and were also responsible for propaganda, the application of new technical and scientific methods in agriculture, the organization of seed production and livestock breeding, land reclamation, the veterinary service, pest control, and assisting the collective farms with their bookkeeping and preparations of their annual and quarterly plans.[111]

It was soon evident that this form of collective farm management was also a failure. The inspectors performed their tasks poorly because they lacked technical equipment and scientific expertise. Many could not even perform simple tasks, such as measuring the temperature and humidity of the soil. Once again the party had to explain that the measures adopted to date had been inadequate and that thorough reorganization was necessary.

The January 1961 plenum of the CC CPSU adopted new measures for the reorganization of agriculture. It assigned the USSR Ministry of Agriculture special responsibility for the work of the scientific research institutes, and ordered it to propagate the results of agricultural research, to make recommendations to the collective and state farms, and to be responsible for the training of agricultural cadres up to specialized secondary and advanced level. The plenum abolished the raion agricultural inspectorates and established a new link in the chain of agricultural management—the experimental farms [*opytnye khoziaistva*]. The Soviet leaders planned to establish scientific-technical councils at these experimental farms to help the region's agricultural specialists and leading workers. Unlike the inspectorates, which dealt almost exclusively with administrative matters, the main aim of the experimental farms was to develop agricultural expertise and to convey this expertise to the collective and state farms.

Several party officials clashed with Khrushchev at the January plenum. Of the Ukrainian representatives, Pidhorny was the most outspoken in his criticism of agricultural policy. One of the greatest obstacles to the development of agriculture, he claimed, was related to the abolition of the MTS. At the time of abolition, he continued, the collective farms had bought up almost the entire stock of machinery, including equipment that was obsolete. Pointing out that industry was unable to meet the demands for agricultural machinery, Pidhorny said:

A lot of manual work is still being done, especially during the corn and beet harvest. The requirement for tractors and other machines remains unfulfilled year in, year out. For example, only half the required tractors has been delivered, and these are hardly sufficient to replace the tractors that are worn out. There is still a shortage of trucks and tractor-trailers, silo-harvesters, corn combines and many other farming machines; there is also a shortage of tires and spare parts.[112]

Khrushchev interrupted Pidhorny at this point, and the following dialogue, reported in *Pravda*, developed:

Khrushchev: Comrade Podgorny, think of the initiative of the tractor operators from Odessa oblast, who drive their tractors at higher speeds. That's progressive because it makes it possible to double the capacity of the same tractor park. Have you read about that?
Pidhorny: Yes, we are doing that sort of thing in the Odessa and Kherson oblasts.
Khrushchev: Tell us about it, please. Otherwise we shall only hear that you need more tractors and nothing about what you already have.
Pidhorny: I mentioned in my speech that we want to increase speed. But we must nevertheless get what we need.

Khrushchev: Then say the word "get" louder.

Pidhorny: Nikita Sergeevich, when I talk about a shortage of machines, I believe I am only confirming what you have said about the abnormal situation in the production of certain farm machines that are lacking today.

Khrushchev: Pay attention to that, comrades, he's trying to drag me into it now.[113]

Khrushchev reacted similarly to other statements made at the plenum, an enlarged session attended by numerous party and state officials and representatives of agriculture, industry and science. When we compare the speech that Khrushchev delivered on this occasion with earlier speeches, it is clear that he had assumed personal responsibility for all fundamental strategic and political goals in agriculture. In December 1959, for example, he declared: "It is a well-known fact that we have enough grain to cover our needs at present."[114] And in a speech to the Twenty-first CPSU Congress, delivered on 27 January 1959, he said:

> The construction of a new grain base in the eastern part of the country makes it possible to embark upon a fundamental restructuring of agricultural production in several republics and oblasts and on a more rational utilization of the rich natural and economic conditions to increase the output of arable and animal farming.... Today we no longer have to buy up grain, for the time being, in the northwestern regions of the RSFSR, in the Baltic republics, in many Belorussian oblasts and in Polissia, Ukraine. These areas will now specialize in the production of milk, bacon and technical crops....[115]

At the January 1961 plenum of the CC CPSU, Khrushchev criticized managers for curtailing the cultivation of grain crops:

> Some managers took the following line: If the state does not impose grain-procurement quotas, that means it does not need our grain. So that means we can cut back on grain farming.... The correct version is: all regions, including the republics, should co-operate rigorously in the creation of the necessary state grain stock.[116]

Such contradictions can be found in many of Khrushchev's statements about agricultural policy, even on controversial questions, such as the remuneration of kolkhoz workers and material incentives for higher productivity. In May 1959, Khrushchev told a joint session of the CC CPU, the Ukrainian Council of Ministers and the Presidium of the Ukrainian Supreme Soviet: "Many leading collective farms want to get as much money as possible per 'work day.' I am by no means a supporter of spending too much money and natural produce for work days." He warned against a "kulak mentality": "How can I grab as much money as possible to put in my piggy bank?"[117]

At the January plenum of the CC CPSU Khrushchev provoked the first secretary of the Armenian CP, I. N. Zarobian, and exclaimed: "Why don't you say anything about the need to give the collective farm peasants more pay? ... No one here talks about additional remuneration for work. Do you want to achieve communism with moral factors alone?"[118]

This agricultural reform was complemented by the creation of *Soiuzselkhoztekhnika*, the all-union association for the sale of agricultural equipment, spare parts, mineral fertilizers and other technical materials. *Soiuzselkhoztekhnika*, subordinate to the USSR Council of Ministers, was also made responsible for organizing the utilization and repair of machinery at the collective and state farms. An equivalent association—*Ukrsilhosptekhnika*—was established in Ukraine, headed by a council to which the chairmen of the oblast branches of *Ukrsilhosptekhnika* and several state farm directors and collective farm chairmen belonged. The oblast branches also had their own councils.[119]

Criticism of agriculture by the Soviet leadership continued after the January 1961 plenum. Now the charge was that the experimental farms could not operate at full capacity because their relation to the producers was too indirect and the gap between the collective and state farm management system was still too great. Despite all the reforms, shortcomings in agricultural management made it impossible to meet all the targets of the 1959–66 seven-year plan. So Khrushchev developed a new approach: the weak point of the reforms was that they had not affected the direct, day-to-day management of the collective and state farms. This problem was discussed at the March 1962 plenum of the CC CPSU, during which Khrushchev suddenly "discovered" that the Soviet Union had no organization dealing systematically with the management of agricultural production:

> There is a kind of autonomy at our collective and state farms. There is no active intervention from the state organs and no day-to-day influence on the development of production.... You can't build the relations between a co-operative and the state on the principle of non-interference!"[120]

He made several proposals: to establish state and collective farm production boards in the oblasts; that each republic, krai and oblast should work out the structure of the production boards, established on an inter-raion basis; that the post of a board inspector with extensive powers should be created; that the boards should determine the production plans for each collective farm and that they be empowered to commission the collective farms to find or develop new reserves to organize the actual production process and to control the collective farms' activities in general.[121]

After the March plenum, the CC CPU and the Ukrainian Council of Ministers issued a joint decree "On Restructuring the Management of Agriculture in the Ukrainian SSR." On the basis of this decree, the republic established 190 regional production boards, run by specialists who were also experienced in party and state work. The most important positions on these boards were those of the instructor-organizers, who maintained close contacts with agricultural specialists and production managers. To strengthen the party's control over agriculture, the decree established party and Komsomol committees within the production boards.[122]

A new problem emerged: who was to co-ordinate all the organizations responsible for agricultural management? On 28 March 1962 the Agriculture Committee of the Ukrainian SSR was created. Its chairman was the first secretary of the CC CPU, while the deputy chairman was the first deputy chairman of the Council of Ministers, the minister for the production and procurement of agricultural produce. The committee consisted of the CC CPU secretary responsible for agriculture, the director of the Central Committee's Department of Agriculture and his deputy, the chairman of *Ukrsilhosptekhnika*, the director of the department of agriculture and procurement at the Ukrainian Gosplan, and the chairman of the council of ministers' state committee for the water economy. The all-union equivalent of the new body—the USSR Agriculture Committee—was established on 30 April 1962. At the local level, oblast committees were created to manage agricultural production and the operations of the organizations working for agriculture. The party was also strongly represented in these organs.[123]

As usual, the newspapers devoted to economic issues gave a positive evaluation of the management reform even before it went into effect. They depicted it as the creation of a unified and tightly knit system for managing agriculture as a whole, an assertion that was supported by the Ukrainian republic's reports of successful plan fulfillment in 1962. However, the reforms survived Khrushchev by only a matter of days.

Notes

1. *Radianska Ukraina*, 17 February 1960.
2. On 2 February 1960, for example, *Robitnycha hazeta* reported the trial of five Ukrainians in the town of Romny, Sumy oblast. The defendants were militiamen accused of complicity in the shooting of Soviet partisans. They were all sentenced to death.
3. *Iunost*, no. 6 (1959).
4. D. Pokhylevych, "Uniatstvo i ioho reaktsiina rol," *Komunist Ukrainy*, no. 7 (1959): 75ff.

5. The "Nachtigall" unit was part of the Wehrmacht and was posted on the front lines in 1941, but does not appear to have seen action. "After the dissolution of Stetsko's government, this unit had been withdrawn from the front, together with 'Roland.' Both detachments were thoroughly reorganized, certain nationalist members were arrested and the remainder sent as a detachment to fight Red partisans in White Russia." J. Armstrong, *Ukrainian Nationalism*, 2d ed. (New York, 1963), 153.

6. For an eyewitness account of the executions in Brygidky Prison, see M. Rosliak, "Masakra v tiurmi 'Brygidky' " in M. Rudnytska, ed., *Zakhidna Ukraina pid bolshevykamy* (New York, 1958), 441–4.

7. For an account of the murder of Polish professors by the SS, see Z. Albert, "Zamordowanie 25 profesorów wyższych uczelni we Lwowie przez hitlerowców w lipcu 1941 r.," *Przegląd Lekarski* (Cracow), no. 1 (1964).

8. *Radianska Ukraina*, 21 October 1959.

9. In his book *Rossiia bez prikras i umolchanii*, the emigre Soviet journalist Leonid Vladimirov [Finkelstein] reports that according to an article published by *Literaturnaia gazeta* on 10 February 1953, Kychko and several others posed as partisans but had, in fact, collaborated with the German occupation force in Vinnytsia. He apparently survived by becoming a Soviet expert on Zionism, on which he wrote his dissertation. It should be noted that *Vinnytska pravda* reported on 12 December 1954 that the party officials Valchuk and Kychko, whose partisan activities during the Second World War had been questioned, were fully rehabilitated. This report stated that they had been in the "Ukraina" resistance movement.

10. *Radianska Ukraina*, 8 October 1960.

11. *Druzhba narodov* (January 1959).

12. M. M. Bilousov, V. I. Klokov, "Falsyfikatsiia borotby ukrainskoho narodu proty nimetsko-fashystskykh zaharbnykiv u burzhuaznii literaturi," *Ukrainskyi istorychnyi zhurnal*, no. 1 (1959): 136ff.

13. I. Kravtsev, *Sblizhenie sotsialisticheskikh natsii v protsesse perekhoda k kommunizmu* (Kiev, 1960), 80.

14. *Ibid.*, 81. During the meeting between a French socialist delegation and Khrushchev mentioned earlier (see Chapter Two, n. 87), the latter confirmed that, in the case of non-Russians (Jews, for example) the cadre selection criteria did not apply. He also remarked: "If Jews wanted to get the top jobs in our republic, the local population would look askance. Esepecially since they don't think they are less intelligent or less talented than the Jews."

15. V. Rusanivsky, "Novi perspektyvy rozvytku natsionalnykh mov v SRSR," *Nasha kultura*, no. 8 (Warsaw, 1959): 5.

16. N. S. Khrushchev, *Stroitelstvo kommunizma v SSSR i razvitie selskogo khoziaistva* (Moscow, 1963), 281ff.

17. *Pravda*, 12 January 1961.

18. *Ibid.*

19. *Ibid.*

20. *Ocherki istorii Kommunisticheskoi partii Ukrainy* (Kiev, 1977), 672.

21. Khrushchev, *Stroitelstvo kommunizma*, 379ff.

22. *Ibid.*

23. *Suchasnist*, no. 12 (1967): 64.

24. *Ukrainski iurysty pid sudom KGB* (Munich, 1968), 34.
25. *Ibid.*, 38.
26. There was no official explanation for Kyrychenko's removal. In Ukraine it was rumoured that he responded to one of Khrushchev's scornful remarks about Ukraine with the words: "Nikita, without us Ukrainians, you would still be small fry."
27. *Radianska Ukraina*, 28 September 1961.
28. *Ibid.*, 23 June 1961.
29. *Ibid.*, 28–30 September, 1 October 1961.
30. *XII sezd KPSS. Stenograficheskii otchet*, 3 vols. (Moscow, 1962), 1: 272.
31. *Ibid.*, 279–80.
32. *Ibid.*, 280.
33. *Ibid.*, 280.
34. *Ibid.*, 3:115.
35. *Ibid.*
36. *Literaturna hazeta*, 24 November 1961.
37. *Ibid.*
38. *Robitnycha hazeta*, 10 November 1962.
39. *Literaturna hazeta*, 12 and 16 January 1962.
40. *Ibid.*, 16 January 1962.
41. *Ibid.*
42. *Ibid.*
43. *Vestnik vysshei shkoly*, no. 2 (1962).
44. A. Skaba, "Zavdannia ideolohichnoi roboty v svitli rishen XXII zizdu KPRS," *Komunist Ukrainy*, no. 3 (1962): 19.
45. *Literaturna Ukraina*, 11 May 1962.
46. *Ibid.*, 2 November 1962.
47. *Radianska Ukraina*, 11 August 1962.
48. *Ibid.*
49. N. S. Khrushchev, L. F. Ilichev, *Die Kunst gehört dem Volke* (Berlin, 1963), 5ff.
50. *Radianska Ukraina.*, 5 March 1963.
51. Khrushchev and Ilichev, *Die Kunst gehört dem Volke*, 118.
52. *Ibid.*, 116, 165.
53. *Radianska Ukraina*, 13 and 14 March 1963.
54. *Ibid.*, 9 April 1963.
55. *Ibid.*, 10 April 1963.
56. *Literaturna Ukraina*, 24 April 1963.
57. *Ibid.*, 23 April 1963.
58. *Ibid.*, 18 April 1963.
59. "Ideolohichnii roboti—nastupatelnist i boiovytist," *Komunist Ukrainy*, no. 5 (1963): 7ff.
60. V. Malanchuk, "Partiina orhanizatsiia i tvorcha intelihentsiia," *Komunist Ukrainy*, no. 6 (1963): 52ff.
61. *Ibid.*
62. *Radianska Ukraina*, 20 April 1963.
63. Vasyl Symonenko, *Bereh chekan*, (New York, 1965), 178ff.
64. See *Ukrainian Herald: Issue IV* (Munich, 1972), 108–20.

65. *Radianska osvita*, 5 December 1962.

66. *Nasha kultura*, (Warsaw) (March 1963): 51.

67. *Vsesoiuznoe soveshchanie o merakh ulushcheniia podgotovki nauchno-pedagogicheskikh kadrov po istoricheskim naukam 18–21.12.1962* (Moscow, 1964), 68.

68. *Ibid.*, 347.

69. "Natsionalnyi vopros nakanune i v period provedeniia Velikoi Oktiabrskoi Sotsialisticheskoi revoliutsii," *Istoriia SSSR*, no. 5 (1964): 215ff.

70. *Ibid.* Founded to promote the right of Ukrainians in Austria-Hungary to self-determination, the council took over the government in Lviv and all Western Ukraine on 1 November 1918. The Lviv historian S. N. Zlubko declared in his contribution that it was necessary to rehabilitate a number of nationalist organizations in Galicia—the Supreme Ukrainian Council (Holovna Ukrainska Rada), for example.

71. I. Dziuba, "'Poiasniuvalna zapyska do Spilky radianskykh pysmennykiv Ukrainy pro vechir pamiati Lesi Ukrainky u Kyevi 17 serpnia 1963 r." *Samizdat Documents*, vol. 18.

72. *Pravda*, 7 April 1964.

73. "Z pryvodu protsesu nad Pohruzhalskym," *Samizdat Documents*, vol. 18.

74. *Radianska Ukraina*, 3 July 1963.

75. *Radianska kultura*, 15 August 1956.

76. *Literaturna hazeta*, 17 May 1957.

77. *Radianska Ukraina*, 1 October 1957.

78. *Ibid.*, 14 February 1959.

79. Several minor "incidents" helped to generate sympathies for China in Ukraine. A baby born in an overcrowded auditorium during a concert given in a Chinese provincial town by the Ukrainian Song and Dance Ensemble was named Chan, which means "Ukrainian dance." The Ukrainian artists became his godparents and, as the "most popular Chinese" in Ukraine, he was flooded with presents. An article on the state of Chan's health appeared in *Robitnycha hazeta* on 10 April 1960. Kiev television and various newspapers carried numerous reports on the baby. Press reports indicate that Chinese was introduced into the curriculum at a Ukrainian school. On 14 March 1958, *Robitnycha hazeta* claimed that many of the pupils were fairly fluent in Chinese and received children's newspapers from China. Textbooks, however, were in short supply. The number of Ukrainian pupils who were studying Chinese was cited as approximately one hundred. The school was later closed.

80. H. Starushenko, "Proty revizii heneralnoi linii Komunistychnoho rukhu," *Komunist Ukrainy*, no. 9 (1963): 10ff.

81. *Vedomosti Verkhovnogo Soveta SSSR*, no. 15 (1950).

82. *Ibid.*, no. 3 (1953).

83. *Ibid.*, no. 10 (1954).

84. *Narysy istorii Komunistychnoi partii Ukrainy*, 571.

85. *Spravochnik partiinogo rabotnika*, (Moscow, 1957), 227ff.

86. *Pravda*, 28 April 1957.

87. *Radianska Ukraina*, 1 June 1957.

88. *Pravda*, 28 April 1957.

89. V. M. Marchuk, *Organy gosudarstvennogo upravleniia USSR na sovremennom etape* (Kiev, 1964): 52.

90. "Novyi etap v rozvytku radianskoi ekonomiky," *Komunist Ukrainy*, no. 5 (1957): 5.

91. "Za dalshyi rozkvit ekonomiky Radianskoi Ukrainy," *Komunist Ukrainy*, no. 6 (1957): 3.

92. "K dalneishemu uluchsheniiu rukovodstva promyshlennostiu i stroitelstvom," *Partiinaia zhizn*, no. 4 (1957): 1ff.

93. "Demokraticheskii tsentralizm—osnova upravleniia sotsialisticheskim khoziaistvom," *Kommunist*, no. 4 (1957): 1ff.

94. *Kommunist* mentions a scientific associate of an industrial research institute, V. Velovich, who made a concrete proposal for recognition of self-management as a principle of economic management. Other authors saw the reform as the expression of an underlying need for a complete decentralization of management. Cf. A. S. Prybluda, *Kompetentsiia Sovnarkhoza i ego otraslevykh upravlenii*, (Moscow, 1970), 7.

95. *Radianska Ukraina*, 8 June 1957.

96. *Ibid.*, 11 June 1957.

97. Marchuk, *Organy gosudarstvennogo upravleniia USSR na sovremennom etape*, 58.

98. *Ibid.*

99. N. S. Khrushchev, *Stroitelstvo kommunizma v SSSR i razvitie selskogo khoziaistva* (Moscow, 1963), 4: 32.

100. *Radianska Ukraina*, 1 July 1958.

101. *Ibid.*, 27 July 1958.

102. *Ibid.*, 7 July 1960.

103. Marchuk, *Organy gosudarstvennogo upravleniia*, 63.

104. I. Kuhukalo, A. Sich, "Ukrupneni ekonomichni raiony Ukrainskoi RSR," *Ekonomika Radianskoi Ukrainy*, no. 1, (1963): 62.

105. *Pravda*, 14 March 1963.

106. *Narysy istorii Komunistychnoi partii Ukrainy*, 573.

107. V. M. Taranenko, "Uchast trudiashchykh Ukrainy v osvoienni tsilynnykh i perelohovykh zemel," *Ukrainskyi istorychnyi zhurnal*, no. 6 (1959): 46ff; *Narysy istorii Komunistychnoi partii Ukrainy*, 573.

108. *Selskoe khoziaistvo SSSR* (Moscow, 1960), 468–75; *Ekonomika Radianskoi Ukrainy*, no. 1 (1962): 127.

109. V. A. Tsikulin, *Istoriia gosudarstvennykh uchrezhdenii SSSR 1936–1965* (Moscow, 1966), 291ff.

110. Cf. Lewytzkyj, *Die Sowjetukraine*, 101.

111. Cf. Marchuk, *Organy gosudarstvennogo upravleniia*, 79 and Tsikulin, *Istoriia gosudarstvennykh uchrezhdenii*, 293.

112. *Pravda*, 12 January 1961.

113. *Ibid.*

114. *Ibid.*, 29 December 1959.

115. *Ibid.*, 28 January 1959.

116. *Ibid.*, 21 January 1961.

117. *Radianska Ukraina*, 12 May 1959.

118. *Pravda*, 15 January 1961.

119. Marchuk, *Organy gosudarstvennogo upravleniia*, 82.
120. *Pravda*, 6 March 1962.
121. *Ibid.*
122. "Za pryskorennia tempiv pidnesennia silskoho hospodarstva Ukrainy" *Ekonomika Radianskoi Ukrainy*, no. 3 (1962): 6
123. Marchuk, *Organy gosudarstvennogo upravleniia*, 89ff.

Chapter Four

Khrushchev's Fall and Shelest's Career

Reaction to Khrushchev's Fall

On 15 October 1964, Khrushchev was released from the posts of first secretary and Presidium member of the CC CPSU, and chairman of the USSR Council of Ministers. Officially, the action was taken "at his own request for reasons of health and on account of his advanced age." Leonid Brezhnev was elected first secretary of the CC CPSU and Aleksei Kosygin became chairman of the Council of Ministers.[1]

There were no extreme reactions in Ukraine to Khrushchev's fall. Not only party officials but also the majority of party members wanted to abolish Khrushchev's reforms. There were, however, fears that the planned dissolution of the economic councils and the return to the traditional system of managing the economy vertically according to branches would again restrict the rights of the republics. It should be remembered that, despite the bureaucratic bungling of the Soviet leaders, the population had reacted positively to the decision to bring economic management closer to home.

The first criticism of Khrushchev in the Ukrainian party press came in an editorial published by *Komunist Ukrainy* in November 1964. Although this article did not mention the former leader by name, it attacked a "leader" who violated the principle of collective decision-making and behaved like an autocrat, a clear reference to Khrushchev:

In our day and age it is unthinkable that leading positions should be held by a communist who ceases to consider the opinion of the masses, the collective, and substitutes his own decisions and actions for their will. The people appreciates leaders who are guided firmly and undeviatingly in all things by the legacy of Lenin. The masses trust them, support them, follow them. However, this support is lost by those leaders who begin to rely on their own experience and their own reasoning, who lose their sense of the new, their sense of existing reality. The party has warned and continually warns its cadres of this danger, educates them unremittingly in the spirit of the Leninist principles, the Programme and the Statutes of the CPSU.[2]

A month later the CPU organ *Komunist Ukrainy* reiterated a question that many Ukrainians, not only communists, were asking themselves: Why had they given their support to Khrushchev's subjective proposals? The article reported on discussions held in 1962 about ways and means of developing industrial output by harnessing reserves in order to increase quality and reduce production costs:

It was under these very conditions that proposals were made in September 1962, in which the task of strengthening party influence on the development of production was linked with the necessity of changing the principles underlying the party's organizational structure. The idea was to reorganize the party organizations and their leading organs from the lowest to the highest level, restructuring them on the production principle, i.e., creating autonomous industrial and agricultural party organizations. However, the draft reorganization proposal included some ideas that could scarcely be repudiated. The point was to increase the party organs' responsibility for economic construction, to bring the party leadership closer to production and make it more qualified.[3]

Two years later, however, expectations had not been fulfilled, and the article cited numerous examples of the mounting chaos caused by Khrushchev's reforms, especially in areas where jurisdiction overlapped. The reform had divided control of the raions between the party and the state administration, without establishing a system for co-ordination and co-operation. The overlapping administration extended to the militia, the courts, the public prosecutor's office and the health services. In all these areas, the regional organizations were subordinated to the agricultural bodies, and the oblast organizations to the oblast committees for agriculture.[4]

In November 1964 a plenary session of the CC CPSU dealt with the unification of the oblast and krai committees for industry and agriculture. It asserted that the existing division—far from involving the party leadership more closely with production—actually had the opposite effect.[5] On 20 November 1964 the CC CPU accepted Moscow's decision and re-established unified party committees in Ukraine's nineteen oblasts. The party committees of the collective and state farm production associations were reorganized as party raion committees and the zonal industrial-production committees of the CPU were dissolved. The Ukrainian leaders decided to re-establish the CPU city committees in Dnipropetrovsk, Kharkiv, Kiev, Lviv, Mykolaiv, Odessa, Poltava and Zaporizhzhia, which had been disbanded after the division of the party organizations.[6]

Elections to the raion and city committees were held in January 1965. Under Shelest's leadership the party tried to use the occasion to improve the committees' "qualitative composition." Ninety per cent of the newly elected first secretaries of the rural raion committees and the agriculture secretaries of the city committees had a higher education; 43 per cent of these officials were industrial and agricultural specialists; 35 per cent were agronomists and livestock experts; and 57 per cent of the newly elected secretaries were under forty.[7]

Shelest Develops his Political Profile as Party Boss

Shelest's public appearances and political activities—especially after Khrushchev's fall—reveal that he was trying both to promote the interests of the Ukrainian SSR by his work in Kiev and to cultivate approval and popularity in Moscow by fostering the image of a peerless party leader with new ideas and concepts. He did not want to condemn out of hand everything that Khrushchev had done—particularly in the economic sphere. At the March 1965 plenum of the CC CPSU, Shelest gave a speech "On Most Urgent Measures for the Development of Soviet Agriculture," which criticized Khrushchev without naming him:

> The violation of the economic laws governing the development of agriculture could lead to an adventurist policy. We are familiar with the following slogans: "We shall soon catch up with and overtake the United States in the per capita production of meat and milk!" and "We have it good today and we'll have it better tomorrow!" And at the same time people have to stand in line outside the bread stores.

Shelest also reproached some of the officials attending the plenum:

> Can we say today that our officials are free of the vice of subjectivism? No, we cannot, because this [attitude] has been drummed into people for years. This vice still occurs in many planning, economic and other all-union and republican organizations, and we should rid ourselves of it as soon as possible.[8]

Shelest tried, in a roundabout way, to convince the plenum that the economic councils had operated successfully. He pointed out that Ukrainian industry had fulfilled its tasks for 1964 ahead of schedule and was overfulfilling the current plans. He attacked shortcomings in the procurement of the agricultural machinery that the republic so urgently needed:

> Is it normal for an automobile like the GAZ-51A to cost 1,080 rubles (which isn't exactly cheap) when a machine as simple as a TVK–80 feed distributor costs 1,400 rubles? The price of a set of tires for a Belarus tractor is almost 25 per cent of the cost of the whole tractor. A tire for a drive wheel on a combine harvester costs 224.50 rubles. A collective farm has to sell over three metric tons of wheat to buy one.[9]

Shelest argued eloquently that Ukraine should be provided with more and better machines and should receive more funds for irrigation projects.

After the September 1965 plenum of the CC CPSU decided to abolish the economic councils, the seventh session of the Ukrainian Supreme Soviet, which convened in the following month, established the following union-republican ministries: Ferrous Metallurgy; the Coal Industry; the Timber, Pulp, Paper and Wood-Processing Industries; the Building Materials Industry; Rural Construction; and Meat and Dairy Industry. The decree also established a republican ministry of Local Industry, created several main administrations and reorganized several state production committees.

The abolition of Khrushchev's economic management reform was a victory for the supporters of centralism. It restored the vertical, centralized system of management, which automatically restricted the powers of the republics. A section of the Ukrainian bureaucracy, especially the lower echelon, opposed the dissolution of the economic councils. Generally, those who supported the restoration of centralism rallied around Shcherbytsky, who had often criticized the work of the economic councils; while Shelest, who had often warned against an unqualified condemnation of the councils, was the rallying-point for the malcontents. Shelest's attitude was expressed clearly in his speech at the plenary session of the CC CPU on 19–20 October 1965. Reporting on the implementation of the decisions taken at the September plenum of the CC CPSU, he endorsed the dissolution of the economic councils but added:

> It would, however, be wrong to see only negative aspects in the activities of the economic councils. The organization of industrial management by the economic councils had some positive features, especially in the organization of co-operation between enterprises, in the provision of material and technical supplies, and so forth. For this reason, those comrades who have

been over-critical have done the economic councils an injustice. We should judge the manifestations of our life objectively.[10]

The Twenty-third CPU Congress was held on 15–18 March 1966. The agenda included the draft directives for the 1965–70 five-year plan, issued in February. The only speaker who dealt with Ukraine's political controversies and the growing social conflicts (these topics received only marginal attention at the congress) without resorting to harsh statements was the writer O. Ie. Korniichuk:

> Heated discussions are in progress among [our] creative youth; they are worried by problems of socialist realism and romanticism. They like to reassess literary and artistic treasures and are looking for new ways. They wouldn't be young people if they didn't engage in keen discussions. We can only welcome it and boldly support all good elements just as the Komsomol and the party supported us when we were still young. However, there are among us younger writers who obstinately maintain that only they know what is white and what is black. [They] and no one else. This is a case of kids playing at Columbus. The affliction passes when a young man becomes more conscious of his responsibility toward the people and begins to understand that no discoveries are possible nowadays without thorough study of the laws governing the development of our society, without acquiring the great heritage of our culture.[11]

Shelest delivered the principal report at the congress and dealt mainly with economic matters. However, as the republic's internal political problems had become so critical, he was obliged to devote part of his report to "The Intensification of the Ideological Struggle—A Militant Task of the Party Organization." Referring to the (alleged) increase of anti-communist activities abroad, notably among certain emigre groups, Shelest declared that the prime target of ideological work should be "all indications of bourgeois ideology." He noted that a large section of the Ukrainian population still practiced religion and demanded greater efforts to educate workers in the spirit of atheism. Concerning the nationality problem, he said:

> Because of the consistent implementation of the Leninist nationality policy, the national disputes and enmities that the exploiting classes and their ideologues—the bourgeois nationalists and the great-power chauvinists—sowed and encouraged throughout the centuries have been completely eliminated in our country.... In the entire history of Ukraine there has never been an important juncture at which the Ukrainian people could not lean on the strong shoulder of its true brother and friend, the Russian people, and rely on the fraternal support of all our country's people....

Nationalism and great-power chauvinism have always been the two faces of
bourgeois policy and ideology on the nationality question. Indeed, it was in
the tenacious and uncompromising struggle against these [policies] that the
unshakeable international unity and fraternity of all Soviet peoples was
forged.[12]

In this speech, Shelest made thrusts not only at nationalism but also at
"great-power chauvinism." As for Shelest himself, the self-confidence he
displayed at the Twenty-third CPU Congress and the delegates' reactions
to his speech indicated that he had succeeded in winning their respect.

Another Attempt to Tighten the Ideological Screws

After Khrushchev's fall, a polarization of the politically active section of
the population occurred and the sections of the party apparatus responsible
for ideology were strengthened considerably. M. A. Suslov, the CC CPSU
member responsible for this area, increased his personal authority after
Ilichev, one of Khrushchev's protégés, lost his position as secretary of
the Central Committee in March 1965. However, Suslov continued to
share responsibility for ideology with P. N. Demichev. Ukraine's chief
ideologist was Skaba, who worked in co-operation with Kondufor, then
head of the Central Committee Department for Science and Culture. The
main "ideological watchdogs" over literature were the critic
M. Z. Shamota, the "historian" I. Kravtsev and his political counterpart,
the writer O. I. Poltoratsky. The work of this trio was complemented by a
Suslov protégé, V. Malanchuk, doctor of historical sciences and secretary
of the Lviv oblast party committee. The ideological apparatus established a
wide network of units down to the raion level and staffed them with new
and loyal officials.

On 16 December 1965, in *Pravda*, an article by Malanchuk made a
strong plea for the rapprochement of the Soviet nations: "This is a mighty
and objective process. To resist it is a sign of national narrow-mindedness.
We sometimes encounter among us immature people who equate local
interests with the interests of the whole state." Returning to the old theme,
he argued that the danger of nationalism was particularly great in Western
Ukraine, because that area had been under a "foreign yoke" for many
centuries. Thus the party paid special attention to the ideological question
in this region. Malanchuk reported that several Lviv historians had tried to
rehabilitate the Western Ukrainian republic created in 1918, and received
a hostile reaction:

The scholarly public of Lviv sharply criticized a few officials who assumed
the role of apologists for the so-called Western Ukrainian People's
Republic.... [These officials] tried to cover up the fact that the "republic"
of the Ukrainian counter-revolution and foreign imperialist circles served as a

weapon to suppress the revolutionary movement of the masses for the creation of a unified Ukrainian Soviet state.

After criticizing "serious" ideological errors made by the editors of the literary journal *Zhovten*, Malanchuk also discussed the question of national language. Here, he said, Lenin had predicted that "the popular masses of non-Russian nationality, liberated from social and national suppression, will themselves recognize the necessity of learning the Russian language voluntarily, [realizing] that this will become a powerful source for the development of the economy and culture of all the peoples, and for the creation of close ties, rapprochement and true fraternity among them." The party organizations, declared Malanchuk, were educating the workers to reject any manifestations of bourgeois ideology and to be vigilant against the "hostile activities of imperialist circles and the Ukrainian bourgeois nationalists."

Adrian Hoshovsky, a former official of the Communist Party of Western Ukraine (CPWU), took issue with Malanchuk's *Pravda* article. Responding in *Nasha kultura*, the literary supplement of the Warsaw *Nashe slovo*, Hoshovsky pointed out that Malanchuk's position was fundamentally different from that of Shelest:

> This is not the right place to talk about the contents of Comrade Malanchuk's article about cadre selection and national narrow-mindedness. Here we only want to point to the radical difference between the spirit of this article and the speeches of Comrade Shelest ... Comrade Honchar and other leading writers at the Fifth Writers' Congress about the attitude toward "our beloved and wonderful Ukrainian language" and about the necessity of protecting this great treasure through the state.[13]

Ukrainian journals, notably *Komunist Ukrainy*, published a series of articles on ideological education from which it was clear that a close-knit and centrally co-ordinated team of ideologists, together with their aides in the CPU, had taken the offensive against the reformers. The purpose of these articles was not to engage in open polemics with reformists and those expressing opposition (within the legal framework), but to link them with dissidents, "bourgeois nationalists" and "imperialists." For example, an article by V. Boichenko, secretary of the Kiev oblast committee responsible for ideology, criticized certain party organizations for tolerating the activities of young members of the cultural intelligentsia such as Ivan Dziuba and Vasyl Stus, and the poetess Lina Kostenko. Boichenko noted the recent activities of foreign radio stations and warned:

> There are still ideologically and morally unstable people who fall for bourgeois propaganda and, under its influence, misinterpret certain events

and manifestations of our social life, become purveyors of alien views and ideas and spread rumours and inventions about our reality.[14]

In an article published by *Komunist Ukrainy*, B. Serhiienko and I. Klymchuk accused Western anti-communist organizations of trying to subvert Ukrainians and described their tactics:

> The nationalists are basing their hopes on the susceptibility of the unstable section of our youth to bourgeois ideology. Like other imperialist ideologues, they try to set youth against the older generation of Soviet people and deny the ideological heritage of the generations in our society. One of the manifest forms of this perfidious plan is the [practice] of inciting creative youth against the glorious traditions of Soviet Ukrainian literature [in exchange] for false praise and the printing of ideologically weak works by young writers in nationalist publications.[15]

Attempts were made to arouse not only anti-Semitic but, in a return to the strategy employed prior to 1953, also anti-German feelings. The press demanded constant vigilance against the threat of West German revisionism and revanchism, and several articles identified the Federal Republic of Germany with "Nazi Germany." On 23 October 1965 Leonid Brezhnev went to Kiev to present the city with the "Golden Star," awarded in connection with the twentieth anniversary of the victory over Germany. The final section of his presentation speech was devoted to foreign policy:

> To this very day, the people on the Rhine have not disavowed [their] revanchist plans; they still want to revise the results of the Second World War and are demanding nuclear weapons to realize this criminal purpose. At a reunion of the former SS divisions, the same divisions that killed and plundered on this Ukrainian soil, members of the Bundestag and ministers of the Federal Republic raised their voices to scream revenge, without a trace of shame.[16]

Brezhnev's speech marked the beginning of a propaganda campaign against Bonn that was connected with the Kremlin's ideological strategy in Ukraine. (The Soviet leaders feared the effects of western propaganda on Ukrainian reformists.) While Brezhnev was in Kiev, Suslov presented the "Golden Star" to Odessa, declaring: "The main pillar of international reaction and aggression is American imperialism. . . . The aggressive forces of imperialism, including West German imperialism, and the revanchists are developing plans to start a new war."[17]

The Broad Anti-Chauvinist Front

The party leadership (especially in Ukraine) was surprised by the degree of resistance to its attempts to curtail the rights of the republics and to all forms of Russification and discrimination, particularly in language and culture. At that time some party members sought a compromise and tried to avoid an open confrontation with dissidents. These communists were found in Shelest's camp and expected Pidhorny, who already enjoyed influence and authority in the Politburo of the CC CPSU, to support them. The militants, mainly young communists, wanted to draw the attention of their comrades abroad, especially in Poland and Czechoslovakia, to the situation in Ukraine. In December 1964 some formed a committee, which drew up an appeal "to all communists of the people's democracies and capitalist countries and to the leading organs of the communist and other parties of the world." The appeal was smuggled to the West, and extracts from it were published in the press.[18] (The Ukrainian communists also appealed to the Canadian Communist Party, whose members included a number of Canadians of Ukrainian extraction, mainly of the second generation.)

The Ukrainian party leadership believed that the leaders of the CPSU, headed by Brezhnev, could still prevent a shift to the right and continue "the return to Leninist norms." It maintained that the dissatisfaction in Ukraine was only a response to Khrushchev's inconsistent and contradictory policies, and that the prospects for eliminating the consequences of the personality cult in the sphere of nationality policy were now better than ever. At a conference of university and college presidents in August 1965, Iu. M. Dadenkov, Ukrainian minister for higher and secondary special education, delivered a report on language problems at the educational institutions controlled by his ministry. The report outlined the extent of Russification of the republic's universities and colleges. Subsequently, the presidents of these institutions received a copy of the report as instructional material.

In an article published in the *samvydav* journal the *Ukrainian Herald* (*Ukrainskyi visnyk*), Viacheslav Chornovil, one of the leaders of the political opposition, reported the measures taken by the CPU (led by Shelest) to de-Russify the republic's system of higher education. It appears that some members of the Presidium of the CC CPSU gave this action some chance of success. Chornovil quoted extensively from Dadenkov's paper in his article. This information surprised many:

> In the fifty higher educational institutes of the ministry (there are higher educational institutes which are not under the jurisdiction of the ministry of the republic), there are only 317,529 students, of whom 177,051 are Ukrainians, that is, 55 per cent.... These higher educational institutes

employ 18,132 staff instructors, of whom 8,932 are Ukrainians (less than 50 per cent!!). The publishing houses of the Universities of Kiev, Lviv and Kharkiv published 2,297 titles of scientific and educational literature during 1960–64, of which 795 titles were in Ukrainian, that is, 35 per cent. . . . An analysis of the situation in the universities of the republic [shows that there are]: 75,207 students, of whom 49,953 are Ukrainians, that is, 61 per cent. . . . The faculties of the universities consisted of 4,400 persons, of whom 2,475 (56 per cent) were Ukrainians. Only 1,497 give lectures in Ukrainian. . . . At the University of Kharkiv, in particular, of 777 lecturers, only 104 (13 per cent) lecture in Ukrainian. At the University of Odessa, where Ukrainian students comprise 55 per cent, of 537 lecturers, only 53 (10 per cent) lecture in Ukrainian.[19]

Dadenkov also reported on various institutes, in which the percentage of staff that lectured in Ukrainian was even smaller than at many of the universities. Chornovil noted that despite the general shortage of Ukrainian-language textbooks—there were none whatsoever for 70 per cent of the subjects taught at the eight universities—no proposals had been made to improve the situation.

Although the centre of political unrest and protest in Ukraine was Kiev, and not Lviv, many party ideologists maintained that it was easier to make the connection between the opposition forces and the "bourgeois nationalists" in Lviv. In April 1965 disturbances broke out at Kiev University after statements made by the Russian writer, V. A. Soloukhin, in defence of the Ukrainians' demands. "If I had been born a Ukrainian," said Soloukhin, "I would never want to be a Russian." On 13 April a group of students at the university discussed Soloukhin's article and decided to continue the discussion. On 20 April a meeting of several hundred young people, including students from other universities and colleges, turned into a demonstration in defence of the Ukrainian language. The participants protested that most lectures were held in Russian and that young Ukrainians had to perform their military service in other Soviet republics. One student who compared the current position of Ukraine with that of former colonies received an ovation. The students decided to form a society for the promotion of Ukrainian culture and elected a provisional board to handle the society's business. A delegation, which requested a meeting with First Secretary Shelest, was received by an official of the Central Committee Department of Science and Culture, Popov, who recorded the names of the delegates. The KGB detained them on the following day for interrogation.[20]

In August and September 1965, KGB agents arrested lecturers, artists and scholars throughout Ukraine. Viacheslav Chornovil documented the KGB operation; he compiled biographies of the victims, and outlined their professional careers and political activities. The documentation included letters that the accused had written to their relatives. It was published in *samvydav* under a title borrowed from Griboedov, *Lykho z rozumu*, the Ukrainian equivalent of *Gore ot uma* [Woe from Wit], and in 1967 it was published abroad.

In his preface Chornovil wrote:

> If it were possible to compile a typical biography of the average person convicted in 1966 for "anti-Soviet nationalistic propaganda and agitation," it would look as follows: The convicted N. was twenty-eight to thirty years old at the time of his arrest. He came from a peasant's or worker's family, graduated with honours from secondary school, entered university (perhaps after serving in the army), where he actively participated in scientific discussion groups. Being an excellent student he obtained a good position, wrote a postgraduate dissertation (or succeeded in defending one), and his articles were published in periodicals (or he even published a book). Even if his profession was a technical one, he took an interest in literature and art and grieved for the state of his native language and culture. He is still unmarried or was married shortly before his arrest and has a small child....
>
> This time [the authorities] were dealing with people of high education who were brought up in Soviet conditions and who were able to grasp the essence of Marxism-Leninism from original sources and not second-hand through quotations. They were dealing with people who had not learned from the bitter experience of the thirties and forties. Notwithstanding the harsh conditions of camp existence, all the convicted continue to develop their intellectual potential and to worry about the same unsolved problems that concerned them before their arrest.[21]

The "Twenty Criminals," as they were called, were convicted and received sentences of up to twenty-five years in labour camps.

The arrests of 1961 were, for the most part, directed against groups that had either founded or—as in the case of Lukianenko—intended to found clandestine organizations. Those arrested in 1965, however, had acted within the framework of the Soviet constitution, and made no effort to conceal their convictions. For example, one of the best known of the "Twenty Criminals," the writer and literary historian Sviatoslav Karavansky, drew up a memorandum on nationality policy and handed copies to the Polish and Czechoslovakian consuls in Kiev, with a request for the convocation of an international conference of communist and workers' parties to discuss the issues involved.

The Fifth Congress of Ukrainian Writers

The Fifth Congress of Ukrainian Writers was held on 16–20 November 1966. The official delegates were complemented by guests from Russia, including high-level party officials, representatives of science and culture, students and officers. At the congress, Petro Shelest delivered a major speech, which dealt with cultural policy and controversial nationality questions:

> Soviet literature and art—these are our party's true helpmates in the formation of a new world outlook among the masses. The party principle (*partiinist*) is the most important source of strength for Soviet literature. The writers must stay in constant contact with the people and with the party.

Shelest denounced "bourgeois ideologues," who had tried to drive a wedge between the Soviet Union's creative intelligentsia and the party. His speech included encouragement for those writers and intellectuals who defended the rights of the national language:

> Our beloved Ukrainian Soviet literature and art are flourishing under these conditions. You are their creators, their builders. The blossoming of the socialist Ukrainian culture and language depends in many respects on the people who are gathered here today. But let us talk not so much about the necessity of such a blossoming as of your creative work. We must treat our beloved and wonderful Ukrainian language with care and respect. It is our treasure, our greatest heritage, which everyone—above all, you writers—should protect and develop. Novels, narratives, novellas and poetry of a high ideological timbre, written in the wonderful Ukrainian language and on a high artistic level—that is what is needed for the further enrichment and development of the national culture and language. Your work in this direction has been and will be supported by the Communist party.[22]

Shelest praised those who promoted Ukrainian culture abroad. Specifically, he mentioned the American tour made by the Ukrainian Song and Dance Ensemble under Virsky, the Korean tour of the H. Veriovka Folk Choir, the Romanian tour of Kiev's Shevchenko Opera and Ballet Theatre, and the foreign tours of Kirovohrad's "Iatran" Dance Ensemble.

Oles Honchar, chairman of the Ukrainian Writers' Union, delivered a balanced and objective critique of the work of young writers. He expressed particular concern about the teaching of Ukrainian in schools:

> It is impermissible for children's schoolbooks to be written in a wooden officialese and for reading texts to be selected in a negligent manner, so that the desire to learn the works of literature and the mother tongue (which, it is rightly said, is a sonorous and melodious language replete with beauty) is not awakened in the children but taken from them. This congress cannot avoid discussing the situation of Ukrainian language instruction at the secondary and higher schools. A people's language is its greatest treasure, and we must all protect it—sometimes with authoritarian state-sponsored measures. [We]

must stubbornly develop, renew and enrich the people's language through our literary activity. It is the sacred duty of an author to polish untiringly the diamonds of the people's words, to make them more lustrous.[23]

Honchar proposed the establishment of a publishing house for foreign literature in Ukraine and reported on the propagation of the Ukrainian language abroad, especially in Czechoslovakia, Romania and Yugoslavia.

The literary critic Leonid Novychenko took issue with Russophile critics and historians in Moscow. His prime target was S. Agaev, who had published several articles in the Moscow journal *Voprosy iazykoznaniia* practically demanding that all writers in the Soviet Union use only Russian and renounce their national languages. Agaev divided the languages into three categories: those with a chance to survive and develop (Russian, Armenian, Georgian, Estonian, Latvian and Lithuanian); those that were doomed to extinction and served only as an instrument of local, day-to-day communication; and those that had a literature, and were used in the press and for primary education but had limited prospects for further development. Agaev's articles provoked protests throughout the Soviet Union. Novychenko decisively repudiated this theory, which was also condemned by a number of the Russian guests at the congress, including Sergei Baruzdin, secretary of the Soviet Writers' Union and editor of the journal *Druzhba narodov*. The latter declared: "I must say that, after you have spoken out so fervidly and with such a sense of involvement...for the purity of the Ukrainian language, I believe that we in Russia will become more concerned about the purity of the Russian language. Your congress will help us in this respect."[24]

Vitalii Korotych was annoyed that the works of some Ukrainian writers were still blacklisted although they had already been published in Czechoslovakia:

> So long as we do not feel at home in our own culture we cannot be others' guests with dignity. For is it not an infamy that the works of Bohdan-Ihor Antonych have been published in Czechoslovakia but his book has not reached us yet? The works of Ievhen Pluzhnyk will soon appear there, too, but when will they be published here? Oles Honchar has already mentioned Panteleimon Kulish. I would like to recall his namesake, the famous Soviet playwright. Where have the works of Mykola Kulish been published in a worthy framework and given their proper due? How much longer are we going to provide our foes with weapons for political speculation, how much longer do we want to rob ourselves?[25]

Korotych endorsed Honchar's proposal for the establishment of a publishing house for foreign literature in Ukraine and pointed out that the republic had no Ukrainian primers for adult foreign students.

The Fifth Congress of Ukrainian Writers was followed with great interest abroad, especially among Ukrainians living in Czechoslovakia, Poland and Romania. Newspapers in these countries printed numerous commentaries, as well as statements made at the congress—especially excerpts from Honchar's speech. *Nasha kultura*, the Ukrainian-language newspaper published in Poland, observed:

> In evaluating the congress proceedings as a whole it must be said that the participants proved themselves to be worthy heirs to the glorious traditions of T. Shevchenko, I. Franko, L. Ukrainka and M. Kotsiubynsky, that the people can entrust them to take the helm in the struggle to maintain the' standards of national literature and culture.[26]

A Canadian Delegation Visits Ukraine

In 1967 the Ukrainian communists achieved a degree of success in their efforts to interest foreign communist parties in developments taking place in the Ukrainian SSR. From 31 March to 24 April of that year a delegation from the Communist Party of Canada visited Ukraine—the first known occasion when a foreign party received official permission to look at internal Soviet problems. It seems likely that Shelest supported the visit and obtained the endorsement of Pidhorny and Brezhnev.

The Communist Party of Canada, neither large nor of major political significance in the international workers' movement, had a special interest in Soviet nationality policy because its members included a relatively large Ukrainian contingent. This group had alerted the Canadian party leaders to the Russification campaign in Ukraine, and these leaders were particularly alarmed that the victims of persecution included members of the CPU. Apart from these patent violations of "Marxism-Leninism," the Canadian communists were also interested in Soviet nationality policy, because their own country had similar problems.

The members of the Canadian delegation were: George Solomon, Tony Bilecki, Bill Ross, Peter Krawchuk, Bill Harasym and Tim Buck. At the outset Shelest told the Canadians that nationality policy was still a problem in Ukraine: "We had problems and we still have problems, but we are overcoming them." Shelest also referred to the Ukrainian language: "Some comrades have, on occasion, expressed mistaken ideas about what they call the merging of languages, but only a fool could imagine that there is any possibility of Russian taking over in Ukraine."[27]

The delegation's report on the visit, published in the Canadian party journals *Viewpoint* and *Zhyttia i slovo* (1 January 1968), was read with great interest both in Ukraine and abroad. Several passages expressed satisfaction that the party leaders in Kiev and Moscow recognized the nationality problems and were attempting to tackle them: "In various other discussions in ministries of the government, in the Academy of Sciences and such, we saw evidence that the problem is recognized and, where necessary, changes are being made to facilitate its solution." According to the Canadian report, "the work of our delegation contributed to this process." This impression (an inaccurate one) was heightened by comments and suggestions made by the Ukrainian Canadians:

> We learned that the debate concerning the role of the Ukrainian language, its meaning to the Ukrainian people and its future, was summed up and its lessons drawn in the position of the Central Committee of the Communist Party of the Soviet Union, which reaffirmed the primacy of the Ukrainian language in the Ukraine. When Comrade Bazhan, the famous writer, told our delegation "I don't think we shall have any more trouble on that question," he did not suggest that there will not be arguments. His point was quite distinctly that the position of the party corresponds with the realities of life and will win overwhelming support because of that. Erroneous opinions will become discredited. It is socialist democracy at work.[28]

The Canadian delegation was given copious statistical material about the status of the Ukrainian educational system, about scientific institutes and about lectures in Ukrainian in post-secondary educational institutions, much of which was provided by P. P. Udovychenko, then minister of public education. When the delegation showed Udovychenko an article by a teacher in Zaporizhzhia who had complained that his colleagues "don't know the Ukrainian language properly [and] don't read Ukrainian literature," the minister replied: "But we have 34,000 schools with 480,000 teachers. One teacher's opinion about his or her fellow teachers does not contradict this, though he or she may have written with very good intentions."[29] The delegation agreed that such articles should be evaluated positively.

The Canadian communists also asked why there were so few schools and other cultural institutions for the large Ukrainian minorities in other republics of the USSR. They received no satisfactory reply. Furthermore, when they asked why so much Russian was spoken in the streets of Kiev (an indication of Russification), they received the cynical reply that people can speak whatever language they like. During talks with members of the Ukrainian Writers' Union, the Canadian delegation raised the issue of the recent political arrests. The author Oleksandr Korniichuk answered: "[These people] were arrested because they were engaged in an attempt to distribute anti-Soviet propaganda printed in West Germany, not because of something they had written." According to the Canadian report, Korniichuk emphasized "that the searching among young people must be dealt with sympathetically, in a positive way, without encouraging the tendency among some of the young people to assume, quite uncritically, that they could solve all the problems of today quite easily." Korniichuk also told the Canadian guests why the Ukrainian Writers' Congress had emphasized the importance of the Ukrainian language:

It is true that there have been arguments to the effect that all the Slavonic languages will merge with Russian in a very short time, but that concept has been rejected. Together with the struggle against Ukrainian nationalism it is necessary to press the fight against Russian chauvinism. Our congress expressed the policy of the Communist Party of the Soviet Union and the October Plenum of its Central Committee. I don't think we shall have any more trouble with that question.

A further exchange on the language issue occurred during a meeting of the delegation and Academician I. K. Bilodid, director of the Institute of Social Sciences. Concerning the latter's assurances about the future of the Ukrainian language, one of the delegation declared:

Yet, when I was on a previous delegation, a Ukrainian comrade told us that the Ukrainian language does not lend itself to describing scientific and technological developments. We have seen in life, including our visit to the academy today, that the Ukrainian language is used to describe the most complex scientific developments. At the same time, after the session of the Supreme Soviet we heard many deputies, Ukrainians, speaking Russian in conversation. Is this an expression of the status of the Russian language within the party? This is a question not of their right, but of the status of the Ukrainian language within the family of the Soviet people.[30]

Bilodid answered evasively that the Russian language received no privileges, but that Ukrainians found it useful. Incidentally, Bilodid must have used this formulation consciously, for he repeated it when the thesis of the Russian language being the only path to the treasures of Russian and world culture and modern technology had gained currency. However, Soviet officials tried to convince the Canadian communists that all theories about merging the languages had been repudiated and that there was no process of assimilation in Ukraine: "The concept of two native languages is scientifically incorrect. The Russian language is becoming the second language in Ukraine as in other republics because it is needed for communication between all peoples in the Soviet Union. But the Russian language has no privileges."[31]

The Canadian delegation's report concluded:

It became evident in the course of our discussions that there are real differences in the understanding of and approach to the language question at various levels of party organization and among different leading comrades, even though they all believe themselves [to be] subscribing [to] the Leninist national policy. In addition to variations of understanding and attitudes between persons, we found instances of gaps between declared policy and practice.

There is, first of all, the attitude, quite common, that the national question has been solved successfully in Ukraine on the basis of Lenin's teachings, that there are no problems of a national character, no pressures whatsoever concerning languages, that the Soviet pople are all united by the common aim of building socialism and that's what counts. . . . The response of our delegation to that attitude was, and is, that if no problem exists, if everything has already been resolved, then obviously there is nothing to be done or said. But, obviously, there was need for discussion and action.

Second, there was the opinion, expressed by the minister of education, that the question of national aspirations does not depend on language. A similar position was advanced by A. D. Skaba, secretary for ideology in the Central Committee, who declared that what is important is the development of technique, not the language in which the textbooks are published. He said that he was not concerned whether in the hydrostation at Burshtyn there were more signs in Russian or in Ukrainian.

The report noted that the thesis of the primacy of technology over the secondary or minor issue of language in the construction of communism was widespread. By way of consolation, it hastened to add:

This concept was, however, contradicted by the statements of P. Iu. Shelest, member of [the] Politbureau, CPSU and first secretary, Central Committee, C.P. Ukraine, who declared emphatically that the development of Communist society must permit the fullest and freest economic and cultural development of every nation. "Patriotism," he went on to say, "is developed in the family and its roots are in the family."

The report pointed out that certain categories of Ukrainian writers and students had been depicted as "bourgeois nationalists," but that the delegation received no precise definition of this anathematized "creed":

Bourgeois nationalism was not defined. There has been a tendency in some quarters to brand as bourgeois nationalism, or some kind of deviation, demands for the greater use of the Ukrainian language in public institutions. Such carry-overs from the Stalin era do not help in correctly resolving the language problem.

The Canadian delegation was dissatisfied with the explanations it received about violations of socialist legality and human rights:

When inquiries were made about the sentencing of Ukrainian writers and others, we were told that they were not recognized writers, that they were not imprisoned for their writings, that they were convicted as enemies of the state. But the specific charges against them were not revealed. Although we do not claim to know what considerations of state security led to the trials of these writers being conducted in secret, we must make the point that such *in camera* trials never serve to dispel doubts and questioning.[32]

The report criticized the limited opportunities for Ukrainians living in the other republics of the USSR to cultivate their native language and culture. Such criticism is understandable when we consider the contrast between nationality policy in Ukraine and in Canada, a country that has made serious efforts to ensure the survival of minority languages.

The official reaction to the report in the Ukrainian SSR was hostile. In September 1969 a letter was published in *Viewpoint* and *Zhyttia i slovo* in which twenty-six CPU officials, civil servants, teachers, scientists, journalists, etc., declared that the Canadian communist delegation had misrepresented the situation in Ukraine, distorted a number of facts and succumbed to the influence of bourgeois nationalists and other enemies of the Soviet Union. The letter defended the political trials: "Actually it is a question of crimes committed by people who flouted Soviet laws, sought to undermine the foundations of the socialist system by illegal activities, harmed the interests of the state and people by their deeds, and were punished for this."[33] The Canadian party leaders backed down under such pressure, apparently lacking the courage of their original convictions. They renewed their pledge of solidarity with the CPSU, and the visit to Ukraine became little more than a minor, if interesting, episode in the history of the Communist parties of Ukraine and Canada.

A Novel Creates a Furor

In January 1968 the literary journal *Vitchyzna* began serializing Oles Honchar's *Sobor* (The Cathedral)—a novel that, initially, was received with enthusiasm throughout Ukraine. It was issued in book form by the Dnipro publishing house in a first edition of 100,000 copies. The critics' first reaction ranged from mere approval to wild enthusiasm.[34] On 29 April 1968, however, a group of dogmatic literary critics, led by V. Kozachenko, the secretary of the writers' party organization, attacked the novel at a party meeting of the Kiev Writers' Union. This marked the beginning of a campaign against *Sobor*.

In *Sobor*, Honchar analyzed the problems of life in an industrial society. Although he set the novel in Ukraine, he dealt with an international rather than a "national" problem. The book consisted of a series of short biographies, combining fiction with social criticism. The scene is a Ukrainian industrial centre and the characters include metalworkers, students, factory workers, housewives, bureaucrats and juvenile delinquents. In this centre, dominated by an ultra-modern metallurgical combine, a monument of the past—the cathedral—has survived. It was built by Cossacks to symbolize their own and future freedoms. In the course of the centuries the cathedral saw the Cossacks lose their liberty, witnessed persecution under the tsars and barely escaped destruction by Makhno's anarchists. It survived war and passed unscathed through Stalin's reign of terror. It withstood industrialization, perhaps because the technocrats' tendency to destroy the past was tempered by the emergence of new forces that sought to preserve its heritage. But the cathedral is depicted not just an edifice, but as a symbol of the persistence of good in man and of the struggle against evil as embodied by the bureaucracy:

> There is such a thing as a drug of greed for power, a heroin of careerism. Once a man takes a fix he is lost. The only gleam in his eye is greed for power. He'd sacrifice his own father for his career. He'd destroy the Cathedral just to climb another rung. Ideals? He scoffs at all ideals. Only power and more power. And if you ask him why? To climb still higher.... Today he manages a factory shop, tomorrow he's a director, and then he sets his sights on a post in the main administration.

Honchar sees these power-seekers, bureaucrats who work alongside the "waste-producers," as the greatest ill of socialist society. He links their constant urge to destroy the cathedral with the grave problems of modern society—the imposition of "progress" at the cost of human welfare; environmental pollution; and the destruction of nature's beauty, of everything that the cathedral symbolizes. The following excerpt, spoken by one of Honchar's characters, shows that the author was concerned with all mankind, not just the Ukrainian nation:

> [The cathedral] does not belong to you; it is not mine and it is not ours, nor does it belong to the nation that created it. It belongs to all the people of our planet. In its defiance of all that is evil and destructive, the cathedral embodies progress, continuity.

Through another of his characters, Honchar demonstrated the contradiction between progress and the vital demands of human welfare: "They wanted to turn Lake Kakhovka, into which half of Ukraine has been sunk, into a sea. And what did it become? A swamp, a rotting swamp that spreads its stench all over Ukraine. Pilots who fly over it have to hold their noses."

In 1968 Honchar described one of the major dilemmas of our age in terms reminiscent of today's environmentalists: our intellect has the capacity for divine discovery, but our emotions and passions are still largely neolithic. In his novel he lashes out at the hypocrisy of the people who live in the vicinity of the cathedral: a group of rowdies who dance to jazz music in the house of God; a married factory foreman who pays lip-service to communist morality and has no qualms about seducing a young girl; a young careerist who gets rid of his "inconvenient" father by sending him to a home for the aged; thieves and black-marketeers; people with neither heart nor conscience. One reason for the angry reaction to Honchar's novel in official circles was its accurate reflection of contemporary Soviet society.

Despite its sombre mood, *Sobor* offered some hope: "You cannot build life on suspicion and distrust; you cannot live by the dogmas of hate. Something higher still lives in man—the need for cohesion, succour and brotherhood."[35]

Ukrainian-language publications in Soviet satellite countries lauded Honchar's novel. The most important review was by Dr. Orest Zilynsky of Charles University, published in Czechoslovakia:

> The novel is a freely narrated account of the life of people in an industrial city in southern Ukraine—metalworkers, housewives, students, party officials, rowdies.... It describes a head-on collision between the old and the new in the life of contemporary Ukraine; it depicts both modern life and the philosophical problems of the content of life for man and society.... It is important to note that the ideal that Honchar develops does not bear the hallmark of a closed national character. It is universal and common to all mankind, for the forces against which the novel fights are the deadly enemies of the whole of human history. It contrasts liberty and naked coercion, the freedom of creative thinking and the trammels of decreed truth, the warmth of human trust and the cold severity of the establishment's inderdictions....
> There is a world-wide philosophical debate about the tragedy of modern man oppressed by the institutions, prohibitions and authorities that he has created. In his work the Ukrainian writer depicts examples of this tragedy, which is carving up man's soul within the framework of socialist practice. In this way he anticipated the spiritual upheaval that is now occurring in our state.[36]

In Ukraine itself, the forces of the right closed ranks against *Sobor*. In their campaign against Honchar's novel, they mobilized the "outraged" workers of Ukrainian industry, especially in the region where the author located his fictional city. They used the well-tried method of setting the workers against the intellectuals. Letters to the press declared that the metalworkers portrayed by Honchar were not those whose achievements had earned them medals and bonuses but eternal malcontents who do not want to face up to life. The letter-writing campaign reached major dimensions in the Ukrainian provincial press.[37]

Reaction to *Sobor* was particularly hostile in the city and oblast of Dnipropetrovsk, as reported in the *samvydav* document "Letter from the Creative Youth of Dnipropetrovsk."[38] At a conference of the secretaries of the oblast's primary party organization, oblast committee secretary O. F. Vatchenko condemned the novel and the positive reviews in such local newspapers as *Zoria* and *Prapor iunosti*. His declaration that the working class of Dnipropetrovsk rejected *Sobor* precipitated a wave of negative criticism. Letters condemning the smear campaign and praising Honchar's novel were passed on to the oblast committee and the KGB. The former vetoed the plans of the Faculty of History and Philosophy at Dnipropetrovsk University to celebrate Honchar's fiftieth birthday, although the event had already been arranged and advertised. Before the veto was imposed, the faculty's dean, Pavlov, had banned discussion of *Sobor* at a university seminar.

The clashes between the supporters and opponents of Honchar's novel led to a purge in the party and Komsomol. The "Letter from the Creative Youth of Dnipropetrovsk" named several journalists and officials who were expelled from these bodies. Those opposed to the novel branded its advocates "bourgeois nationalists," a label that ensured the persecution of those young writers who refused to dance to the party's tune. During a counter-protest, the CPU leadership was inundated with letters condemning the arrests, and the controversy threatened to involve the entire country.

Shelest came under pressure from the ideological apparatus. In March 1968 the CPU tried to assert control by transferring Skaba from the post of Central Committee secretary for ideology to the directorship of the Institute of History of the Ukrainian Academy of Sciences. He was replaced by a chemist, Professor F. D. Ovcharenko, formerly head of the Central Committee Department for Science and Culture. The choice of successor was surprising, because this post was usually reserved for a professional historian with a thorough knowledge of the history of Ukraine and, above all, of its Communist Party.

The new appointment did not bring about any real change. It demonstrated only that Shelest had sufficient authority to convince the Politburo of the CC CPSU of the need for change, for, under the nomenclature system, he had to get this body's approval for a nomination to so high a post. His probable argument was that a man who had not been involved with the ideological apparatus would have the best chance of defusing the conflict among the intelligentsia and between the intelligentsia and the party in a manner most favourable to the party.

On 12 June 1968 the party members of the Ukrainian Writers' Union held a meeting, in which Oles Honchar participated.[39] The meeting declared that the campaign against *Sobor* had been overzealous, and rehabilitated Honchar. The victims of the campaign, who, for the most part, were young writers and students from Dnipropetrovsk, were less fortunate, however.

A Wave of Protest and More Political Unrest

In the 1960s (especially after Khrushchev's fall), Ukrainians believed that direct appeals to the authorities or to Shelest himself would redress injustices and solve problems. One petition—a letter to Brezhnev, Kosygin and Pidhorny in which 139 scientists, writers, artists, students and workers protested the Ukrainian trials of 1965 and 1966 became something of a cause célèbre. The letter was drafted in April 1968, shortly after Skaba's transfer. Describing illegal arrests in Ukraine, the authors wrote:

All these and other facts show that the recent trials have become a form of suppressing dissidents, a form of suppressing all kinds of civil action and social criticism—activities that every society needs to maintain its health. They confirm the increasingly patent trend toward the restoration of Stalinism against which I. Gabai, Iu. Kim and P. Iakir struggled so energetically and courageously in their appeal to the scientists, cultural workers and artists of the USSR. In Ukraine, where the violation of democracy is compounded and intensified by distortion of the nationality problem, the symptoms of Stalinism manifest themselves more patently and crudely.

After criticizing the state security organs, the letter continued:

We consider it our duty to express our profound concern about what has happened. We call upon you to apply your authority and power to ensure that the courts and the office of the state prosecutor adhere strictly to Soviet laws and that the difficulties and differences of opinion that arise in our public and political life be resolved in the ideological domain instead of being left to the competence of the office of the state prosecutor and the state security organs.[40]

Like so many of its predecessors and successors, the letter failed to achieve its aim. The party leadership showed more interest in preventing further protest than in clarifying, let alone solving the real problem. The matter was passed on to the security organs. The signatories were interrogated, some by the KGB, some by the party apparatus, and urged to withdraw their signatures or sign a declaration that they had been persuaded to sign on the basis of false information. Nevertheless, the protests continued. Most of these letters were distributed in *samvydav* and later published in the underground journal, the *Ukrainian Herald*, which began appearing in January 1970. Reports about these protests and their consequences also appeared in the Moscow samizdat journal *Chronicle of Current Events* (*Khronika tekushchikh sobytii*). As testimony of the political situation in Ukraine, all these letters are important historical documents.

The protests sometimes turned into tragedy. On 5 November 1968, the eve of the fifty-first anniversary of the October Revolution, Vasyl Makukha, a 50-year-old man who had spent years in Stalin's labour camps, immolated himself on the main street of Kiev. He drenched his clothes with gasoline, delivered a brief speech about Russification and the colonial status of Ukraine, and then set himself on fire. He ran like a human torch toward the Kalinin Square, shouting repeatedly "Long Live Free Ukraine!" Makukha died in the Zhovtnevy Hospital in Kiev.[41] Another attempt at self-immolation occurred near Kiev University in March 1969. Bereslavsky, from Berdiansk (Zaporizhzhia oblast), attached posters protesting Russification to the walls of the university. When he saw that he was being observed he poured gasoline over his clothes and ignited them. He was rescued and later sentenced to two-and-a-half years' imprisonment.[42]

A central figure in these political events was the talented Ukrainian literary critic Ivan Dziuba, who was popular for his courageous reviews and public speeches. He achieved particular renown with the speech he delivered on the anniversary of the tragedy of Babyn Iar, the gorge near Kiev where the Germans shot several thousand Kievan Jews and Ukrainians in 1941.

Toward the end of 1965 Dziuba completed *Internationalism or Russification?*, a study of Ukraine's status in the USSR. Suggestions that Dziuba wrote his study at the request of Ukrainian party officials have some credibility, since the original manuscript was addressed to P. Shelest, First Secretary of the CC CPU and member of the Presidium of the CC CPSU, and to V. V. Shcherbytsky, Chairman of the Ukrainian Council of Ministers and alternate member of the Presidium of the CC CPSU. Dziuba completed the manuscript in December 1965 and circulated a few copies among his closest friends. When the addressees failed to react, it was distributed in *samvydav*. It was published abroad, first in Ukrainian and subsequently in Italian, English, French, Chinese and Russian.[43]

In this study, Dziuba, who avowed loyalty to Marxism-Leninism, criticized the deviation of Soviet nationality policy toward chauvinism and Russification. He substantiated his arguments with quotations from Lenin, copious statistics and documentary evidence of the extent of Russification. He came under attack in the USSR in 1969, after his study appeared in the West. According to the first issue of the *Ukrainian Herald*, the KGB first suggested that he write a suitable refutation of this "bourgeois propaganda." Dziuba refused on the grounds that his work was a Marxist analysis of Soviet nationality policy and that he had had nothing to do with its publication abroad. The first public criticism came from the writer L. Dmyterko.[44] It was followed immediately by a monograph of Bohdan

Stenchuk entitled *Shcho i iak obstoiuie Ivan Dziuba?* (The English edition, published in 1970, was called *What I. Dzyuba Stands For, And How He Does It.*) Published by the Association for Cultural Relations with Ukrainians Abroad, the book was intended exclusively for Ukrainian readers outside the Soviet Union. According to the *Ukrainian Herald,* although Stenchuk was credited with its authorship, the book was in fact co-authored by the head of the CC CPU's Department of Propaganda and Agitation, H. H. Shevel, and the scholar V. Ievdokymenko. A number of *samvydav* writers responded to Dziuba's critics, one of the first of whom was the Kievan, Vasyl Stus.

The Dziuba "case" posed a very delicate problem for the leaders of the CPU. Dziuba himself enjoyed considerable popularity and his line of argument in *Internationalism or Russification?* was supported by detailed evidence. When the Kiev Writers' Union dealt with the case in the fall of 1969, many members opposed the move to expel Dziuba from the association. Even writers like A. Holovko, P. Panch and Iu. Smolych, who did not share Dziuba's political views, came to his defence. D. Pavlychko, for example, declared that it was "necessary to give serious consideration to the shortcomings of nationality policy and to acknowledge the fact that it is not Dziuba who has created the problem but the problem that has created Dziuba."[45] Under pressure, mainly from the Board of the Writers' Union, Dziuba dissociated himself from "certain circles" of the Ukrainian emigration:

> At times certain people—with whose anti-communist views I have never had, and am not prepared to have, anything in common—"sympathize" and "solidarize" with me.... At times this political prattle goes so far as to declare me, no more nor less, a leader of an allegedly existing nationalist underground in Ukraine.

Dziuba went on to affirm that as a Soviet literary figure he had always represented positions opposed to the ideology of Ukrainian bourgeois nationalism and the concepts of misanthropy or enmity between peoples:

> I have always strived to approach the nationalities question—as any other question—from the standpoint of the principles of scientific communism and the teachings of Marx-Engels-Lenin, perceiving the prospects for their resolution by way of fulfilment of Lenin's testaments and communist construction.[46]

Here the campaign against Dziuba ended. He was, however, unable to publish his writings.

The Ukrainian intelligentsia had mixed reactions to Dziuba's comments. Some defended him and believed that, after a while, his articles would be printed again and he would regain his position as one of the republic's most talented and influential literary critics. Others, however, condemned his statement on the following grounds:

> Under the conditions existing in Ukraine, Dziuba's authority as a critic and public activist of high principles and steadfast nature did not entitle him to enter a compromise that did not give him anything except the temporary right to retain his membership in the Ukrainian Writers' Union. Further concessions will be demanded of him. When he attacked "nationalism" Dziuba forgot that both he and those who shared his views—be they at liberty or under duress—are themselves called nationalists, regardless of their Marxist positions. There are situations when it is not ethical to oppose openly even that with which one does not really agree in principle.[47]

The Ukrainian party hard-liners were already trying to convince Moscow that Shelest was responsible for the "liberal" treatment of dissidents in Ukraine. As usual, they invoked the spectre of nationalism. They claimed that Shelest and his chief ideologist, Ovcharenko, underestimated the dangerous upsurge of "bourgeois nationalism," which, they alleged, was flourishing in Western Ukraine. As a result of their efforts, the first secretary of the Lviv oblast committee, V. S. Kutsevol, a Shelest supporter, was ordered to Moscow to answer reports about the situation in Lviv and the surrounding oblasts at a plenary session of the CC CPSU. On 7 October 1971 the Central Committee adopted a resolution "On Political Activity among the Population of Lviv Oblast." The text of the resolution was never published in the press, but a résumé was published in a collection of documents dealing with the ideological work of the CPSU.[48]

The resolution criticized various social groups in the city and oblast of Lviv, above all scholars and university instructors:

> In their books and articles, [these people] glorified some of the ideologues of Ukrainian bourgeois nationalism, violated the party principle in their treatment of the historical past ... tried to defuse the class struggle and to idealize the old past. By this they caused particular harm to the education of youth. There are [also] shortcomings in atheist work among the population.... Among some of the teachers and students there are signs of an apolitical attitude, nationalist views and violation of the norms of socialist morality.[49]

The resolution berated the quality and quantity of the ideological and political work of the Lviv city and oblast committees. The CC CPSU called for an oblast-wide educational campaign, to be conducted in the spirit of internationalism, of fraternal friendship among peoples, and for a struggle against all manifestations of bourgeois nationalism and national narrow-mindedness. It also demanded that the party, state, Komsomol and trade-union organizations begin a "cultural-educational" offensive. It was essential, it declared, "to propagate socialist traditions and customs and to wage an implacable campaign against religiosity among communists and Komsomol members."

This resolution may be viewed as an ideological thrust against the policies of Shelest and his supporters. The whole affair tends to support the view that Shelest was a "liberal" on the questions of national culture and the defence of Ukrainian interests in science, literature and art.

At this time, Kiev was the scene of several impressive actions in defence of Ukrainian culture. The demonstration at the Shevchenko Monument and the protests against anti-Semitism at Babyn Iar are but two examples. Meanwhile, the attitude of ordinary people in Western Ukraine, the workers and peasants who categorically rejected Russification and clung to their national traditions, remained an insoluble problem for the party. The resolution of the CC CPSU continued to trouble the CC CPU, even after Shelest's fall.

The *Ukrainian Herald* gave a very general report on the CPSU resolution, which merely confirmed that Kutsevol reported to the November 1971 plenum of the CC CPSU on the status of party work in Lviv oblast. The *Herald* did mention, however, that Suslov's proposal to dismiss Kutsevol from the post of first secretary of the oblast committee was rejected thanks to Shelest's intervention. The journal also noted that, after the Central Committee's resolution, the target of the press campaign was modified from "Ukrainian bourgeois nationalism" to "nationalistic tendencies, national narrow-mindedness, and outdated national customs."[50]

The resolution was followed by a wave of persecution: mass arrests, disciplinary actions, expulsions from colleges and universities. According to the *Ukrainian Herald*:

> The scum of society was beginning to rear its ugly head; the KGB completely slipped out from under the control of the CPU leadership. The number of KGB men and undercover agents increased sharply. The head of the Republic's KGB, Fedorchuk, sent off reports to Moscow, [charging] that the leadership of the CPU was not helping the KGB in carrying out its work effectively. Shcherbytsky and Malanchuk, pursuing their careerist ambitions, tried to convince Moscow's Politburo that P. Shelest was a nationalistic deviationist. Under such circumstances, the CC CPSU saw Shelest as an obstacle to the implementation of their pogrom policy in Ukraine.[51]

The Invasion of Czechoslovakia Casts a Shadow

The reaction to the suppression of the Prague Spring by Warsaw Pact forces in August 1968 was especially strong in Ukraine, which shares a border with Czechoslovakia and has a long tradition of cultural and economic links with that country. These links were broadened and intensified after the Second World War with the encouragement of both Moscow and Kiev, a development to which no little contribution was made by the Ukrainian minority in Czechoslovakia, a small but active ethnic group with its own schools, press, cultural institutions and official representation. The Ukrainians in Czechoslovakia were sympathetic toward the reformist aspirations of communists and intellectuals in Ukraine from the time of their first emergence in 1953. They also supported Alexander Dubček's efforts to establish "socialism with a human face." Representatives of the Ukrainian minority issued several declarations of solidarity with Dubček's policies during the critical period preceding the intervention of the Warsaw Pact forces. Contacts between Ukraine and Czechoslovakia were also furthered by their close economic relationship within the Council for Mutual Economic Assistance (Comecon). After the Twenty-second CPU Congress, Ukrainian-Czechoslovak relations were enhanced by a programme for increased contacts between Ukrainian and Czechoslovak students. This included Ukrainian-Czechoslovak clubs, individual and collective pen-friendships, and exchanges of student delegations. Ukrainian school children and students had more connections with their peers in Czechoslovakia than in any other country.

The Soviet leaders took a different view of these links when the Moscow–Prague conflict began to escalate. However, articles sympathetic toward Czechoslovakia continued to appear in the Soviet Ukrainian press up to July 1968—only one month before the invasion. On 2 July, for example, the first reports on the "Ukrainian Days in the CSSR" under the title "More Friendship and Fraternity" were published.[52]

The Ukrainian press took particular note of the popularity enjoyed by the works of Taras Shevchenko in Czechoslovakia; the fact that Shevchenko had been well-informed about the national struggle of the Czechs and Slovaks, according to *Literaturna Ukraina*, was appreciated in Czechoslovakia. The paper hinted at the Soviet leadership's lack of understanding for the developments in that country by quoting the following passage from a Czech newspaper: "As for his attitude to Czechs and Slovaks, Shevchenko knew them better than many of our contemporaries."[53]

On 17 July 1968 *Pravda* published an article by O. P. Botvin, secretary of the Kiev CPU city committee, which caused a flurry of excitement both in the East and in the West. Botvin confirmed that there had been a wide-ranging and impassioned debate in Ukraine over the possible reform or democratization of the Soviet system. According to Botvin, "Some people are even inclined to ruminate on the putrid 'theories' of the necessity of 'democratization' and the 'liberalization of socialism' thrown to them by enemy propaganda." The party, reported Botvin, had to "correct" the work of various organizations in Kiev to achieve the proper "ideological direction" and to institute changes in cadre policy.

The party leaders in Moscow and Kiev, including Shelest himself, tried to minimize the impact of the programme and practical measures adopted by the Czechoslovak reformist communists before the decision to invade that country was taken. They were only too aware that the USSR and, especially, Ukraine offered fertile soil for such a programme. Ukrainian press reports published shortly before the intervention show that the invasion was prepared with the utmost efficiency and precision.

Initially, however, Ukrainian party leaders did not know how to react. The Ukrainian press commentaries on Czechoslovakia were limited to reprints from the central press. There are two possible explanations: either the CPU had not yet received precise instructions from Moscow or, more likely, the Ukrainian apparatus needed time to assess the mood of the Ukrainian population. Eventually, it made every effort to convince party activists of the necessity of suppressing the Prague reforms and to provide them with the necessary propaganda. The party press began to depict the Czechoslovak reform communists as "revisionists." In *Komunist Ukrainy* we read:

> Nowadays revisionism is more closely related to nationalism than at any time in the past. And it is not just that the narrow national interests of today's revisionists often take precedence over the proletarian international interests of the movement as a whole. In the case of some comrades, including those at the top of individual fraternal parties, there is a manifest tendency to ignore the experience of other parties and socialist countries and the international experience as generalized by Marxist-Leninist experience.[54]

The propaganda campaign gradually increased in intensity; it began to portray Czechoslovak reform communists as the "henchmen of imperialism," especially West German "imperialism," their aim being to destroy the socialist community. During the campaign, parallels were drawn between the factional struggles in the CPU during the 1920s and the demands of the Czechoslovak reform communists. In an article for *Komunist Ukrainy*, P. Bachynsky outlined the "nationalist deviation" movement led by Shumsky and Khvyliovy in the mid-1920s. Then, recalling the slogan "Away from Moscow," he described how the party commissioned all its theoreticians "to mobilize the masses against revisionism."[55]

Courses, seminars and lectures on ideology in the context of current events were held in Ukraine. The most important of these was a seminar for propagandists of the party organizations, the Komsomol, the *Znannia* Society and the Ukrainian military districts. Moscow sent several professors and ideologists to the seminar, held on 24–29 June 1968. The main contributions were papers on such topics as "The Leninist General Line of the CPSU and the Struggle Against Contemporary Revisionism," "The CPSU—The Leading Force in Soviet Society" and "Nationalism—The Greatest Danger for the Communist Workers' Movement."[56]

The Western press published numerous, often contradictory reports about Shelest's role in the negotiations between the CPU and the Communist Party of Czechoslovakia. In the opinion of Vladimir Horský: Shelest, Ulbricht and Gomułka had supported military intervention in Czechoslovakia, because they were afraid that the political ideas of the Prague reform were contagious. The Polish slogan "All Poland is Waiting for its Dubček!"[57] and the sale of tattered copies of *Rude pravo* for a ruble on the Ukrainian black market[58] showed that these fears were justified. According to Horský:

> If you consider that, apart from Gomułka and Ulbricht, it was Ukraine and the other non-Russians who insisted in the Kremlin that force be used against Prague, then the theory of "fear of a focus of infection" is sufficiently valid.[59]

The invasion provoked many protests in Ukraine. Some Ukrainians were arrested and given long terms of imprisonment. The *Chronicle of Current Events*, for example, reported that the 40-year-old Oleksandr Serhiienko, who was accused of having denigrated the "international aid to Czechoslovakia," was sentenced in Kiev to seven years in strict-regime labour camps and three years of internal exile. In July 1972, the 54-year-old teacher Ivan Kovalenko was put on trial for criticizing the invasion of Czechoslovakia in the presence of his colleagues and pupils.[60] The full scope of the protests and public expressions of sympathy for Dubček's experiment will never be known. If the closeness of relations between Ukraine and Czechoslovakia prior to the invasion is any measure, it must have been considerable.

Another Writers' Demonstration

The repercussions of the Fifth Writers' Congress had not died down when, in January 1970, the Board of the Ukrainian Writers' Union met in plenary session to discuss "the international ties of Ukrainian literature." Shortly before the plenum, *Literaturna Ukraina* published an article by Oleh Mykytenko, the son of the liquidated writer Ivan Mykytenko, which stated:

> We have something to say to the world. To tell of the historical path of the Ukrainian people, which rose from colonial oppression to socialist statehood;

to show this people's spiritual world: its art, culture, science, creations and language. This is not only the internal task of Ukrainian literature but also its highest international duty.[61]

Oleh Mykytenko proposed that all existing institutions and organizations for relations with foreign countries should be commissioned to propagate Ukrainian literature and art. He suggested that foreign philologists should be trained as translators at Kiev University and that foreign students in Kiev should be drawn into the project. The meeting was convened on the initiative of the CPU leadership, which wanted to curb the Ukrainian intelligentsia's insistent demands for closer ties with foreign countries.

The plenary session of the Board of the Ukrainian Writers' Union commenced with a brief address delivered by Oles Honchar. The main report was read by the union's secretary, Pavlo Zahrebelny, who mixed an apologia for the party line on art and literature with objective criticism of those official bodies that systematically impeded the contacts of Ukrainian writers with other countries. He claimed that the journals and books published in Moscow paid little attention to Ukrainian literature. In fact, declared Zahrebelny, *Sovetskaia literatura*, the official organ of the Soviet Writers' Union that also printed in foreign languages, boycotted publications in the Ukrainian language, as did *Progress*, the foreign-language publishing house in Moscow.[62]

Ukrainian writers and intellectuals claimed that closer ties with foreign countries were in the interest of the party and the best means of refuting nationalistic falsifications. Accordingly, the plenum of the Board of the Ukrainian Writers' Union charged that "bourgeois nationalists" were trying to disparage loyal Ukrainian writers in other countries while promoting the works of "dissident" authors. Many speakers pointed out that very few works of Ukrainian literature were published abroad. Zahrebelny called for more translations of foreign works into Ukrainian and suggested the creation of a special prize for outstanding translations.

The poet Rostyslav Bratun urged his colleagues to learn foreign languages and proposed that translators be trained at Ukrainian universities. "Where," he asked, "are the phonograph records, where are the dictionaries, guides and textbooks for learning our language?"[63] The representatives of the Moscow literary journals at the plenum supported their Ukrainian colleagues' demands but pointed out potential difficulties. The CPU was represented by I. A. Peresadenko, the head of the Central Committee Department for Ties with Foreign Countries.

The Board of the Ukrainian Writers' Union held another plenary session on 18–19 November, this time in Kharkiv. The subject, "The Working Man in Soviet Ukrainian Literature," was chosen apparently in response to party pressure. V. Kozachenko, secretary of the party organization at the Writers' Union, warned against the illusion of "creating a literature that stands above classes." On the whole, this plenum, which was held on the eve of the Twenty-fourth CPU Congress and was apparently designed to prepare Ukrainian writers for this event, was a routine affair.[64]

The party leadership's efforts to curb the Ukrainian reformists included a low-key campaign to remove wilful persons from the editorial boards of literary journals and publishing houses. Marharyta Malynovska, an open-minded and talented literary critic who, as deputy chief editor, had enhanced the sophistication and candour of *Literaturna Ukraina*, was removed from her post. Her name disappeared from the masthead on 1 January 1970. In the middle of that year personnel changes were also made in the editorial board of the literary journal *Prapor*, which is published in Kharkiv. The journal *Vsesvit*, specializing in translations of foreign literature, bore the brunt of a more open attack. Among its sins were: publishing the works of second-rate authors, particularly the proponents of modernism; haphazardness in the selection of the works it published; disregard for relations with foreign communist parties; and failure to respond adequately to the false representation of Ukrainian literature abroad. An enlarged plenary session of the Board of the Ukrainian Writers' Union held on 24 April 1970, discussed *Vsesvit* in the presence of representatives of the Ukrainian Society for Friendship and Cultural Ties with Foreign Countries.[65]

Ukrainian Scientists Voice Their Demands

Until the mid-1960s, the CPSU leadership discussed major problems by means of "expert" opinions in newspapers, journals and magazines. In November 1951 it used this technique for a wide-ranging "economic discussion" that subsequently served as a basis for Stalin's last work, *The Economic Problems of Socialism in the Soviet Union*. Later, the press published the opinions of military experts on nuclear warfare. *Voprosy istorii* was used as an experts' forum on the concept of nationhood. Such discussions had to be approved at the highest political level, which gave the participants a relatively freer rein to express their opinions, and, more important, enabled the Politburo to keep abreast of the current viewpoints and thereby maintain control.

In mid-1970, Petro Shelest initiated a discussion of the status of the natural sciences in Ukraine, the training of scientific personnel and the impediments to the exchange of scientific information. It began with an article by Shelest's son Vitalii, who was then deputy director of the Institute of Theoretical Physics at the Ukrainian Academy of Sciences.[66] The discussion ended suddenly at the end of July, because the participating scientists overstepped "the rules" and transformed it into a political demonstration that set off repercussions in the scientific centres of the Soviet Union and the West.

Several scientists drew attention to the shortcomings of the Ukrainian scientific establishment, particularly its relatively primitive level. Iu. O. Mytropolsky, a member of the Ukrainian Academy of Sciences, asserted:

> Mathematics and basic research have not yet acquired the authority they deserve in our country. Clear proof of this is the fact that, year in, year out, we always get fewer applicants for the universities than for the road-construction, building, polytechnic and other institutes. Why? Because everyone knows that, after graduation from the university, most young specialists are assigned to work in the schools.[67]

The study of physics or mathematics, according to Mytropolsky, promised no sure return for the graduate's intellectual investment. Those who, despite the absence of appropriate reward, chose these subjects, received neither stimulus nor support during their studies.

Mytropolsky also complained about the low salaries received by teachers and the low standard of high-school education: "Because of the poor pay, as a rule only the mediocre go into pedagogical work. The state must raise the general level of education... in the high-schools and in the basic subjects, especially physics, mathematics and foreign languages." Vitalii Shelest called for a thorough reform of the educational system and the creation of special study centres for leading scientists:

> Incidentally, in the United States there is such a branch for physicists, the Institute for Advanced Studies, at Princeton.... The creation of such teaching establishments in the Soviet Union and, especially, Ukraine is a realistic and realizable undertaking. Indeed, it is more than that: it is a duty.[68]

Shelest also noted that "a considerable proportion of our scholars do not become doctors of science until they reach pension age." In the words of the physicist V. Klymeniuk:

> At present the situation in Ukraine and in the Soviet Union as a whole is such that just about every fourth doctor received his title at retirement age; the average age of experts who defend their candidate's thesis is almost forty. The excessively high age structure of the cadres is a permanent and continually worsening phenomenon.[69]

The Ukrainian scientists pressed for more contacts with their Western colleagues. In the words of O. H. Ivakhnenko, a corresponding member of the Ukrainian Academy of Sciences: "Twenty years ago anyone, especially a scholar, could visit any scientific establishment.... Today this is practically impossible." Ivakhnenko also complained that it was difficult to obtain foreign scientific literature. It took two or three years, he said, for important foreign publications, including specialized articles, to reach Ukraine, by which time they had lost their topicality. Moreover, there were no Ukrainian translations of these publications.[70] In November 1970, several months after the scientists' debate had come to a premature end, the CC CPSU accepted a resolution "On the Work of the Party Committee at the Lebedev Institute of Physics of the USSR Academy of Sciences." This resolution, which established a number of new guidelines for scientific work, was a substitute for the final analysis that usually ended such discussions.[71]

The Twenty-fourth CPU Congress

The Twenty-fourth CPU Congress was held on 17–20 March 1971, when the Soviet leadership had begun to promote détente. Among the leadership there was a consensus that initiatives such as the projected Conference on Security and Co-operation in Europe (CSCE) could lead to an expansion of East–West scientific and technological co-operation, negotiations on the limitation of strategical weapons, and talks on the reduction of armed forces in Central Europe. At the same time the Kremlin believed that détente would have to be accompanied by an intensification of the ideological struggle between East and West. Indeed, this was the leitmotif of the Ukrainian and other republican party congresses. In this context the foremost questions were the ideological and political education of youth, the dissident problem, law and order in "socialist reality," and labour discipline. Accordingly, Shelest began his speech to the CPU Congress by attacking the ideological enemy:

> During recent years the forces of imperialism have tried repeatedly to test our strength and our determination to defend the achievements of the socialist system. But, on each occasion, all these attempts of the imperialists suffered a humiliating defeat. We have exposed and will continue to expose the deceitful actions of the imperialists and their agents.[72]

Shelest devoted the main part of his report to the Ukrainian economy. Although the republic had fulfilled the 1966–70 five-year plan, he said, many branches of the economy were still falling short of the required standards. Shelest criticized several ministries, and castigated the light and food industries. In 1970, he declared, Ukraine could no longer be held up as an example for the solution of economic problems. Shelest's comments on artists, writers and scientists were his harshest to date:

Individual scientists commit breaches of the principles of the party when they evaluate social phenomena and events in their works. They resort to the construction of fictitious models that have no relation to real life and concern themselves more with so-called cerebral acrobatics than the creative analysis of contemporary problems. The Central Committee detected great shortcomings in the work of the Institute of Philosophy at the Ukrainian Academy of Sciences and of several social-science faculties at institutions of higher learning, and called on the institute directors and the scholarly collectives to adhere strictly to the Leninist principles of party allegiance in scientific analysis. We must always remember that the socio-economic sciences are a potent weapon in the struggle against bourgeois ideology.

Criticizing artists and officials, Shelest declared:

The achievements of art and literature deserve high marks, but we cannot fail to notice the continued occurrence of painful ethical miscalculations and ideological deviations. Politically immature and artistically defective works sometimes appear. This applies not only to a few young and inexperienced people but also to some well-known artists. It happens that they lose the clear ideological orientation in their creative work and that they do not distinguish between healthy, just criticism of shortcomings and nihilistic carping. There are also people who, instead of providing a profound and accurate representation of our people's great deeds, are effusive over petty subjects and formalistic fumblings, who overlook the fact that what are most important are developments in all spheres of the life of Soviet society. Such artists need a clear reminder of their civic and professional responsibility toward the readers and viewers, toward their people. Can a true master really find satisfaction in the role of a purveyor of shoddy verbal goods and, especially, ideological rubbish?

Shelest exhorted his listeners to "intensify the ideological struggle" and painted a menacing picture of the imperialist threat against the Soviet Union:

All reactionary forces of the present time, from the troubadours of imperialism to the remnants of the White-Guardist and bourgeois-nationalist scum, the Trotskyites, and all kinds of defectors and traitors, are united under the black banners of anti-communism. In the filthy anti-Soviet crusades a special role is reserved for the damned enemy of our people, the Ukrainian bourgeois nationalists, those perfidious foes of the fatherland, those renegades that the wind has scattered like dust throughout the world. The Zionists are displaying a special form of activity. Zionism is a reactionary, racist and nationalist ideology that serves the cause of imperialism, lock, stock and barrel. The Zionists, who represent their lords' lust for conquest, use fascist methods of struggle against the progressive movement.

Only a few of the party officials endorsed this anathematization; for example, the first secretary of the Dnipropetrovsk oblast committee, O. F. Vatchenko, and his Kievan colleague, V. M. Tsybulko. The writer Iu. Smolych also attacked the "bourgeois nationalists" and accused a number of young writers of being apolitical and tending toward formalism and modernism. At the same time he praised Shelest for speaking "quite correctly of the necessity of cultivating the mother tongue and its folk characters." Smolych declared: "Our literary youth loves the Ukrainian language, and that is wonderful. For it is the duty of men of letters to honour, develop and propagate the mother tongue." O. S. Kapto, the first secretary of the Ukrainian Komsomol Central Committee, warned the youth against succumbing to the influence of any foe, especially "the anti-communists, revisionists, opportunists, bourgeois nationalists and malevolent Zionists."[73] Like other speakers, he condemned apolitical attitudes among Ukrainian youth.

The Twenty-fourth CPSU Congress, which took place in Moscow from 30 March to 9 April 1971, also discussed the nationality question. In his report to the congress, Brezhnev touched on a new characteristic of nationality policy:

All the nationalities and peoples of our country, but, above all, the great Russian people, have played their role in the creation, consolidation and development of this mighty union of peoples with equal rights. [The Russian people's] revolutionary energy, its willingness to make sacrifices, its love of work and its internationalism have justly earned it the sincere respect of all the peoples of our socialist homeland.[74]

Brezhnev's words came as a surprise, since after the Twentieth Party Congress it had been considered improper to use such phrases as "the great Russian people" or "the great Russian brother." Brezhnev's terminology echoed Stalin's May 1945 toast to the "great Russian people" that signalled the glorification of Russia and the beginning of all-out Russification.

Shelest avoided this kind of statement in his speech and spoke only of further consolidation of the moral and political unity of Soviet society and the "friendship of the peoples of our fatherland." The representatives of some other union republics, however, did not follow his example. The Uzbek party chief, Sh. R. Rashidov, for example, proclaimed: "The Russian people is the elder brother and true friend of all Soviet peoples. It has deservingly acquired warm love and deep respect." T. Usubaliev, the first secretary of the Kirghiz Central Committee, thanked "the great Russian people and its heroic working class, the bearer of socialist internationalism and the fraternity of peoples." His praise for the Russian people exceeded even that of Stalin:

> Profound internationalism, great talent, a clear understanding, a generous heart, selflessness, constant readiness for self-sacrifice, and magnanimity—all these are the outstanding characteristics of the great Russian people that have earned it the deepest respect of all Soviet peoples, including the people of Kirghizia.[75]

Brezhnev repeated the thesis that the Soviet Union had become a new historical community of people—the Soviet people.[76] This signalled the rapid integration of the peoples of the USSR.

The Ukrainian party apparatus soon began to propagate this idea, but, initially at least, avoided the cult of the "elder brother" and the view that the Russian language should be a second mother tongue. For example, an article by P. P. Bachynsky stressed Russian as a means of communication in a multinational state and gave the following assurance: "In the Soviet Union conditions have been created to permit each citizen to speak and to rear and educate his children in any language he wishes. Special rights for or compulsion to use one language or another are impermissible."[77] The campaign emphasized the complexity of the Soviet economy and the benefits of greater integration within the Soviet state. It implied that Ukraine should make a major contribution to overall economic development and put less emphasis on its own economic rights. The articles seemed designed to reassure the masses that there would be no violation of "Leninist principles" in nationality policy. This in itself was sufficient to generate uncertainty about the future.

Ukraine and the Sino-Soviet Conflict

The rapid deterioration of relations between China and the USSR in the late 1960s also affected Soviet nationality policy. Peking decided to emphasize the failings of Soviet nationality policy in its attacks on Moscow, often focusing on Ukraine. For example, Radio Peking reported on dissident trends and arrests in Ukraine to attract the sympathies of Ukrainians and other non-Russian peoples. In a programme broadcast on 6 June 1969 under the title "The Bourgeois Dictatorship of the New Soviet Revisionist Tsars," Radio Peking told its listeners:

> In Ukraine there are various kinds of psychiatric clinics, concentration camps and prisons for the persecution of the Soviet people. It is known that in Dnipropetrovsk oblast with a population of 2.5 million, there are ten prisons with 50,000 inmates. That is more than in tsarist times. The Soviet revisionist renegade clique has transformed the first socialist state into a great fascist prison.... In recent years the people in southern Siberia and

Russia, in Ukraine and in Uzbekistan, in the Kazakh city of Chimkent and in other cities, have organized strikes, uprisings and demonstrations; they have attacked and burned the offices of the fascist dictatorship and thus resisted the fascist tyranny established by the renegade clique of the new· tsars. In more than one case the Soviet revisionist renegade clique has called in military units, tanks and even warplanes to...suppress and massacre the striking workers and revolutionary masses and to establish a regime of White terror in the country. Such national minorities as the Tatars, the Georgians and the Latvians are subjected to bloody reprisals and persecuted by the renegade clique. The proletariat and the peoples of all nationalities in the Soviet Union continue to live under the yoke of misery and slavery.

Similar accusations appeared in an article entitled "Soviet Revisionism Hard Pressed by the Revolutionary Peoples of the Soviet Union and the World," published in the 17 June 1969 issue of *Peking Review*: "The Soviet revisionist renegade clique is rabidly pursuing a Great Russian policy in the treatment of the national minorities in the Soviet Union and exposing millions of people from the national minorities to ever-mounting subjugation and exploitation." The article referred to mass arrests in Kazakhstan, Ukraine, Georgia and Lithuania and noted that the majority of the inmates of the concentration camps were non-Russians whom the "Soviet revisionists" had "branded as bourgeois nationalists." "As in the times of the old tsars," the article concluded, "the Soviet Union has become a vast prison for the masses of all nationalities."

Peking escalated its propaganda, playing heavily on the theme of national discrimination and creating a headache for those responsible for Soviet counter-propaganda. Soviet publications began to bracket the Chinese with the "imperialists," and to claim that Peking's aim was to split the international communist movement. In an article for *Komunist Ukrainy* in the summer of 1968, Shelest charged that the "imperialists" were putting their stakes on revisionist and nationalist elements:

In the struggle against the CPSU and world communism they are exploiting the chauvinist great power policy and the divisive activity of Mao Tse-tung and his group, the slightest deviation from Marxism-Leninism, the symptoms of opportunism in the ranks of communists in individual countries, and certain tendencies that find their expression in an infamous "neutrality" with respect to common problems of world communism and the workers' movement.[78]

The party reacted to the Chinese propaganda campaign by emphasizing the cruelty toward the population of Chinese units that had fought in the Red Army during the revolution. Most Soviet people, in fact, thought that China was experiencing its own *Zhdanovshchina*. Thus the Chinese campaign had little influence on the Ukrainian "opposition." Nevertheless, the Kremlin was concerned about the Chinese campaign, especially once the border conflict began to escalate. The Chinese encouraged recalcitrants in the Soviet Union to exercise their constitutional right to secede from the USSR. The most fertile soil for such propaganda was Ukraine, Armenia and the Baltic republics.

Military-Patriotic Education: A Means of Ideological Tempering?

After Khrushchev's fall the military, political circles and representatives of the older generation wanted to educate youth in the virtues displayed by their fathers and grandfathers during the Second World War and the October Revolution. Leonid Brezhnev supported these demands. The older generation believed that a "continuity of virtues" would ensure a continuity of political attitudes. The demands themselves were motivated by what party leaders viewed as the "moral decay" of youth, as manifested in an increasingly critical attitude toward the past and the present. The proclaimers of the old virtues also saw the danger of foreign, particularly Western, influences and of "revisionist" trends in the communist parties of other countries. In his speech to the Twenty-third CPSU Congress, Brezhnev said:

> Sometimes certain party and Komsomol organizations forget that the present generation of boys and girls have not passed through the hard schools of revolutionary struggle and trial experienced by the older generation. Some young people would like to circumvent the fullness of life; they are dependent on others, demand a lot from the state, but forget their duties to society and the people.[79]

In May 1969 a conference of Ukrainian Komsomol city and raion committees was held in Kiev. Before a thousand officials, newspaper, radio and television journalists and activists from the Kiev Komsomol City Committee, O. S. Kapto, then first secretary of the Ukrainian Komsomol's Central Committee, delivered a report "On the Further Improvement of the Activities of the Komsomol Organizations for Ideological Tempering of Youth." The CPU Politburo viewed the report as especially significant, because Kapto gave a detailed analysis of the Komsomol.

Kapto noted that there had been a shift in the age structure of the Ukrainian Komsomol and that 75 per cent of the members were now under 20. This meant that three-quarters of the membership had been born after the Second World War. Furthermore, 39 per cent were in the 14–17 age group. It was a time when the profile of the young generation had undergone a radical change: its knowledge, cultural level and aspirations had grown. Seventy-seven out of 100 Ukrainian Komsomol members who had already left school had a complete or partial secondary or higher education. In the last ten years, Kapto said, the number of Komsomol members with a secondary education had tripled, while the number with a higher education had doubled. Kapto noted, however, that "it would be wrong to conclude from this that the level of education automatically improves the [standards of] ideological training desired by the party. On the contrary, new difficulties and problems are emerging."[80]

Ideological control over young people had become more difficult because of the increase in the sources from which citizens could obtain uncensored information. Before the war, young people had access to three or four sources of information at the most; now they had as many as fifteen.[81] One of the major threats to the party's monopoly of education was "Comrade Transistor," who enhanced "bourgeois" ideological influences. Both young and old sought information from such sources as the Voice of America, Radio Liberty, Radio Vatican and other foreign broadcasters.

The counter-measures proposed by the party included: clubs for the study of Lenin's works; special awards for diligent Komsomol members; schemes for improving work morale; and (most important) plans for the improved training of youth in the military and patriotic virtues. At the Kiev conference, Kapto appealed vehemently for better military-patriotic training. Although Komsomol organizations had created the "Eagle" Youth Regiment in Donetsk, the "Military-Patriotic Schools" in Odessa, the "Young Friends of the Border Forces" in Rivne oblast and similar groups in Bukovyna and Transcarpathia, the party was not satisfied with the level of military-patriotic training. Kapto complained:

> The present international situation demands that the republic's Komsomol organizations intensify the military-patriotic training of youth. It is the task of the Komsomol organization to persuade all young men and women, especially the young workers and urban youth, to march on "the paths trod by their famous forebears."[82]

In contrast to Khrushchev's policies, which had encouraged local initiative, the party's policy under Brezhnev was to strengthen constantly the "party core" of the youth organization, i.e., to put full party members in all the key positions. As early as 1968 the Ukrainian party press reported the success of this policy:

> The strengthening of the party cores is of great importance for improving the party management of the Komsomol. The party has always paid great attention to this matter. After the Twenty-third CPSU Congress and the Twenty-third CPU Congress there was a significant increase in the number of communists elected to the republic's Komsomol organs. Now all the first secretaries of the Komsomol city and raion committees are communists.

Almost half the secretaries of the primary Komsomol organizations in industrial, construction and transport enterprises, at state and collective farms are members or candidate members of the CPSU. It is the duty of the party organizations to ensure the further consolidation of the party core in the Komsomol.[83]

The strategy could hardly have been described more explicitly. Not only were party members being "elected" to the key Komsomol posts, they were also dictating the youth organization's entire cadre policy. They were responsible for implementing the measures defined as "party management of the Komsomol." The success of the strategy can be measured by the increase in the number of party members in key Komsomol posts, from 37,987 in 1966 to 109,308 in 1972.[84]

The Ukrainian press had noted the growing influence of "enemy propaganda" on youth well before the conference in Kiev. At the Komsomol plenum held in July 1969 to mark the organization's fiftieth anniversary, Shelest warned of the dangers from "foreign circles":

Imperialist propaganda is trying to distract the young generation from the problems of the present time, to poison the minds of young men and women with the venom of apolitical attitudes, scepticism and "neutrality in the class struggle." In trying to curry favour as the "friends of youth" they speculate on the inexperience of the young. Some of the politicos abroad are trying to exploit the unstable section of youth for their own political ends and to turn it against socialism. This makes it necessary to maintain political-revolutionary vigilance, mobility, the ability to recognize the enemy despite all his attempts at camouflage and to act decisively against all symptoms of enemy ideology, of rightist and leftist opportunism and nationalism.[85]

Military-patriotic training was promoted with particular intensity at Ukrainian schools after 1969. The methods employed were described in *Radianska shkola*, the official journal of the Ukrainian Ministry of Public Education. The system of military-patriotic education was governed by a law of 1 January 1968. It involved military instruction in the clubs for young pioneers, cosmonauts, pilots, border guards and sailors. School children were taught marksmanship and basic military knowledge. Especially popular forms of military education were military sports camps, "Young Soldiers' Schools," "Universities of Tomorrow's Soldiers," military museums, "Halls of Heroes," meetings with veterans of the October Revolution and the Second World War, conferences on patriotic themes, and visits to famous battlefields. Many schools in Kiev held "courage courses" during which the students met with old Bolsheviks, war veterans and prominent politicians.[86]

Military training was not an effective substitute for genuine political education. Many school children were more interested in technological development than military education. Consequently, the Ukrainian Komsomol put the question of improving military-patriotic training on the agenda of its December 1969 plenum. Kapto proposed to replace DOSAAF [Voluntary Society for the Promotion of Co-operation with the Army, Navy and Air Force] with a republican "Scientific and Technical Youth Society." As conceived by Kapto, this society would have a wide network of local branches and would establish youth sections in the Society of Inventors and Rationalizers.[87]

The CPU found the military-patriotic education of students in higher education particularly problematic, especially in Kiev. The institutes and universities were centres of political ferment. Students took part in demonstrations and protests and attended meetings organized by representatives of the Ukrainian intelligentsia. At that time Kiev University's president, Shvets, banished many students and dismissed a number of professors. The following incident was characteristic: on 19 March 1969 General Shulzhenko, deputy chairman of the Ukrainian KGB, held a lecture at the university on "Some Questions of the Ideological Struggle." During the lecture (delivered in Ukrainian), he spoke scornfully of Bereslavsky, who had tried to immolate himself in front of a university building. His comments were reported in *Chronicle of Current Events*.[88]

In Ukraine's secondary schools, the teachers, many of whom were not well-educated, were confronted with increasingly well-informed and self-confident pupils. Many schools tried to introduce student self-management. Pupils were interested in social problems. They wanted to make their own decisions and develop their own views, both in their private lives and at school. *Radianska shkola* noted these developments and urged the teachers to adapt to the new situation. "Don't be afraid," the journal said, "of the tough questions that youth is concerned about."[89] But this advice went unheeded, and many pedagogues—particularly the weaker ones—believed military-patriotic education to be the best means of restoring "order."

The Ukrainian Herald: the Uncensored Voice of Ukraine

The appearance of the *Ukrainian Herald* in January 1970 represented a major initiative of the Ukrainian dissidents. Until then the only regular *samvydav* journal in the Soviet Union was the Russian *Chronicle of Current Events*, published in Moscow since 1968. Although *Chronicle* reported most major developments, its coverage of Ukraine was sporadic. The *Herald*, on the other hand, concentrated on events in Ukraine.

The introduction to the first issue declared that the authors considered it necessary to publish a periodical free from the trammels of censorship. The *Ukrainian Herald*, they emphasized, was neither anti-Soviet nor anti-communist. Its contents and aims were legal and in keeping with the Constitution. The criticism of persons and institutions, the introduction stated, was not an anti-Soviet activity but one based on the principles of socialist democracy. Criticism was a constitutionally guaranteed right and the honourable duty of any citizen, especially when the targets of criticism—however highly placed—had committed errors in their attempts to solve internal political problems and violated the rights of people and the nation. Furthermore the *Herald* saw itself as a public forum, not an organ of specific groups or organizations.

The *Herald* reported the growing movement against Russification and the measures taken to contain it. It published poetry as well as political analyses. Altogether six issues of the *Herald* reached the West—issue five was never received. (The editor of the first four issues was Viacheslav Chornovil, sentenced in 1973 to a long prison term).[90] The *Herald* is the most important source of information about a brief but stormy period in the history of Ukraine—from the end of 1969 to the spring of 1974. It is also invaluable for an understanding of events and processes that occurred prior to 1969, and which are unfolding today.

Petro Shelest's Fall

Several *samvydav* articles by Ukrainian intellectuals depicted the post-Stalin period in Ukraine as an era of struggle for popular and national rights, a renaissance. A milestone of this period was the exposure of Stalin's excesses at the Twentieth CPSU Congress. The party leadership had resolved to eliminate the consequences of the personality cult but failed to carry out the necessary measures. Various historical factors affected the course of developments in Ukraine: UPA's resistance to Soviet power after the war; the testimony of prisoners released from the camps, which proved an important source of information about the purges of the 1930s; and the events of the postwar period up to 1953. It would, however, be incorrect to view the Ukrainian "renaissance" as a continuation of the earlier resistance movement in its efforts to defend the republic's national rights. It is hard to equate the wave of demands and protests in the second half of the 1950s with the concept of an "opposition," which implies political organizations and the formulation of political programmes. Furthermore, the Ukrainian renaissance did not display the tendency of the opposition that developed in Moscow and other Russian centres in the early 1960s toward programmatic statements and concepts (e.g., the "Democrats' Movement"). Nevertheless, the aims pursued in Ukraine were formulated clearly: the elimination of the consequences of the personality cult meant, first and foremost, the elimination of all forms of discrimination in nationality policy as a whole, and more specifically, equality in the areas of national language, education and economy. The centre of this movement was Kiev, where intellectuals, students and workers were actively involved. A significant part of the party apparatus sympathized and played a major role in the movement, and most of the activists were party members.

What role did Shelest and his supporters play in this tense situation? The answer is uncertain because the evidence is incomplete. It is nevertheless possible to describe and analyze Ukraine's historical development under Shelest's leadership. Petro Shelest's loyalty to the party and its leaders is not in doubt. Born in 1918 in Andriivtsi (now in Kharkiv oblast), of Ukrainian poor peasant stock, he joined the party in 1928. He developed an interest in engineering and technology during the 1920s and, in 1935, graduated from the Mariupil Metallurgical Institute. He was a Komsomol activist for many years. Before completing compulsory military service, from 1935 to 1937, he was a managing engineer of a factory shop. His party administrative career began in 1940, and during the Second World War he held executive posts in the defence industry in Cheliabinsk and Saratov, after which he was director of various factories in Leningrad and Kiev. Unlike many Soviet leaders, Shelest was not involved in the purges or the terror shortly before Stalin's death. His party work in Ukraine began in the 1950s. He was elected an alternate member of the CC CPU in 1952 and a full member in 1956. His election to the post of second secretary of the Kiev City Committee in 1954 proved the turning point in his career.

Shelest's rapid ascent in the Ukrainian party began at a time when many party officials (especially those who held the top posts) were "discovering" that their power depended not only on Moscow but also on the Ukrainian people and the course of events in the republic. A specifically "Ukrainian" party organization emerged that was obliged to recognize the justice of many of the demands being made by the political "opposition": intellectuals with a sense of national identity, "reformist" communists, and representatives of various levels of society who supported the "elimination of the consequences of the personality cult in Ukraine" and an end to the "distortion" of "Leninist" nationality policy. Thus, the party opposed the Russification of the educational system (cf. Dadenkov's letter), the falsification of the history of the Ukrainian people and the CPU, and the glorification of the tsars and famous Russian generals (a demand to which, as we have shown, even Skaba subscribed). It was also determined to defend the republic's economic rights, and was relatively successful in this under Khrushchev's administration. In this context Shelest and his supporters tried to create a strong basis within the party in order to contain and defuse the conflicts within Ukrainian society.

Under Brezhnev, however, events took an opposite course. Russophiles raised the spectre of a "nationalist threat" in Ukraine by sending a stream of denunciatory letters and reports to Moscow. After a troubled period in the mid–1950s, this group had gained strength. It began to form a "counter-movement" while Khrushchev was still in power and awaited the right time to play its card. The denunciations of nationalism by Lviv oblast committee secretary Malanchuk, which were received eagerly in the Kremlin, became more vehement after Shelest ousted Skaba from the post of Central Committee secretary with responsibility for ideology and replaced him with Ovcharenko. In his new position as director of the Institute of History of the Ukrainian Academy of Sciences, Skaba joined in accusations that the "opposition" in Ukraine was made up of "bourgeois nationalists" and "henchmen of imperialism." Two of Skaba's associates were the historian Iurii Rymarenko, a Halan Prize winner who worked at the History Institute and later joined the Ukrainian Academy of Sciences' Institute of Philosophy; and Vitalii Cherednychenko, then a Candidate of Historical Sciences. The two men co-authored an article on Ukrainian bourgeois nationalism that accused the "nationalists" of maintaining contacts not only with anti-communist and imperialist circles but also with Maoists:

> In latter years the Ukrainian bourgeois nationalists have been striving to establish and strengthen contacts with the Maoists. They are tempted primarily by the Maoists' anti-Soviet course, the efforts made by Peking's propagandists to compromise the CPSU and the USSR, to shake the unity of the socialist countries and the communist and workers' movement.... The propaganda from Peking often tries to utilize the "arguments" of the Ukrainian bourgeois nationalists for various anti-Soviet actions.[91]

Two major figures in the anti-Ukrainian trend were Mykola Shamota and Liubomyr Dmyterko. The former was director of the Institute of Literature attached to the Ukrainian Academy of Sciences. The latter, an editor of *Literaturna Ukraina*, had earlier denounced "bourgeois nationalists" and "Zionists" during the last year of the Stalin era, thereby incriminating many innocent Ukrainian-Jewish writers. (See his libellous article in *Literaturnaia gazeta*, 9 March 1949.) The lower ranks of the Ukrainian KGB, especially in the provinces, still harboured the "stalwart Chekists," who also opposed the Ukrainian renaissance. Nevertheless, there are signs that, in a certain sense, the KGB leadership and the Shelest group found a kind of "common language," a circumstance that is confirmed by several *samvydav* publications.

The relatives of many victims of persecution wrote directly to the State Security Committee attached to the Ukrainian Council of Ministers, asking for direct intervention and help. One such letter from the writer Vasyl Stus, dated 28 July 1970, said:

> The last decade was a period in which the material and spiritual conditions of life deteriorated almost systematically. The general devaluation of values—ranging from the ruble exchange rate to the many economic, political, ethical and aesthetic standards—is continuing. I am sure that there

are many questions today for which the need for a solution is felt equally by A. Solzhenitsyn and Iu. Andropov, V. Nikitchenko and V. Moroz, V. Kozachenko and I. Dziuba, I. Svitlychny and M. Shamota. The urge to hold a healthy dialogue is growing stronger and stronger. We need a referendum on many questions. Unfortunately a healthy discussion of many questions is forbidden.[92]

The *Ukrainian Herald* reported at least one case where a "dialogue" occurred. After his release in 1969, Chornovil, one of the most important representatives of the Ukrainian opposition, met with KGB chief Nikitchenko to discuss the reasons for his arrest.[93] However, such discussions ended abruptly after the death of KGB deputy chairman B. S. Shulzhenko (June 1970) and Nikitchenko's replacement by V. V. Fedorchuk (20 July 1970).[94] There was a change of attitude which was of paramount importance for Ukraine. Shelest, Ovcharenko and many other party officials began to speak of the "anti-Soviet activities of the bourgeois nationalists" and of their collaboration with Western anti-communist organizations or "imperialist" intelligence services. But the KGB (under Fedorchuk) was obliged to construct the "evidence," since the political opposition in Ukraine rejected any contact with anti-Soviet and "imperialist" organizations categorically. The aim was to end the opposition's semi-legal status and drive it into clandestine operations, so that its activists could, technically, be tried as criminals. This was not the course desired or expected by Shelest and the other CPU leaders.

In January 1972 KGB agents arrested Iaroslav Dobosh, a Belgian citizen of Ukrainian extraction, and charged him with engaging in anti-Soviet activities on Ukrainian territory. Under investigation, Dobosh confessed that he had been sent to Ukraine by the Bandera OUN. He allegedly requested permission to address representatives of the public and the press so that he could make a statement on the "subversive activities of the Ukrainian bourgeois nationalists" and his own mission. A press conference was organized on 2 June 1972 in Kiev and attended by representatives of the Ukrainian and central press, radio, television, the creative unions, public organizations and workers' collectives. After an opening statement by V. I. Horkun, the director of RATAU, the Ukrainian news agency, Dobosh described the tasks that the Bandera OUN had commissioned him to perform. Upon his arrival in Kiev, he said, his first task was to establish contact with representatives of the opposition. He was expected to arrange meetings with Ivan Svitlychny, Zinoviia Franko, Anna Kotsur, Leonid Seleznenko and Stefaniia Hulyk, from whom he would receive information. This information was to be smuggled into the West and used "against the Soviet Union." Dobosh stated that he was to inform these persons about the work of the nationalist organizations in the West and to attempt to establish nationalist cells in Ukraine. He claimed that his contact man in Belgium, a certain Koval, had supplied him with a list of addresses, passwords and other information needed for the assignment. In his own words:

> During my stay in Kiev from 29–31 December 1971, I called Ivan Svitlychny, Zinoviia Franko and Leonid Seleznenko from phone booths. We met at agreed places. Seleznenko helped to set up a meeting with Anna Kotsur. I informed all these people about the anti-Soviet activities of Ukrainian organizations in the West.... From them I received all and more than the information and corresponding documents that I required. I gave Svitlychny and Zinoviia Franko an allowance of 50 rubles each, and I gave Anna Kotsur another 50 rubles for the negative of a document.... On 3 January 1972 I arrived in Lviv, and stayed in the Intourist Hotel. On 4 January I visited Stefaniia Hulyk in her apartment on 5 Descartes Street. I also informed her about the anti-Soviet organizations in the West and received information from her. As commissioned by Koval, I gave her an allowance of 30 rubles.... After I had performed all my tasks, I left Lviv on 4 January and was arrested at the Chop border station.... Now I understand that I have committed a grave crime against the Soviet state...and assure the Soviet government that I shall never again engage in anti-Soviet activities.[95]

In response to the Soviet press correspondent, Dobosh said that his treatment during arrest had been exemplary, and that he had been given the opportunity to speak to representatives of the Belgian embassy. Concerning the manuscripts Koval had told him to bring out of the USSR, he said: "The material included a manuscript by S. Karavansky, whom the nationalists consider a great martyr unjustly punished by the Soviet government. They would certainly have used this manuscript to slander the Soviet Union again." This statement sufficed for the authorities to impose an additional punishment on Karavansky.

The Soviet authorties sent Dobosh back to Belgium as a *persona non grata* soon after this press conference, and on 11 February 1971 the Ukrainian press reported that I. Svitlychny, V. Chornovil, Ie. Sverstiuk, Leonid Pliushch, Zinovii Antoniuk, Volodymyr Rokytsky, Kovalenko, Oleksandr Serhienko, Mykola Plakhotniuk, Vasyl Stus, Leonid Seleznenko, Danylo Shumuk, Mykola Kholodny and others had been punished for "engaging in activities inimical to the socialist order."[96]

Radianska Ukraina returned to the Dobosh case in connection with an attack on a "pro-Chinese" group. It ignored the fact that the Bandera OUN sympathized with Chiang Kai-shek and presented the Dobosh case in a way that suggested that Peking backed the OUN. According to *Radianska Ukraina*: "It does not matter one whit to the Peking leaders that the Ukrainian bourgeois nationalists pin such hopes on imperialist intelligence services and serve them body and soul."[97] The newspaper thus implied that the nationalists were also being supported by American intelligence services.

Immediately after Dobosh's meeting with several dissidents, authorities prepared to expel Ivan Dziuba from the Ukrainian Writers' Union, even though Dobosh's deposition did not incriminate him directly. (In fact, Dziuba was careful to avoid direct contact with emigrés.) The Presidium of the Writers' Union, which met to discuss Dziuba's case, issued the following communiqué:

I. Dziuba has been expelled from the Ukrainian Writers' Union for [his] grave violation of the principles and precepts of the Union's statutes, for compiling and propagating material of an anti-Soviet and anti-communist nature that expresses nationalist views, libels the Soviet order and the party's nationality policy, and is being used energetically by our class enemies in their struggle against the Communist Party and the Soviet state. The decision was accepted unanimously by the Presidium.[98]

Less than half of the twenty-nine Presidium members attended the session. Iu. Smolych declared that he had a cold. B. Oliinyk, one of the Union's three deputy chairmen, and ex-chairman Oles Honchar were absent without an excuse. The absences may be interpreted as a silent protest against the Presidium's policy.

Another victim of the authorities' crackdown was Zinoviia Franko, granddaughter of Ivan Franko, who had originally been dismissed from her position at the Institute of Linguistics (Ukrainian Academy of Sciences) in 1968 for co-signing various letters to the CPU from Ukrainian intellectuals. Although reinstated, she was dismissed again at the beginning of 1969, and accused of sending information about the situation in Ukraine to a friend in the United States. Since she sent her letters to America via the regular post, KGB members edited them so that they could be construed as anti-Soviet.[99] Soon after the Dobosh affair, *Radianska Ukraina* published a statement by Franko in which she "confessed her sins" and begged forgiveness: "The recent events—I mean the arrest of the Belgian subject Iaroslav Dobosh—have opened my eyes to many things. I have given thought to what kind of game is really being played here."[100] The text of the statement was broadcast by the foreign service of Radio Kiev. Therefore, Franko said, she had decided to address the public in full awareness of having committed acts that "the criminal code rightly denotes as anti-Soviet activity." She described how she had compiled and distributed "anti-Soviet" material, and admitted having contacts with tourists of Ukrainian extraction to whom she had also given information.

In my political blindness I did not realize that I had begun to pass on information to the undercover agents of hostile foreign nationalist centres, [to people] who were in contact with the intelligence services of imperialist states. Iaroslav Dobosh was one of these.... I have also realized why the enemies of the Ukrainian people cling to the name Franko and to what purpose they used me. They were trying to exploit that name of my grandfather, the great Ivan Franko, a passionate internationalist and revolutionary democrat, in their anti-Soviet struggle. If I can be forgiven all this, I will do my utmost to expiate my guilt before the people by honest toil.[101]

On 5 April 1972, Radio Kiev broadcast a recantation by M. Iu. Braichevsky, Candidate of Historical Sciences and associate of the Ukrainian Academy of Sciences' Institute of Archeology. In 1966, Braichevsky had written a study entitled "Annexation or Reunification?" Although refused publication by the Soviet authorities, since it maintained that Russia had annexed Ukraine, the study appeared in *samvydav* and was subsequently published in the West. As a result, Braichevsky was dismissed from his position at the Institute of Archeology. In his recantation he protested against attempts to represent his study as a critique of Soviet historiography and declared: "Scholarship cannot develop without creative discussion, for it is well known that the truth emerges from controversy—naturally, only when it is based on firm foundations and a corresponding scholarly standard."

Braichevsky, who said that he had written over forty articles and a monograph in the previous four years, called the attempts to use "Annexation or Reunification?" for political ends "disgraceful" and averred that he had not asked anyone to publish it abroad.[102] In the study itself, however, he spoke of a massive distortion of the history of the peoples now united in the Soviet state and criticized Soviet historiography for calling the non-Russian peoples' struggle to throw off the yoke of tsarism "reactionary," whereas Marx and Lenin had considered this progressive.[103] Several years passed before Braichevsky's works were accepted for publication again.

The Dobosh affair gave the Ukrainian organs their biggest "success" since Stalin's death, since it supplied "proof" of close links between the internal opposition and foreign anti-communist centres. It provided material for triumphant reports to the Kremlin and enabled Shelest's opponents to depict him as the protector of political dissidents or, at the very least, a politically blind man who could not or did not want to see the danger emanating from the "bourgeois nationalists." The CPSU Politburo decided it was time to call Shelest to account.

On 19 May 1972 Brezhnev delivered a report on the international situation at a plenary session of the CC CPSU.[104] At the discussion, the Ukrainian SSR was represented by Vatchenko, first secretary of the Dnipropetrovsk oblast committee, who was a vehement opponent of Shelest, and by B. Paton, president of the Ukrainian Academy of Sciences.

The report gave no indication of whether Shelest attended the plenum. The next day the Presidium of the USSR Supreme Soviet published a decree demoting him to a deputy chairman of the USSR Council of Ministers.[105]

The *Ukrainian Herald* issues 7–8 gave a more specific account of what actually happened in Moscow. According to this source, Shelest was summoned to a session of the Politburo by telephone only hours before it began. The atmosphere in the assembly hall was icy and hostile. Shelest was told to sit on a back bench, and was then informed he was to be made a deputy chairman of the USSR Council of Ministers. Before the meeting was officially opened he was accused of localism [*mestnichestvo*] and pursuing narrow national interests, policies which allegedly had encouraged the emergence of a nationalist movement in Ukraine. Shelest reportedly left the hall with the words: "Everything is finished now!"[106]

An Assessment of Shelest's Personality

Petro Shelest's period on the stage of Ukrainian history began with a tempestuous period during Khrushchev's term of office and ended eight years and seven months later. He tried to preserve and expand Ukraine's achievements during this period. Shelest published several books, but his most interesting and politically most successful book was *Ukraino nasha Radianska* (O Ukraine, Our Soviet Land).[107] Published in 1970 in an edition of 100,000 copies, it was "sold out" soon after it went on display in the bookstore windows, which suggests that "certain organs" had engineered immediate "bestsellerdom." Vsevolod Holubnychy felt that the book's value was that it stressed the continuity of Ukrainian history and culture.[108] Shelest constantly emphasizes that Ukraine is a "state" and never mentions a "union." Ukraine-Moscow relations are portrayed as one-sided, with the consistent national suppression of Ukraine. Such issues as Valuev's injunction and the ban on Ukrainian schools during the nineteenth century are described in detail. Further, there is nothing in the book to suggest that the oppression had ended. Much is made of the social liberation of Ukraine as a result of the October Revolution, and of social and cultural development, but Soviet nationality policy is ignored.

Ukraino, nasha Radianska also reviews the current status of Ukrainian culture, and glorifies the mother tongue. In the chapter about literature, Shelest was silent on the achievements of contemporary Soviet Ukrainian literature, but in an earlier chapter he declared that: "Unfortunately, the progressive role of the Zaporozhian Sich and its significance are not given adequate treatment in our present-day historical literature and fiction, in films and fine arts." Shelest recalled the classical authors who had written about it: "Aren't our artists capable of continuing the tradition of which I have spoken? They are capable of it and must do it." He quotes Marx's statements about the democracy of the Sich and Shevchenko's bitter denunciation of Catherine II for disbanding the Sich.

Shelest's chapters on architecture, the fine arts and music represent a *de facto* recommendation for a programme of "mute" national culture, to compensate for the enforced stagnation of literature. Thus he criticizes the "eclectic mixture of different architectural styles" and calls on the architect to "seek the best contemporary Ukrainian national style" so that the "Ukrainian ornament" will be preserved in the new towns and villages. He appeals for "the preservation of the inimitable originality and highly artistic national character in artifacts made from glass, ceramics, textiles, etc." Each chapter on a given subject begins with a reference to a "specific, original and inimitable" Ukrainian culture that had existed since the time of Kievan Rus. At the same time he criticizes "shirking and bragging," a thinly veiled attack on the Ukrainian intelligentsia.

Shelest emphasized that despite attempts by the German fascists to destroy the Ukrainian nation and its culture, "our strength waxed and the love of our fatherland, of our great achievements, of our mother tongue flamed still higher." Later in the book he again stressed that "The rape of a nation does not destroy it, it only multiplies its strength."

Shelest explained why he had decided to write the book:

We did it to underscore once again that today's new socialist Ukraine and its great achievements did not come to be of their own accord. They were won at the cost of great human sacrifice, by the heroism and steadfastness of the popular masses. The simplest and most mundane things often prevent us from seeing and understanding the miracle that has occurred in Ukraine under Soviet power and to experience all this in the depth of our being. It is really a miracle! Downtrodden and maltreated by conquerors for centuries, travailing under the heavy yoke of tsarism, in the past a backward and illiterate land; yet today Ukraine is one of the most progressive, well educated and most cultivated countries in the world.

The closing words of the book were: "Follow Lenin... [for] the Leninist epoch in Ukraine has had its beginning but it will never have an end."

One question remains: Why was this book written? It did not appear on any anniversary (it was after the 100th anniversary of Lenin's birth and long before the 50th anniversary of the USSR), nor was there any word of an anniversary in it. So it may have been written as a policy statement, or a programme for the prevailing restrictive conditions (especially in the arts). The book provides an answer to the "common citizen, the man in the street" who asks: "What is Ukraine and where does it come from?" It is also admirably optimistic in its historical perspective, an attempt to instil belief in Ukraine's invincibility, to show how developed and potentially powerful the Ukrainian republic really is compared with its backward past. Notably, Shelest ignores the much-cited Russian aid to the people of Ukraine. At various junctures he also points out the magnitude of Ukraine's contribution to the economy of the USSR.[109] Months later, his book was attacked in *Komunist Ukrainy*.

Immediately after Shelest's fall many publications, especially in the West, printed various rumours and allegations about him, some of which were certainly planted by the KGB's disinformation specialists. As Holubnychy noted: "Shelest is now the target of a covert campaign; a lot of *provocateur* allegations are being spread abroad, e.g., that he obtained a visa for Dobosh, etc. You have to be very cautious in the face of this disinformation campaign. In this case the machinery is steadily increasing its workload."[110]

The *Ukrainian Herald* also averred that "certain bodies" had spread defamatory reports about Shelest in the second half of 1972 and at the beginnning of 1973, such as the report that he had encouraged corruption in Ukraine. Thus in March and May 1972, KGB operatives organized two pogroms against Jews near the Kiev synagogue. Later they planted the rumour that the pogroms had been initiated by Shelest personally. At the same time, in order to promote anti-Semitism, they started a rumour that the Jews were again demanding national autonomy.[111]

The most widespread piece of disinformation was the assertion that Shelest was an opponent of détente.[112] In fact, he had supported détente since the policy's inception. This is borne out by an article that he wrote for *Komunist Ukrainy*:

> The activities of the Soviet Union have played a decisive role in the positive changes on the European continent. The treaties concluded between the Soviet Union, the People's Republic of Poland and the Federal Republic of Germany, and the four-power agreement on West Berlin, deserve a special mention in this context. The proposal submitted by the Soviet Union and other socialist states for the convocation of an all-European conference and the creation of a European security system is receiving increasingly widespread support among the public and the governments of many countries.... The Leninist foreign policy of peace and peoples' friendship that the CPSU and the Soviet government are conducting is bearing abundant fruits and gaining convincing victories over the reactionary forces. It is necessary to use all the information media to recount in depth and breadth the support given to the Communist Party's domestic and foreign policy by the Soviet man, by our entire people.[113]

Shelest gave his full support to the official interpretation of Brezhnev's détente policy. However, Western reports that Shelest formulated the policy of a simultaneous escalation of the ideological struggle between East and West, which the Soviets considered a necessary concomitant of détente, are mistaken. Although this was a plank of the party leadership, Shelest placed no more emphasis on the concept than was demanded.

Petro Shelest was a product of the political developments in Ukraine after 1953 with all their hopes, expectations, demands and disappointments. His rapid rise to political prominence followed the course of these developments, for which he felt a large degree of responsibility. The end of this phase, which spanned almost twenty years, was also the end of his political career in Ukraine. In the interests of the republic he tried to save much that was, in reality, already lost. He could achieve no more, not even with the support of the ever-dwindling and increasingly harassed circle of reformists and activists from the ranks of the intelligentsia, youth, the workers and the party.

Notes

1. *Pravda*, 16 October 1964.
2. "Leninski pryntsypy—nepokhytna osnova partiinoho zhyttia," *Komunist Ukrainy*, no. 11 (1964): 5.
3. "Leninskym kursom," *Komunist Ukrainy*, no. 12 (1964): 6ff.
4. *Ibid.*, 8.
5. *Ocherki istorii Kommunisticheskoi partii Ukrainy*, 693.
6. *Ibid.*, 694.
7. "Pidvyshchuvaty kerivnu rol partiinykh organizatsii, zmitsniuvaty zviazok z masamy," *Komunist Ukrainy*, no. 2 (1965): 3ff.
8. *Plenum TsK KPSS 24–26.3.1965* (Moscow, 1965), 37.
9. *Ibid.*, 39.
10. *Radianska Ukraina*, 20 October 1965.
11. *Ibid.*, 17 March 1966.
12. *Ibid.*, 16 March 1966.
13. A. Hoshovsky, "Z pryvodu 'Narysiv istorii KPZU'," *Nasha kultura* (supplement to *Nashe slovo*), Warsaw, no. 12 (December 1966): 5.
14. V. Boichenko, "Partiini organizatsii ta ideolohichne zahartuvannia tvorchoi intelihentsii," *Komunist Ukrainy*, no. 6 (1966): 17.
15. B. Serhiienko, I. Klymchuk, "Pid chornym praporom antykomunizmu," *Komunist Ukrainy*, no. 2 (1966): 45.
16. *Radianska Ukraina*, 24 October 1965.
17. *Ibid.*, 31 October 1965.
18. *Sobranie dokumentov samizdata*, vol. 18, AS Nr 912, Munich.
19. *Dissent in Ukraine: The Ukrainian Herald Issue 6*, (Baltimore-Paris-Toronto, 1977), 32–4.
20. See I. V. Koliaska, *Osvita v Radianskii Ukraini*, (Toronto, 1970), 173ff.
21. See English edition of *Lykho z rozumu* published as: V. Chornovil, ed. *The Chornovil Papers* (Toronto, 1968), 81, 89.
22. *Radianska Ukraina*, 17 November 1966.
23. *Ibid.*
24. *Literaturna Ukraina*, 23 and 25 November 1966.
25. *Ibid.*, 23 November 1966.
26. *Nasha kultura*, no. 12 (December 1966): 3.
27. "Report of Delegation to Ukraine. Central Committee Meeting, September 16, 17 and 18, 1967," *Viewpoint* 5, no. 1 (January 1968): 1, 2.

28. *Ibid.*, 7.
29. *Ibid.*, 2.
30. *Ibid.*, 7.
31. *Ibid.*, 9.
32. *Ibid.*, 9–11.
33. *Viewpoint* 1, no. 4 (September–October 1969): 60.
34. *Literaturnaia gazeta*, 23 March 1968; *Literaturna Ukraina*, 19 January and 29 March 1968.
35. *Sobor* is analyzed in our "Die Ukrainische Sozialistische Sowjet-republik. Die politische und wirtschaftliche Entwicklung in der Ukraine in der ersten Jahreshälfte 1968." An analysis prepared for the *Studiengruppe für Ost-West-Fragen* (Düsseldorf) 8 (1968): 8.
36. *Duklia*, no. 3 (1968): 221ff.
37. *Robitnycha hazeta*, 28 April 1968, reported on part of this letter-writing campaign.
38. "Lyst tvorchoi molodi Dnipropetrovska" *Suchasnist*, no. 2 (1969): 78ff.
39. *Literaturna Ukraina*, 18 June 1968.
40. *New York Times*, 4 May 1968.
41. *Ukrainskyi visnyk*, no. 1–2 (January 1969–May 1970) (Paris-Baltimore, 1971): 13.
42. *Ibid.*, 14; *Suchasnist*, no. 8 (1969) reported the self-immolation of the Ukrainian, Vasyl Didukh, in Moscow in 1967.
43. I. Dziuba, *Internatsionalizm chy rusyfikatsiia?* (Munich, 1968).
44. *Literaturna Ukraina*, 5 August 1969.
45. *Ukrainskyi visnyk*, no. 1–2, 19.
46. *Literaturna Ukraina*, 6 January 1970.
47. *Ukrainskyi visnyk*, no. 1–2, 20.
48. *Ob ideologicheskoi rabote KPSS. Sbornik dokumentov* (Moscow, 1977), 328ff.
49. *Ibid.*, 331.
50. *Ukrainian Herald Issue 7–8: Ethnocide of Ukrainians in the USSR*, (Baltimore-Paris-Toronto, 1970), 126.
51. *Ibid.*, 126–7.
52. *Literaturna Ukraina*, 2 July 1968.
53. *Ibid.*
54. V. Mazur, "Pro deiaky rysy suchasnoho revizionizmu," *Komunist Ukrainy*, no. 7 (1968): 64.
55. P. Bachynsky, "KP Ukrainy u borotbi za torzhestvo idei druzhby narodiv i proletarskoho internatsionalizmu," *Komunist Ukrainy*, no. 7 (1968): 26ff.
56. *Radianska Ukraina*, 2 July 1968.
57. V. Horský, *Prague 1968. Systemveränderung und System-verteidigung* (Stuttgart-Munich, 1975), 135.
58. *Die Zeit*, 19 June 1968.
59. Horský, *Prague 1968*, 135.
60. *Khronika tekushchikh sobytii*, no. 27 (15 October 1972), 7.
61. *Literaturna Ukraina*, 13 January 1970.
62. *Ibid.*, 16 January 1970.
63. *Ibid.*, 20 January 1970.

64. *Ibid.*, 20 November 1970.
65. *Ibid.*, 28 April 1970.
66. *Radianska osvita*, 17 October 1970.
67. *Literaturna Ukraina*, 9 June 1970.
68. *Radianska osvita*, 17 October 1970.
69. *Literaturna Ukraina*, 19 June 1970.
70. *Ibid.*, 28 July 1970.
71. *Partiinaia zhizn*, no. 21 (November 1970).
72. This and subsequent quotations from Shelest's speech are cited from *Radianska Ukraina*, 18 March 1971.
73. *Ibid.*, 19 March 1971.
74. *XXIV Sezd KPSS. Stenograficheskii otchet* (Moscow 1971), 1: 100ff.
75. *Ibid.*, 459.
76. *Ibid.*, 101.
77. P. P. Bachynsky, "Radianskyi narod—nova istorychna spilnist liudei," *Komunist Ukrainy*, no. 12 (1972): 39.
78. P. Shelest, "Boiovyi zahin KPRS," *Komunist Ukrainy*, no. 7 (1968): 12.
79. *XXIII Sezd KPSS. Stenograficheskii otchet* (Moscow, 1966), 1: 95.
80. *Molod Ukrainy*, 14-15 May 1969.
81. *Ibid.*
82. *Ibid.*
83. *Komunistychna partiia Ukrainy—boiovyi zahin KPRS* (Kiev, 1976), 135.
84. *Ibid.*
85. *Radianska Ukraina*, 2 July 1969.
86. "Leninski zapovity molodi pro zakhyst Batkivshchyny," *Radianska shkola*, no. 10 (1969).
87. *Molod Ukrainy*, 20 December 1969.
88. *Khronika tekushchikh sobytii*, 2, no. 7 (30 April 1969). The Bereslavsky incident was reported in *Ukrainskyi visnyk*, no. 1–2, 28.
89. V. S. Shevchenko, "Rol komsomolskykh i pionerskykh orhanizatsii u komunistychnomu vykhovanni uchniv," *Radianska shkola*, no. 1 (January 1969).
90. *Ukrainske slovo*, 12 July 1981.
91. Iu. I. Rymanenko and V. P. Cherednychenko, "Ukrainskyi burzhuaznyi natsionalizm—znariaddia antykomunizmu," *Komunist Ukrainy*, no. 10 (1972): 72.
92. *Ukrainskyi visnyk*, no. 3, 28.
93. *Ibid.*, 48.
94. *Radianska Ukraina*, 5 June and 21 July 1970.
95. *Ibid.*, 3 June 1972.
96. *Ibid.*, 11 February 1972, and *Ukrainskyi visnyk*, no. 6 (March 1972): 7ff.
97. *Radianska Ukraina*, 26 February 1972.
98. *Literaturna Ukraina*, 3 March 1972.
99. *Ukrainskyi visnyk*, no. 1 (1970): 68.
100. *Radianska Ukraina*, 2 March 1972.
101. Reported by the Foreign Service of Radio Kiev, 3 March 1972.
102. Radio Kiev, 5 April 1972.
103. M. Braichevsky, *Annexation or Reunification?* (Munich, 1974).

104. *Radianska Ukraina*, 20 May 1972.
105. *Ibid.*, 21 May 1972.
106. *Ukrainian Herald, Issue 7–8*, 127ff.
107. Shelest's other books were: *Istorychne poklykannia molodi* (Kiev, 1967); *Komunist—aktyvnyi borets partii* (Kiev, 1969); *Idei Lenina peremahaiut* (Kiev, 1971).
108. Vsevolod Holubnychy, private correspondence with author.
109. P. Shelest, *Ukraino nasha Radianska*, (Kiev, 1970), 72.
110. Holubnychy, private correspondence with author.
111. *Ukrainian Herald, Issue 7–8*, 128.
112. Many Western journalists accepted this. When Shelest was ousted, a West German television commentator declared: "The great opponent of Brezhnev's policy of détente has been overthrown. The road to détente is now open!"
113. P. Shelest, "Napolehlyvo borotys za zdiisnennia rishen partii," *Komunist Ukrainy*, no. 12 (1971): 16.

Chapter Five

Shcherbytsky Heads the CPU

The Purge of 1972

Shelest's metamorphosis into a *persona non grata* was relatively swift. On 21 May 1972, two days after the plenary session of the CC CPSU described earlier, Shelest's removal to the post of deputy chairman of the USSR Council of Ministers was made public. There is no indication of what Shelest did in this position, but he formally held the job until 8 May 1973.

The CC CPU held a plenum on 25 May, but evidently did not discuss the CPSU decision. In fact, only seven people participated in the proceedings, two of whom—V. M. Tsybulko (Kiev) and V. F. Dobryk (Ivano-Frankivsk)—were first secretaries of oblast committees. Both men were, incidentally, protégés of Shcherbytsky, who was unanimously elected CPU first secretary. It is probable that the majority of secretaries were not invited to the plenum because they were known to be supporters of Shelest.[1]

A purge of Shelest's sympathizers was initiated on 10 October 1972, when the CC CPU transferred his supporter Ovcharenko, the secretary responsible for ideology, "to scientific work and replaced him with V. Iu. Malanchuk."[2] This was a signal for a widespread purge. In November 1973 V. S. Kutsevol, first secretary of the Lviv oblast committee, who had incurred Moscow's disfavour earlier and had only held on to his post with Shelest's support, was demoted to chairman of the Ukrainian Committee for People's Control.[3] (He was succeeded in Lviv by

V. F. Dobryk, formerly first secretary of the Ivano-Frankivsk oblast committee.) The purge engulfed many institutes of the Ukrainian Academy of Sciences, and was concentrated in the technical institutes, evidently in order to curtail the development of the scientific and technical vocabulary of the Ukrainian language. The purge also encompassed the higher party schools and the party rank and file.[4]

A wave of arrests and house searches throughout Ukraine preceded and followed the fall of Shelest. According to the *Ukrainian Herald*, thousands of such cases occurred in Lviv oblast as early as January and February 1972. There were similar reports from Kiev and other towns. Writers such as Z. Krasivsky, A. Lupynis and V. Ruban were committed, without grounds, to special psychiatric clinics, causing panic among members of the Writers' Union.[5] The universities of Lviv and Kiev were also badly hit by the purges, both at the staff and student level. Shcherbytsky also banned events such as the annual commemoration of Shevchenko by the "Club of Creative Youth" [*Klub tvorchoi molodi*] in Kiev. According to the *Ukrainian Herald*:

> The organizing of literary evenings in honour of Shevchenko has been forbidden. One or two official evenings are held by those hypocrites who really despise Shevchenko and the Ukrainian people most and who constantly strive to falsify the works of Shevchenko. Those evenings are held exclusively for propaganda purposes. On orders from the KGB, the collaborators in the Writers' Union of Ukraine will bring a wreath to Shevchenko's monument, while at the same time the KGB will be taking photographs of those who bring Shevchenko flowers and their hearts. Afterward, students will be expelled from the institutes and intellectuals from their place of work.[6]

The purge also saw the removal of Skaba as director of the Institute of History at the Ukrainian Academy of Sciences—a man who, under Shelest, had been a notorious and, as the Canadian ex-communist Kolasky described him, a detested party ideologist. But his fall was temporary, since he later became a full member of the Ukrainian Academy of Sciences.

The Fiftieth Anniversary of the USSR

The main point on the agenda of the enlarged plenary session (attended by non-members) of the CC CPU on 27 July 1972 was: "Preparations for the Fiftieth Anniversary of the USSR." The keynote speech was delivered by Shcherbytsky, and others were presented by his close associates: O. F. Vatchenko, first secretary of the Dnipropetrovsk oblast committee and I. V. Degtiarev, first secretary of the Donetsk oblast committee.

In his first major speech before this forum, Shcherbytsky described the creation of the Soviet Union as "a great historical event to which all the nations and peoples of our country made their contribution, especially the great Russian people, who justly deserve the sincere and great gratitude of all the fraternal peoples." Although most of his speech was devoted to economic questions, he warned writers and social scientists of the "subversive activities of foreign Ukrainian bourgeois nationalists and Zionist organizations who are in the service of foreign intelligence services and are endeavouring to unite their actions."[7] Enemies, he stated, were trying to discredit the nationality policy of the CPSU and shake the alliance among the Soviet peoples. He castigated signs of "liberalism" in the Ukrainian intelligentsia and the inadequate struggle against "nationalist anti-Soviet attitudes." Such comments, although not in keeping with the plenum's predominantly economic theme, may have influenced the subsequent heavy sentences imposed on Ukrainian dissidents.

At this time there was a widespread hope throughout the Soviet Union that Brezhnev would use the occasion of the 50th anniversary of the world's first Soviet state to declare an amnesty for political prisoners. Indeed, fifty-one Soviet scholars and artists of various nationalities, including the well-known physicist Mykhailo Leontovych, a Lenin Prize winner and son of the famous Ukrainian physiologist and neurohistologist, academician Oleksandr Leontovych, petitioned the party leaders to this end. They received no reply. In Ukraine, the official reaction was brutal. There were reportedly eleven trials in Ukraine, which sentenced dissidents to a total of 77 years in strict-regime labour camps and 33 years of internal exile.[8]

The Attack on Shelest: Its Functions and Limits

The CC CPU met in plenary session in April 1973 to discuss the improvement of cadre policies on the basis of decisions adopted at the Twenty-fourth CPU Congress. The main speech was delivered by Shcherbytsky and was a statement of major importance.

Shcherbytsky devoted the first part of his speech to the cadre problems in Ukraine. Noting that many of the 3.8 million specialists working in the republic's economy came from other parts of the USSR, he said that, since the network of higher and specialized secondary educational establishments was so well developed in Ukraine, there was no real need for a large number of helpers from outside. Nevertheless, he maintained that the influx of specialists and skilled workers from other republics was an important demonstration of the friendship and unity of the peoples of the Soviet Union.[9] He also criticized the republic's skilled workers and accused all the ministries of "grave shortcomings" in cadre policy, such as conservatism, inertia, the retention of outdated work methods, excessive bureaucratization, and inadequate technical training. He made several proposals for improving cadre management of agriculture.

In the second part of his speech, Shcherbytsky attacked Shelest without mentioning him by name:

Great shortcomings were recently detected in ideological work. In a number of publications there were deviations from class and party criteria in the evaluation of social events and processes. The authors displayed national hubris and parochialism and idealized the "golden" past. They illuminated the historical past of the Ukrainian people from ideologically false positions of a national character. Some authors gave a distorted description of Ukraine's struggle for union with Russia, of the events during the October Revolution and the Civil War, and of the socialist reconstruction of society. In their works some of them avoid the theses of the present time, display narrow national views and pollute the Ukrainian language with archaic words and other artificial expressions.[10]

Shcherbytsky also maintained—in another veiled criticism of Shelest—that some of the authors writing for *Komunist Ukrainy* had permitted nationalist sentiments, which should have been rejected on principle.

The plenum was a prelude to a particularly important event in the history of the CPU. In April 1973 *Komunist Ukrainy* published an editorial entitled "On the Serious Shortcomings and Errors of a Certain Book."[11] At issue was Shelest's *Ukraino, nasha Radianska*. The editorial was clearly intended as a directive, to make explicit what was permissible and what was impermissible in nationality policy. Its main point was that even those parts of a people's history that have nothing to do with nationalism should not be glorified. Shelest had violated this principle by eulogizing the democratic Cossack state—the Zaporozhian Sich—and ignoring the class struggle in this intrinsically feudal society. The editorial pointed out that the idealization of the Sich by the Ukrainian national bard Taras Shevchenko, the novelist N. V. Gogol and the painter I. E. Repin did not mean that contemporary writers and artists should also glorify this part of Ukraine's past. The authors of the editorial took particular offence at the following passage from Shelest's description of the Cossack Sich:

> To consolidate its power in Ukraine the tsarist government pursued a hard-line policy of great-power suppression and even liquidated those remnants of autonomy that Ukraine had been granted in the Treaty of Pereiaslav. The tsars were especially worried by the Zaporozhian Sich with its autonomous status. The tsarist government was not able to understand that the Sich was a powerful centre of the anti-feudal movement, one of the most important centres of the Ukrainian people's struggle against social and national oppression.[12]

The editorial stated that it was misguided to represent the historical development of a part of the Soviet Union in isolation from the overall development of the country, or, as Shelest had done, to depict Ukraine's union with Russia as a simple and straightforward fact. Shelest, it declared, should have stated that this union had saved Ukraine from foreign subjugation. Shelest was also chided for playing down the beneficial and enriching influence of Russian culture in the formation and development of Soviet Ukrainian literature, art and music. He had allegedly de-emphasized the role of the Communist Party, especially in art and literature, its contribution to socialist construction and to the Marxist education of the creative intelligentsia, its active involvement in the consolidation of communist ideals. The editorial declared that the Soviet communist should view his homeland's economic development within the context of the Soviet economy as a whole:

> In *Ukraino, nasha Radianska*, however, the republic's economic develop-ment and achievements are, to a certain extent, examined separately from the overall successes of the Soviet Union. The fact that the flourishing of the Ukrainian SSR is not only a result of the heroic work of the toilers of Ukraine but also of that of all the peoples of the USSR is not shown. The author summarizes his report on the republic's economy with the conclusion: 'Thanks to the exertions of millions, the Soviet Ukraine has achieved unprecedented heights. The Ukrainian Soviet Socialist Republic has become one of the most highly developed countries in the world. Our republic's mighty economy, advanced agriculture and its unprecedented cultural and scientific boom—these are the heroic deeds of all the toilers of Soviet Ukraine.' As we can see, this passage does not even hint at the co-operation and mutual assistance of the fraternal peoples, does not take into account the fact that these achievements are a part and an expression of the successful development of the whole Soviet state.[13]

The editorial also noted that the development of co-operation between the Ukrainian, Russian and other peoples was ignored in Shelest's book, and that he had not even mentioned the military and political alliance that led to victory in the Civil War. Shelest's work, then, was criticized as part of an attempt to lay down Soviet nationality policy. The inclusion of various other stipulations indicates that the editorial had a broader aim than the settling of accounts with Shelest.

Reprisals and Protests

Information about the reprisals in Ukraine quickly reached the West through the reports of foreign correspondents working in Moscow and through the *Chronicle of Current Events*. There was even some relatively detailed information about life and conditions in the strict-regime "corrective" labour camps. The vehemence of protests from the West surprised party leaders in Moscow and Kiev.[14] Well-known politicians, sci-entists and artists, including Nobel Prize winners, signed appeals on behalf of persecuted dissidents, and the protests intensified when the abuse of psychiatry for political ends became known.

The news from the camps in the Mordovian ASSR and from jails (in particular Vladimir Prison) was disturbing. According to reports that reached the West in January 1974, many of the prisoners in Vladimir (in which were interned Valentyn Moroz, Zinovii Antoniuk, Mykhailo Osadchy and Danylo Shumuk) were refused medical aid even though they were seriously ill. There were also reports that many of the political prisoners were transferred from the camps in Mordovia to Perm.[15] Other dissidents were subjected to "treatment" in special psychiatric clinics. A successful campaign was mounted in the West for the release of one of the best-known victims of this practice, the mathematician Leonid Pliushch, a former associate of the Institute of Cybernetics at the Ukrainian Academy of Sciences. Pliushch's wife, Tatiana Zhitnikova, mobilized human-rights activists in Ukraine, Moscow and abroad and kept them informed of her husband's condition. The fates of Ivan Svitlychny (sentenced to seven years in labour camps and five years of exile in a remote part of the USSR in March 1973) and Valentyn Moroz also received wide publicity.

On 5 September 1973 the inmates of Camp VS 389–35 (Ukrainians, Russians, Jews, Balts and representatives of other nationalities) "celebrated" the anniversary of the establishment of concentration camps in the USSR with hunger-strikes and protests. They proposed that 5 September be proclaimed an international "Day of Protest against Persecution." (At this time the camps had existed for 54 years.) Reports of arrests and reprisals in Ukraine revealed that repression had assumed massive proportions.[16] Although detailed description of the persecution is beyond the scope of this book, it is pertinent to describe the techniques and mechanisms used by the Soviet authorities to handle dissidents.

The most common charge was "anti-Soviet propaganda," which the Soviet Criminal Code classifies as a serious crime against the state. According to the Soviet definition, anti-Soviet propaganda is the dissemination of slander or libel (public or "non-public") against the Soviet state and social fabric in order to undermine or weaken Soviet power, and the preparation, dissemination or possession of anti-Soviet literature for this same end. Punishment for such transgressions ranges from six months' to seven years' loss of freedom, and may include 2–5 years' internal exile. The punishment for people with previous convictions for crimes against the state and for first offenders in time of war is 3-10 years' loss of freedom and (optionally) five years' internal exile.[17]

The law against "anti-Soviet propaganda" permits a wide variety of judicial interpretations. Single words or phrases taken out of context may suffice for a conviction. KGB investigations have two standard methods. One is to "prove" that the accused has founded "an illegal anti-Soviet organization" or "maintained contacts with anti-communist organizations abroad." To date, Ukrainian authorities have never provided genuine proof of contacts between the accused and foreign intelligence services. The dissidents have refused such contacts on principle, because they consider their political activities legal and do not wish to compromise themselves.

The second method used by the KGB to combat dissent is intimidation. The techniques have been refined to the point that a number of Ukrainian intellectuals have recanted. They include: dismissal of the dissident from his place of work; deprivation of income; removal of the dissident's children from their place of study; and (a traditional KGB method of combatting "enemies of the people") incitement of friends and acquaintances against the dissident. The latter practice has now become an "educational method," for use against the population as a whole, and is applied, for example, in work collectives, against individual teachers at staff meetings, against members of the Academy of Sciences, and against ordinary workers. The official euphemism for this practice is "the indignation of the masses."

Let us examine some sample cases. After the prominent dissident Ivan Dziuba was sentenced to five years in prison, the KGB pressured him into a recantation with the promise of a remission of punishment. Several "orthodox" intellectuals, including Zinoviia Franko (herself a victim of this method) and Ivan Khmil (who had spent several years at the Soviet Ukrainian diplomatic mission in New York), visited Dziuba in jail and urged him to recant. After an initial refusal Dziuba capitulated and made a declaration (published in *Visti z Ukrainy* (21 May 1975), a weekly for Ukrainians living abroad) in which he stated:

> I showed a false understanding of the present stage of national relations in the USSR and permitted public attacks on the nationality policy of the CPSU. All this was reflected in the deplorable study *Internationalism or Russification?*, which I wrote in 1965 and which was nothing but an assault on the party's nationality policy. Foreign enemies, especially the Ukrainian bourgeois nationalists, used it for their propaganda in the political fight against Soviet Ukraine.[18]

Dziuba conferred that he had "not broken with his earliest failings," nor "taken a completely principled stand against those who usurped my name." Neither "[have I] really done anything to make reparations for the damage I caused to the interests of my society." Dziuba's declaration was sufficiently contrite for his sentence to be suspended.

Subsequently, he was again permitted to engage in literary activities, although with restricted themes. His declaration sparked strong reactions among dissidents and political prisoners. Leonid Pliushch, in an article written after his expulsion from the Soviet Union, even called him a "traitor."[19] We should recall, however, that *Internationalism or Russification?* remains one of the most important scholarly analyses of Soviet nationality policy. His recantation could not refute the quotations from Lenin or the statistical data on the Russification of the Ukrainian school system and the publishing industry, since Dziuba had listed several Soviet sources. In 1976, Dziuba published a booklet entitled *Hrani krystala*, which adopted the most primitive propaganda and stands in stark contrast to *Internationalism or Russification?*

A similar case to Dziuba's was that of Ievhen [Helii] Sniehiriov (a writer, film director, former head of the scenario department of the Kiev film studios and an active communist). In a statement distributed in *samvydav*, he declared that the Soviet constitution was a falsehood, especially in its claims of the right of the constituent republics to free development and secession from the Union. His document closed with the words: "Today I am sending my [internal] passport to the Department of Internal Affairs for the Lenin District of the city of Kiev and from now on no longer consider myself a citizen of the Soviet Union."[20] At the same time Sniehiriov sent a manuscript entitled *Nenko moia, nenko* (Mother, Mother of Mine) to the West. The manuscript described the trials of members of the League for the Liberation of Ukraine [*Soiuz vyzvolennia Ukrainy*] and the Ukrainian Youth League [*Soiuz ukrainskoi molodi*] in 1930. At these trials several Ukrainian intellectuals were "persuaded" to plead guilty and sentenced to long terms of imprisonment.

Sniehiriov's work was severely criticized in some emigre circles, which believed that these organizations had in fact been founded by Ukrainian patriots. Sniehiriov argued that Soviet security organs had invented artificial links between them and the advocates of Ukrainian independence who were subsequently put on trial.[21] In mid-1978 Sniehiriov fell seriously ill, and was obliged to recant his statement in order to receive hospital treatment. At the time he was too ill to write the required declaration himself, and reportedly withdrew it before he died on 28 December 1978.[22]

A major event in this period was the publication in the West in 1974 of *Za skhidnim obriiem* (Beyond the Eastern Horizon) by Danylo Shumuk, who has spent many years in camps and prisons. The book consists of reminiscences from the time of the Nazi occupation of Ukraine, when Shumuk was a member of UPA. Some emigres felt that his denunciation of certain UPA operations and policies had been inserted into the manuscript by the KGB. In 1978, however, when a new version of the original manuscript reached the Smoloskyp information service, it was established that the passages had in fact been written by Shumuk.

In June 1977, Iosyp Terelia's 31-page letter to Iurii Andropov, the Soviet KGB chief, in which the author declared: "It is a crime to be a citizen of the Soviet Union!,"[23] reached the West. Terelia, 33, had spent fourteen years in prisons and psychiatric clinics. In his letter he described in precise detail the sadistic treatment to which the inmates of the special psychiatric clinic in Sychevka (near Smolensk) were subjected. The letter, dated 21 December 1976, was translated from Ukrainian into Russian by Petro Hryhorenko [Grigorenko] in March 1977. It was also translated into

English and circulated widely in the West. Terelia was rearrested soon after its publication.

The human-rights movement achieved a major success with the release of Pliushch from the special psychiatric clinic in Dnipropetrovsk. Pliushch, who was subsequently deported to the West, gained his freedom largely through the concerted efforts of Ukrainian and Russian activists and supporters in the West. The Soviet leadership was surprised, for example, when left-wing and socialist groups organized a mass demonstration on behalf of Pliushch in Paris on 23 October 1975. It is reported that over 3,000 people, including many prominent cultural and academic figures, took part in the demonstration. The chief editor of the French Communist Party newspaper *L'Humanité* wrote:

> If it is true (and, unfortunately, no proof to the contrary has been supplied so far), if it is correct that this mathematician was committed to a psychiatric clinic solely because he uttered critical remarks about certain aspects of Soviet power or about Soviet power itself, then we have no other choice but to state unequivocally our total rejection of these methods and our demand for his immediate release.[24]

Once in the West, Pliushch began to enlighten the public about the abuse of psychiatry by the Soviet authorities. As a result, many in the West, including those on the left of the political spectrum, are now better informed about Soviet methods.[25]

Further details about the abuse of psychiatry in the USSR were provided by a special commission of the Moscow Helsinki group headed by Alexander Podrabinek, which sent to the West extensive documentation concerning the commitment of sane people to special psychiatric clinics in Ukraine.

New Elements in the Ideological Offensive

On 16–17 May 1974 a CC CPU plenum discussed ideological work in the light of the decisions of the Twenty-fourth CPSU Congress. Of special concern was the "international education of the workers." Evidently "ideological education" was still in a state of crisis, and the Soviet leadership still viewed a "military-patriotic" education as the best means of averting the threat of "subversion." According to Shcherbytsky:

> The military-patriotic education of youth and its preparation for service in the armed forces is an integral part of ideological work. We must continue to improve the work standards of the Voluntary Society for the Promotion of Co-operation with the Army, Navy and Air Force (DOSAAF) and of the Red Cross, to strengthen the sponsorship of military units and sections by workers' collectives and educational establishments, and show a constant

concern for improving the working conditions of the military commissariats.[26]

Military-patriotic education in the USSR is concatenated with the "international education of the workers." The military establishment remains adamant that a thorough mastery of Russian is essential for military training as well as for the cohesion of the Soviet armed forces. Thus it supports the Russification of schools.

In his discourse about the international education of the workers, Shcherbytsky criticized the party organizations of Chernivtsi, Transcarpathia, Odessa, Crimea, Lviv and Ternopil oblasts. In his review of ideological work, he demanded more effort from social scientists, but surprisingly, praised the Ukrainian creative intelligentsia for standing "firmly behind popular folk and party principles." Nevertheless, he said, "individual literary workers and artists are committing errors in their work, some uncritical authors are trying to imitate foreign "modernism," and literary works of a low artistic standard are constantly appearing."[27] The criticism, however, was restrained. Evidently the Ukrainian party chief was trying to enlist the sympathies of the writers and artists. Elsewhere in his speech Shcherbytsky warned that "imperialist circles, bourgeois nationalists and Zionist centres" were stepping up their activities against the Soviet Union: "Enemy propaganda is trying to influence various strata and categories of the Soviet people by glorifying the bourgeois life-style, promoting the ideology of private ownership and reviving religious relics."[28]

The plenum was devoted to strengthening the party apparatus and improving "party management." Shcherbytsky noted improvements in ideological work, but criticized cadre policy in culture, science and education in Kiev, blaming the Kiev city and oblast committees. He accused the Donetsk oblast committee of erroneous cadre-political decisions in science, teaching and journalism, and attacked the committees of Odessa and Kharkiv oblasts, where the intelligentsia were reported to be working "superficially."[29]

On 18 October 1974 Ukraine celebrated the thirtieth anniversary of its "liberation" from German occupation. In his speech at the official ceremony, Shcherbytsky emphasized the role played by the Russians in defeating the enemy: "The great heroic deed of the Russian people is immeasurable." He also praised the role of Brezhnev, who had served as a senior political officer during the war.

In 1974 Shcherbytsky's popularity was at a low ebb in Ukraine. Of all the chiefs of the Ukrainian Communist Party after Stalin's death (Kyrychenko, Pidhorny, Shelest), Shcherbytsky has had the greatest difficulty in building up his image as leader of the second largest Soviet republic. He is knowledgeable about economic problems, but lacks charisma. Further he is the stereotyped party official: totally servile to the leaders in Moscow and fearful of deviating from the party line. As part of a campaign to increase his popularity, Moscow journals published his articles on nationality questions. An important article on Soviet nationality policy appeared in *Problemy mira i sotsializma* (reprinted in *Komunist Ukrainy*), Moscow's platform for definitive articles on nationality policy. Shcherbytsky's basic thesis was that current Soviet nationality policy was rooted in "Leninist principles." He stated that the right of the nationalities to self-determination had been realized in the USSR; every nationality had achieved statehood; and a balanced regional economic development had been achieved. While admitting that "one of the most important natural laws of Soviet society" is "the further rapprochement of all nations and ethnic groups," he added:

> The party is against forcing this process artificially, because it has an objective character and is dictated by the overall course of social development. It is natural that the communist's first duty in this situation is loyalty to Lenin's heritage: maximum attention to the interests and development of each nation. At the same time the party considers inadmissible all efforts to retard the process of the rapprochement of all nations and ethnic groups or to increase national isolation no matter what the pretext. This would undoubtedly contradict the interests of the country as a whole and the interests of each republic, along with the interests of communist construction and those of the internationalist ideology of the communists, and the Soviet people.[30]

On 6–7 February 1975 a republican conference in Kiev dealt with the "international education of the workers." As revealed at the conference, which was attended by representatives from several republics, the "internationalization" of social life presupposed the leadership of the CPSU in the "internationalization" of cadre policies. In practice, this meant giving preference to Russian immigrants over local candidates for key jobs. As one delegate put it: "The objective process of internationalization of social life is reflected in cadre policy."[31] The two most important speeches at the conference were delivered by L. P. Nahorna, a specialist on "Ukrainian bourgeois nationalism" from the Institute of Party History and L. Iu. Berenstein, dean of the Faculty of the History of the CPSU at the Ukrainian Academy of Agricultural Sciences, who "revealed the reactionary and anti-Soviet thrust of the imperialist propaganda of Ukrainian bourgeois nationalism and Zionism."[32]

At this time there were three main characteristics of the political situation in Ukraine: the campaign against dissidents; the strengthening of the party's control over society; and the expansion of ideological education, in particular "military-patriotic and international" education.

Prior to the Twenty-fifth CPU and CPSU Congresses, one of the party's most important aims was to remove unwanted members by an exchange of party cards. Overall responsibility for the exchange lay in the hands of I. K. Lutak, a Politburo member and second secretary of the CC CPU. Lutak delivered a report on the matter at a plenary session of the CC CPU on 20 May 1975, which revealed that those members who had supported the defence of national rights had now been excluded from the party:

> The measures for the improvement of ideological work, the strengthening of the class, patriotic and international education of the workers, and the eradication of examples of a conciliatory attitude towards national narrow-mindedness and glorifying the past received full support. Ideology had thus become more vigorous, richer and more motivated.[33]

It is not known how many dissident communists were expelled. The expelled group evidently included some alcoholics: Lutak remarked that "We cannot ignore the fact that some party members not only fail to campaign stubbornly against a social evil like alcoholism but even tend toward it themselves."[34]

At the Twenty-fifth CPU Congress on 10–13 February 1976, Shcherbytsky spoke about Shelest's dismissal:

> As you know, P. Iu. Shelest, the former first secretary of the CC CPU, was criticized for serious shortcomings in the management of the republican party organization. In 1972 he lost all rapport with the republic's party organization and failed to live up to the high responsibility vested in him, thus losing the moral right to belong to the CC CPU. Comrade Shelest was expelled from the CC CPU by unanimous vote following a motion by the Politburo of the CC CPU.[35]

Shcherbytsky reported that V. I. Dehtiarev had been dismissed from the CC CPU for "lack of discipline" in the implementation of party decisions. (Dehtiarev was the former first secretary of the Donetsk oblast committee who lost his position in January 1976, after Shcherbytsky accused him of violating the principles of cadre work and collective decision-making.) Shcherbytsky also spoke of a decline in the standards of socialist morality in Donetsk oblast, where he detected widespread abuse of alcohol and negligence in the education of the young.[36] Following his demotion from the Donetsk party organization and the Central Committee, Dehtiarev was made chairman of the State Committee for Industrial Safety and Mine Supervision attached to the Ukrainian Council of Ministers.[37]

The Ukrainian Helsinki Group

The signing of the final documents of the Helsinki Conference on Security and Co-operation in Europe (CSCE) in August 1975 was widely discussed in the Soviet Union. Perhaps the most important immediate effect of the Helsinki Conference was that it stimulated the Soviet population to think about human rights and motivated many to campaign for implementation of the provisions of the accord in the USSR and other countries. Dissidents of widely different political opinions agreed that the struggle for human rights should have priority over the task of informing Soviet society about current events at home and abroad. By the end of 1976 the human-rights movement in the USSR had become organized.

The first major step was the establishment on 13 May 1976 in Moscow of the Public Group to Promote the Implementation of the Helsinki Accords in the USSR, led by Professor Iurii Orlov. The Ukrainian human-rights movement was represented in the Moscow Group by the retired general, Petro Hryhorenko. Similar groups were soon founded in other republics.

The Ukrainian Helsinki Group was established on 9 November 1976 in Kiev. It was headed by the writer Mykola Rudenko. Born in 1920 in Voroshylovhrad oblast, Rudenko served as a political officer during the Second World War and was seriously wounded during the siege of Leningrad. He was later discharged as a war invalid. He joined the CPSU in 1946, and from 1947–50 was editor-in-chief of the journal *Dnipro*. His writings on economic and philosophical subjects eventually led to his expulsion from the CPSU and the Ukrainian Writers' Union. Later Rudenko, also a member of Amnesty International, worked as a watchman.[38] The Ukrainian Helsinki Group worked actively for the implementation of the accords. Hundreds of Soviet citizens who had learned the addresses of the group's members through foreign radio broadcasts asked them for help. The group registered numerous violations of civil rights and appealed to the authorities for redress.

The Ukrainian Helsinki Group operated strictly within the law. The authorities knew the names and addresses of its members and could easily obtain information about its activities. In its first public report, Memorandum no. 1, the group stated explicitly that its work was humanitarian, rather than political, and added:

We realize that the entrenched governmental bureaucracy, which continues to grow, can take countermeasures against our legitimate aspirations. But we also understand that the bureaucratic interpretation of human rights does not reflect the full meaning of the international agreements signed by the government of the USSR.[39]

Memorandum no. 1 reported on arrests and trials that had taken place in Ukraine in 1972, noting that those arrested included several young people who had sympathized with Ivan Dziuba. It referred to the case of Vasyl Lisovy, a communist and candidate of philosophical sciences, who had not been politically involved prior to the arrests of Dziuba and others. Incensed by the injustice of these cases, Lisovy wrote a letter to the Ukrainian party and government leaders, which ended: "If these people are criminals, then I am a criminal, too, for I defend their point of view." In reply to this letter, the authorities sentenced Lisovy to seven years' internment in labour camps and three years' exile.[40]

The memorandum also provided a list of political prisoners in labour camps, with their names, professions, dates of arrest, sentences and dates of release; reports on Ukrainians in Vladimir Prison; and information on the cruelest punishment for dissidents: commitment to special psychiatric clinics. Vasyl Ruban, for example, was sent to a clinic in Dnipropetrovsk for possession of the manuscript of "Ukraine—Communist and Independent." The manuscript's author, Iosyp Terelia, has been in a psychiatric clinic in Vinnytsia since November 1976. His commitment, which followed fourteen years in prisons, camps and clinics, triggered a wave of international protest.

In 1977 Soviet security organs arrested numerous activists of the Helsinki group on (trumped-up) charges of rape, theft and trafficking in narcotics. Despite massive protests from the West, those arrested were given severe sentences, especially in Ukraine. Mykola Rudenko and Oleksii Tykhy, two leading Helsinki group members, were arrested on 4 February 1977—the former in Kiev, the latter in Donetsk. Tykhy, a teacher who promoted the Ukrainian language, was a department head at a secondary school. In the West, a number of U. S. senators called on the State Department and President Carter himself to intervene on behalf of the victims of political persecution in Ukraine. These protests were parallelled by actions in other Soviet republics. The trial of Rudenko and Tykhy was held from 23 June to 1 July 1977. Rudenko was sentenced to seven years in camps and five years' exile; Tykhy to ten years in camps plus five in exile.[41]

Further reprisals forced the Helsinki groups to reduce their activities to a minimum. Those members who, despite their desperate situation, still tried to campaign for their cause, were arrested and tried. The Kiev physician Volodymyr Malynkovych, a member of the Ukrainian Helsinki Group, emigrated to the Federal Republic of Germany on 31 December 1979. He maintains that of the 35 members of the Ukrainian Helsinki Group, 27 have been imprisoned, 5 have emigrated, and only 3 are still free. The arrests are now conducted almost exclusively on the basis of the Criminal Procedure Code of the Ukrainian SSR. According to Malynkovych, the arrests are now based on the following articles of the Criminal Code: 84 (theft), 117 (rape), 187 (defamation), 188 (resistance to the militia), 196 (violation of passport regulations), 206 (hooliganism) and 229 (possession of narcotics).

Ukraine Gets a New Constitution

Following a period of public debate, the USSR Supreme Soviet approved
the CC CPSU's draft for a new constitution of the USSR in October
1977. In his address, Brezhnev declared that the new Basic Law would de-
fine the authority of the Union more clearly than the Stalin Constitution
of 1936. He noted, however, that a handful of "comrades" had drawn false
conclusions from the party's thesis of the "Soviet people" as a new
historical community of peoples:

> They proposed the inclusion in the constitution of the concept of a unified
> Soviet nation, the elimination of the union and autonomous republics or
> sharp curtailment of the sovereignty of the union republics, depriving them of
> the right of secession from the USSR and the right to conduct foreign
> relations. The proposals for the dissolution of the Soviet of Nationalities and
> the formation of a unicameral Supreme Soviet aim in the same direction. I
> think that the erroneousness of such proposals is clear. The social and
> political unity of the Soviet people does not imply that national differences
> have disappeared. Thanks to the consistent implementation of Leninist
> nationality policy, we have—in building socialism—successfully resolved the
> nationalities question for the first time in history. The friendship of the
> Soviet peoples is indestructible; their rapprochement and the mutual
> enrichment of their spiritual life is taking place in the process of communist
> construction. We would, however, be treading a dangerous path if we were to
> start forcing this objective process of the rapprochement of the nations
> artificially. V. I. Lenin warned expressly against this, and we shall not depart
> from his heritage.[42]

Shcherbytsky reported on the draft Ukrainian constitution and the
public debate at a session of the republic's Supreme Soviet on 19 April
1978. He, too, mentioned the proposal to abolish the right of secession
from the USSR, but in contrast to Brezhnev, he listed the motives of the
supporters of this proposal:

1)   The republic's economy is an organic part of the unified all-Soviet
     economic complex, and only in this framework can it best realize its
     possibilities and potential;

2)   The consistent implementation of the CPSU's Leninist nationality
     policy in our country has resulted in the liquidation of all forms of
     social and national oppression, inequality and alienation among the
     nations and peoples; a new historical community of peoples—the

Soviet people—to which the Ukrainian people also belongs has emerged;

3)   A new culture has developed, a culture which is socialist in content, national in form, internationalist in spirit and Soviet in alignment, a culture which is a mighty source for the development of each person in the socialist society and of that society's aesthetic and moral education.[43]

Before the proclamation of the new constitution, the concept *edinoe gosudarstvo* [unitary state] was a major topic of dispute among Soviet legal experts. Some argued that the term *edinoe gosudarstvo* should be written into the constitution because it described the true nature of the Soviet state. Brezhnev and his associates found a compromise formula. Thus, Article 70 of the new Basic Law defines the USSR as "*edinoe mnogonatsionalnoe soiuznoe gosudarstvo*" [a unitary multinational federal state]. In practice, the new constitution stresses the increased authority of the Union, part of the trend toward greater centralization that Brezhnev endorsed. It represented a victory for Russian chauvinism, and was another major step away from Lenin's legacy. Shortly before his death, Lenin had surveyed Soviet society and warned against excessive centralism, against the dependence of the union republics on Moscow, and against the Russians' disregard of other national languages. The following statement by Lenin was prophetic:

It is necessary to issue extremely strict regulations governing the use of the national languages in the non-Russian republics...and to control the observance of these regulations with particular care. There is no doubt that, with our apparatus in its present shape, there will be a lot of truly Russian abuses under the pretext of the unified railroad system, under the pretext of the unified treasury, and so forth. Considerable ingenuity will be required to combat such abuses—not to speak of the special kind of rectitude that will be required of those who enter such a combat. Here we need a detailed code that can be compiled only by the representatives of the nation living in the republic concerned. Therefore we should not by any means preclude the possibility that, because of this entire undertaking, we will take another step backward at the next Congress of Soviets, i.e., let the Union of Soviet Socialist Republics exist only militarily and diplomatically and restore the complete autonomy of the individual people's commissariats in all other aspects.[44]

Many of Lenin's comments have since been echoed—to no avail—by dissidents.

Discussion about the new constitution indicated the degree of solidarity among Russian nationalist groups in the various union republics. In his speech to the USSR Supreme Soviet on 4 October 1977, Brezhnev noted that many comrades wanted the concept of a "unified Soviet nation" written into the constitution. Others wanted to abolish the union republics.[45] Similar demands were made in the Ukrainian SSR by representatives of the Russian minority. In a speech to the session of the republican Supreme Soviet held on 19 April 1978, Shcherbytsky remarked that "The Commission [for Draft Legislation] has received letters referring to the undesirability of retaining the passage on Ukraine's right of secession from the Soviet Union in the text of the republic's constitution."[46] Shcherbytsky did not criticize the calls for abolition of the right of secession, but argued for its retention as a "glorious example of the truly democratic nature of the multinational Soviet state."

Following the proclamation of the 1978 constitution, the central and republican press published a series of articles about the nationality problem in the context of the new Basic Law. V. S. Shevtsov, a doctor of legal sciences from Moscow, was the first author to write a study of the problem of "statehood" as it affects Ukrainians under the new constitution. But the article, which appeared in a Ukrainian journal, said nothing new. Shevtsov depicted Soviet national statehood as an important mechanism designed "to regulate national relations and promote socio-political union, the unity of society, and the blossoming, rapprochement and, in the historical perspective, coalescence of the socialist nations."[47]

Another characteristic of the new community, according to Shevtsov, was its "internationalist" nature: "In a multinational socialist society the unitary federal state expresses the basic national interests and needs by its social class essence. Thus, the mechanisms of the federal state are so constructed that they can consider, reflect and secure national interests and requirements."[48] Neither Shevtsov nor the constitution specifies what these "national interests and requirements" are. In practice, they are formulated by the party—not by the people—in all fields of national life—politics, culture, science, education, the economy.

Shevtsov's article, typical of many written about the nationality problem after the issuing of the new constitution, elaborated on the division of authority between the Union and the republics. According to Shevtsov, the new constitution had introduced a new element: "It involves the participation of the (individual) republic in the solution of questions that fall under the authority of the federal state."[49] This implied the integration of the central and republican apparatuses, since the republics could only make maximum use of their rights by co-operating more closely with the central apparatus. However, the republics' participation under the new constitution is limited to those central organs in which the they are represented, e.g., the USSR Supreme Soviet and the USSR Council of Ministers.[50]

A *"Little Russian" Anniversary*

The tercentary of Ukraine's "unification" with the Russian Empire in 1954 had been celebrated with great pomp. Thus the authorities decided to make the 325th anniversary in 1979 an event *ne plus ultra*. The CC CPU adopted the enabling decree and published the plans for the celebrations:[51]

1) Gala meetings attended by representatives of the workers, public organizations, the armed forces, the party and the government to be held in January.

2) Special sessions of the Institute of History of the Ukrainian Academy of Sciences, the Social Science Section, the Gorky Institute of Literature, and the Shevchenko Institute of Literature to be held at Kiev and Dnipropetrovsk universities.

3) A meeting of workers from Briansk (RSFSR), Homel (Belorussian SSR) and Chernihiv (Ukrainian SSR) oblasts to be held at the point where the borders of the three republics meet.

4) Special events to be arranged at factories, building sites, collective farms, state farms, etc., including lectures, discussions, seminars, meetings with writers and artists, etc. Representatives of the RSFSR to participate in these events.

5) A special media campaign to demonstrate the friendship between the Ukrainian, Russian and other peoples of the USSR and their "common struggle for implementation of the decisions of the Twenty-fifth CPSU Congress."

6) The entire propaganda and agitation apparatus is commissioned to devote special campaigns to the anniversary. "Znannia" Publishing House is instructed to publish anniversary books devoted to the "eternal friendship between the Ukrainian, Russian and all other peoples of our land, the victory of the Leninist nationality policy of the CPSU, and the achievements of the Ukrainian people in its socio-economic and cultural development and in the family of the fraternal peoples of the USSR."

7) The Ukrainian state broadcasting service is instructed to prepare a special series of broadcasts about Bohdan Khmelnytsky and a television series about the "fraternal friendship of the Russian and Ukrainian peoples," along with a number of on-the-spot reports from

the historical locations where the agreement on unification was sealed.

8)   Gala meetings of Ukrainian and Russian artists to be held in Moscow and Kiev, together with other special events (film festivals, literary soirées, exhibitions etc.). Special showings of the film *Bohdan Khmelnytsky.*

This list reveals the wide scope of the celebrations and their penetration of all spheres of life.

The celebrations of 1954 and 1979 were an an attempt to to "prove" by massive demonstrations of "people's friendship" that the official policy of "internationalism" has gained general acceptance and approval. But there were significant differences between the two events. One of the purposes of the 1954 celebration was to build up Ukraine's image as the second most important of the otherwise "equal" republics. It was argued that the Ukrainian people, by choosing unification with Russia in 1654, saved itself initially from the Polish and Turkish yokes and eventually from subjugation by Hitler's Germany. Following the elimination of the consequences of the personality cult, the argument continued, a new phase in the enlargement of the rights of the republics had begun. Thus, in 1954 the authorities became conciliatory toward Ukraine, offering inducements to make membership in the multinational state attractive. One such inducement was the cession of the Crimea to the Ukrainian SSR as a "present."

The aims of 1979, however, were claimed to be the following:

1)   To demonstrate the unshakeable fraternal friendship of the Ukrainian people with all the other peoples of the Soviet Union.

2)   To further strengthen the unity of the Soviet peoples and to improve "the patriotic and international education of the workers."

3)   To improve the political activities and the work morale of the workers in the task of implementing the decisions of the Twenty-fifth CPSU Congress and the plans for communist construction.[52]

Thus, the new trend is to accelerate the integration of the republic in the new historical community of the peoples. The efforts to enlarge the rights of the republics have have been superseded by the strict subordination of the member states to the Union—a relationship that has been written into the new constitution and confirmed in Brezhnev's commentaries.

Thanks to Shcherbytsky and his associates, Moscow has succeeded in cultivating a following of loyal "Little Russians" in Ukraine, who are willing to subordinate the republic's interests to those of the centre. As the leader of this group, Shcherbytsky may well go down in history as the *maloros par excellence*.

Notes

1. *Ukrainian Herald, Issue 7–8*, 127.
2. *Komunist Ukrainy*, no. 11 (1972): 3.
3. *Radianska Ukraina*, 27 November 1973.
4. *Ukrainian Herald, Issue 7–8*, 131–51.
5. *Ibid.*, 137.
6. *Ibid.*, 50.
7. *Radianska Ukraina*, 27 July 1972.
8. *Khronika tekushchikh sobytii*, no. 28 (1974): 18ff.
9. *Radianska Ukraina*, 20 April 1973.
10. *Ibid.*
11. "Pro seriozni nedoliky ta pomylky odniei knyhy" *Komunist Ukrainy*, no. 4 (1973): 77ff.
12. Shelest, *Ukraino*, 29.
13. "Pro seriozni nedoliky ta pomylky odniei knyhy," 80.
14. An example of such protest was "An Open Letter to the Members of the Communist Party of the Soviet Union," published in the *The New York Review of Books*, 28 June 1973. Among the signatories were: Joan Baez, Philip Berrigan, Heinrich Böll, Noam Chomsky, Ramsey Clark, Harvey Cox, Erich Fromm, Nat Hentoff, Julius Jacobson, Antonin Liehm, Robert Jay Lifton, Norman Mailer, David McReynolds, Gunnar Myrdal, Paul O'Dwyer, Margaret Papandreou, Alan Paton, Jiri Pelikan, Meyer Schapiro, Arthur Schlesinger Jr., Ivan Svitak, Alexander Yesenin-Volpin, Günther Grass and Leonard Bernstein.
15. *Suchasnist*, no. 1 (1974): 122–4.
16. See, for example, reports in *ibid.*, no. 7–8 (1974): 245–52.
17. *Iurydychnyi slovnyk* (Kiev, 1974), 29.
18. I. Dziuba, "Shliakh obrano nazavzhdy" reprinted in *Suchasnist*, no. 9 (1975): 96ff.
19. L. Pliushch, "Trahediia Ivana Dziuby," *Diialoh*, no. 1 (1977): 53–73.
20. *Suchasnist*, no. 9 (1977): 106ff.
21. Cf. "Bulletin of the 'Smoloskyp' Ukrainian Information Service," 19 April 1977, and H. Sniehiriov, "Nenko moia, nenko," *Suchasnist*, no. 6 (1977): 39ff. The author, who examined documents on the activities of the Soviet security organs (see *Terror i revoliutsiia*, [Paris, 1965]) has advocated this thesis for some time. It is significant that, during the time period encompassed by Sniehiriov's work, the security organs used the same

methods in trials against the "League for the Liberation of Belorussia" and the "League for the Liberation of Uzbekistan." This was a high-return method of "helping" nationally-minded elements to set up an "organization" that could subsequently be used as a pretext for a mass trial with severe sentences. These show trials helped to intimidate the non-Russian peoples.

22. According to a press release of Smoloskyp Ukrainian Information Service, 24 July 1978.
23. *Suchasnist*, no. 7–8 (1977): 216–19.
24. *Khronika zashchity prav v SSSR* (New York), no. 17 (1975): 7.
25. See L. Plyushch, *History's Carnival: A Dissident's Autobiography*, (New York-London, 1979) and *An Interview with Leonid Plyushch* (Toronto, 1976).
26. *Komunist Ukrainy*, no. 6 (1974): 26.
27. *Ibid.*, 20.
28. *Ibid.*, 34.
29. *Ibid.*, 40.
30. V. V. Shcherbytsky, "Mizhnarodne znachennia dosvidu natsionalnykh vidnosyn v SRSR," *Komunist Ukrainy*, no. 12 (1974): 31.
31. "Aktualni pytannia internatsionalnoho vykhovannia trudiashchykh," *Komunist Ukrainy*, no. 3 (1975): 38.
32. *Ibid.*, 41.
33. "Pro pidsumky obminu partiinykh dokumentiv u partiinykh orhanizatsiiakh respubliky i zavdannia po dalshomu polipshenniu partiinoi roboty," *Komunist Ukrainy*, no. 7 (1975): 23.
34. *Ibid.*, 28.
35. *XXV Zizd Komunistychnoi partii Ukrainy* (Kiev, 1976), 6.
36. *Radianska Ukraina*, 27 December 1975.
37. *Ibid.*, 11 January 1976. Dehtiarev's removal led to much speculation. Without any factual basis, many "Kremlinologists" asserted that this was the fall of "Shelest's last protégé." Yet Dehtiarev was involved in manoeuvres against Shelest before his removal. The *Ukrainian Herald Issue 7–8* describes him as a firm opponent of Shelest's who put all his support behind Shcherbytsky whenever there was a confrontation.
38. For biographical information on other members of the Ukrainian Helsinki Group, see: *The Ukrainian Helsinki Group: Five Years of Struggle In Defense of Rights* (Baltimore-Washington-Toronto, 1981).
39. *Declaration and Memorandum No. 1*, (Washington, D.C., 1977), 8.
40. *Ibid.*, 16.
41. *Suchasnist*, no. 1 (1978): 90–111.
42. *Pravda*, 1 October 1977.
43. *Komunist Ukrainy*, no. 5 (1978): 25ff.
44. V. I. Lenin, *Werke*, (Berlin, 1964), 6: 595ff.
45. *Pravda*, 5 October 1977.
46. *Komunist Ukrainy*, no. 5 (1978): 25.
47. V. S. Shevtsov, "Radianska natsionalna derzhavnist," *Komunist Ukrainy*, no. 7 (1978): 32ff.
48. *Ibid.*, 34.
49. *Ibid.*, 37.

50. *Ibid.*, 37–8.
51. *Radianska Ukraina*, 17 September 1978.
52. *Komunist Ukrainy*, no. 10 (1978): 10ff.

Chapter Six

Society

Social Structure

In the second half of the 1960s the political shift to the right under Leonid Brezhnev gave rise to the concept of the "Soviet people" and a reinterpretation of the role of nations in this new community. The party argued that the differences in the level of development of the Soviet peoples had disappeared. Soviet sociologists argue that the Soviet working class is not merely the sum of the working classes of the Soviet nations but rather a single all-union entity. Theoretically, a quantitative or qualitative enhancement of the level of development of one nation automatically entails improvements for the partially underdeveloped nations. This argument is used, for example, to justify preferential treatment of workers, specialists and scientists in the Russian republic, for—according to this line of thought—their advancement benefits the other republics.

This theory has had a catastrophic effect on the social structure of the Soviet nations, particularly concerning their modernization. In Ukraine this is reflected in the differences that exist between the social structure of all national groups and that of the ethnically Ukrainian contingent. In 1970, for example, white-collar staff represented 23 per cent of Ukraine's population, but only 16 per cent of the ethnically Ukrainian population of the republic (see Table 6.1). The lack of advancement of the ethnic Ukrainians illustrates the success of Moscow's migration policies. (There are similar trends in other non-Russian republics.)[1] A comparison of the class composition of the USSR and the Ukrainian SSR shows that the

TABLE 6.1 Ukrainian SSR: Differences Between the Social Structures of the Total Population and the Titular Nation (Ukrainians) 1939–70 (per cent)

Social Class	1939[a]		1959		1970	
	Total Population	Ukrainian	Total Population	Ukrainian	Total Population	Ukrainian
Working Class	33	29	41	34	52	47
White-collar Staff	17	13	17	13	23	16
Collective Farmers	49	55	42	53	25	37

[a] Artisans and private farmers excluded.

SOURCE: 1939 data from Iu. V. Arutiunian, "Izmenenie sotsialnoi struktury sovetskikh natsii," *Istoriia SSSR*, no. 4 (1972): 6; 1959 data from Iu. V. Arutiunian, *Sotsialnaia struktura selskogo naseleniia SSSR* (Moscow, 1971), 84; 1970 data from *Sovremennye etnicheskie protsessy v SSSR* (Moscow, 1977), 131.

development levels of the various social classes in Ukraine—the indicators of a modern economic structure—lie well below the levels of the USSR as a whole (see Table 6.2).

TABLE 6.2 The USSR and Ukraine: Class Structure 1939–70 (per cent)

Social Class	1939[a]		1959		1970	
	USSR	Ukraine	USSR	Ukraine	USSR	Ukraine
Working Class	33.5	32.6	49.5	41.0	56.8	52.0
White-collar Staff	16.7	17.6	18.8	17.0	22.7	23.0
Collective Farmers	47.2	48.7	31.4	42.0	20.5	25.0

[a] Artisans and private farmers excluded.

SOURCE: As for Table 6:1 with the addition of *Narodnoe khoziaistvo SSSR za 60 let* (Moscow, 1978), 8.

According to data for 1967, Ukrainians accounted for 69 per cent of the industrial workers, 72 per cent of the chemical workers, 72 per cent of the light-industry workers and 74 per cent of the food-industry workers in the Ukrainian republic. The percentage of Ukrainians in the leading industrial branches is lower: 59 per cent in iron and steel, 56 per cent in coal, and 65 per cent in machine-building and metal-working. In 1959, 69.5 per cent of the republic's industrial workers were Ukrainians.[2]

Ukraine's working class grew from 3.1 million in 1939 to 11.6 million by 1970, including 3.4 million employed in the countryside.[3] However, throughout that period Ukrainians were underrepresented in this group (see Table 6.3). The differences were even greater in the other republics,

TABLE 6.3 Ukraine: Representation of Titular Nation in the Working Class 1939–70

	1939	1959	1970
Total number of workers (1000s)	3,133	7,938	11,602
Ukrainians (1000s)	1,690	5,515	8,533
Ukrainians (per cent)	54.5	69.8	73.6

SOURCE: *Rabochii klass SSSR i ego vedushchaia rol v stroitelstve kommunizma* (Moscow, 1975), 405.

particularly in Kirghizia, Tadzhikistan, Turkmenia and Moldavia. In 1970 the representation of the titular nation in the working class was highest in the RSFSR (86.3 per cent Russian) and the lowest in Kazakhstan (24.1 per cent Kazakh). These figures reflect the effect of the "fraternal aid" of the "great Russian people." Some Soviet writers do not acknowledge any imbalance, and maintain that the "multinational" structure of the work force is a sign of "internationalism" in practice. Their analysis, however, often conceals the fact that Russians make up the largest group among the white-collar staff and the working class in many national republics, although only a minority of the population. The (incomplete) data on the national composition of specialized blue-collar workers suggest that Russians are also overrepresented in skilled occupations (see Table 6.4).

TABLE 6.4 Proportion of Skilled Personnel in the Agricultural Work Force
of a Given Nationality in the USSR 1959–70 (in per cent)

	Proportion of skilled personnel in the agricultural work force of given nationality		Managers and Specialists		Machine Operators	
Nationality	1959	1970	1959	1970	1959	1970
Russians	15.7	27.9	4.5	6.8	11.2	21.1
Ukrainians	10.6	17.4	2.9	4.6	7.7	12.8
Tadzhiks	4.5	7.3	2.0	2.4	2.5	4.9

SOURCE: Iu. V. Arutiunian, *Sotsialnaia struktura selskogo naseleniia SSSR* (Moscow, 1971), 85.

Those persons with a higher or a specialized secondary education form a particularly important economic group. Soviet statistics, which offer detailed data according to nationality, state that in 1970, Russians made up 59 per cent of specialists with higher education and 64 per cent of those with specialized secondary education (see Table 6.5). Since Russians represented only 52 per cent of the total population of the USSR in 1970, the Soviet authorities evidently made a disproportionate investment in the training of Russian specialists. In Ukraine, Russians, who represented 21 per cent of the population, made up 27 per cent of the "leading cadres."[4]

The Soviet system gives preference to Russians in almost all fields, especially in education and training. The development of the social structures of the individual nations is considered secondary to the development of the social structure of the USSR. Indeed, many Soviet sociological studies no longer deal with the social structure of the titular nations. Some writers speak of the "national structure of the USSR" and the necessity of "overcoming every element of national (and ethnic) character that disturbs the process of overturning national barriers and transforming the entire process of the nations' development into a powerful instrument of co-operation."[5] The overriding principle in relations between the elements of the overall structure (between nations, peoples, national and ethnic groups) is their closest possible unity, their "continuous rapprochement in economic, political, social, intellectual and spiritual life."

Soviet analysts also tend to view the Soviet economy as a unit in which the economies of the individual republics are only of secondary importance. Projects in the interest of a given republic usually have no chance of realization unless they make a contribution to the Soviet economy as a whole.[6] A related problem is planned migration of Russians to the Ukrainian SSR and other republics, even though the latter possess an adequate indigenous labour force. The Institute of Economics at the USSR Academy of Sciences published an in-depth study of labour resources and

TABLE 6.5 Number of Specialists in the USSR 1970–5

Number employed in economy	1970				1975			
	With higher education		With specialized secondary education		With higher education		With specialized secondary education	
	1000s	per cent	1000s	per cent	1000s	per cent	1000s	per cent
Total	6,852.6		9,988.1		9,477.0		13,319.3	
Russians	4,033.6	58.8	6,425.9	64.3	5,570.4	58.7	8,447.3	63.4
Ukrainians	1,031.2	15.0	1,613.7	16.1	1,409.1	14.8	2,178.3	16.3

SOURCE: *Narodnoe obrazovanie, nauka i kultura v SSSR* (Moscow, 1977), 296.

labour migration in 1971. It pointed out that most of the migration was from the RSFSR, the republic with the greatest labour shortage. An average of 150,000 people had reportedly left the RSFSR each year during the preceding eleven years. Russians made up 84 per cent of those from other republics who moved to the Ukrainian SSR. The percentages for Kazakhstan, Belorussia and the Central Asian republics were 66, 62 and 54, respectively.[7] The authors of the study predicted that a continuation of this trend would have serious consequences for the economy of the RSFSR:

> If the departure rate in the period 1971–5 remains at the 1959–69 level, the RSFSR will lose about 750,000 people through the exchange of population with other republics. Of these as many as 600,000 will be of working age. One of the reasons why this drain of population from the RSFSR is especially undesirable is the fall in the labour reserves. In 1970, 14 out of every hundred people capable of working were employed in households or in the private subsidiary economy; now the number is only 3–4. Between 1959 and 1970 some 6.3 million people were drawn from households and the private subsidiary economy to work in the public production sector.[8]

Some Soviet sources maintain that the majority of migrating Russians are pensioners who want to move to a better climate. The Council for Research on Productive Forces of the Ukrainian Academy of Sciences, however, established that only about 5 per cent of the immigrants were in the higher age group.[9] The Soviet Academy's study noted that almost 50,000 people migrated to Ukraine each year, which "cannot be viewed as a positive phenomenon." Moreover, the authors said, the migration of Russians on such a scale complicated the distribution of labour, reduced manpower efficiency and necessitated increased investments in public services and housing.[10]

Population Trends

Between 1926 and 1970 the Ukrainian people suffered two demographic catastrophes. Between 1926 and 1939 the number of Ukrainians in the Soviet Union reportedly fell from 31,195,000 to 28,111,000 (excluding 7.5 million Ukrainians in Western Ukraine),[11] a drop of 9.9 per cent. The total population of the USSR, on the other hand, increased by 15.7 per cent and the number of Russians in the USSR rose by 28 per cent over the same period. The official explanation for the decrease in the Ukrainian population is that during the 1939 census a large number of Ukrainians living in North Caucasia gave their nationality as Russian. In reality it reflected losses incurred during the collectivization and as a result of the grain requisition campaigns of the 1930s, when several million peasants starved to death. Other losses resulted from the Stalinist purges of 1936–8, deportations and imprisonments.

TABLE 6.6 Ethnic Structure of the Ukrainian SSR 1926–79[a]

	1926		1959		1970		1979	
	1000s	per cent	1000s	per cent	1000s	per cent	1000s	per cent
Total population	38,569.0	100.0	41,869.0	100.0	47,126.5	100.0	49,609.0	100.0
Ukrainians	28,625.6	74.2	32,158.5	76.0	35,283.8	74.9	36,489.0	73.6
Russians	3,164.8	8.2	7,091.3	16.9	9,126.3	19.4	10,472.0	21.1
Jews	2,491.9	6.5	840.3	2.0	777.1	1.6	634.0	1.3
Belorussians	85.7	0.2	290.9	0.7	386.8	0.8	406.0	0.8
Poles	2,193.8	5.7	263.3	0.9	295.1	0.6	258.0	0.5
Moldavians and Romanians	454.4	1.2	342.5[b]	0.8	378.0	0.8	294.0[c]	0.6
Bulgarians	223.1	0.6	219.4	0.5	234.4	0.5	238.0	0.5
Hungarians	124.3	0.3	149.2	0.4	157.7	0.3	164.4	0.3
Greeks	120.7	0.3	104.4	0.2	106.9	0.2	104.1	0.2
Tatars	22.3	0.1	60.9	0.1	76.2	0.2	90.5	0.2
Armenians	21.1	0.1	28.0	0.1	33.4	0.07	—	—
Gypsies	—	22.0	—	30.0	0.06	—	—	—
Gagaus	22.1	0.1	23.5	0.1	26.5	0.05	—	—

[a] Only ethnic groups that consist of over twenty thousand persons have been listed.
[b] 1959: Moldavians 241.6; Romanians 100.9; 1970: Moldavians 265.9; Romanians 112.2.
[c] 1979: Moldavians only; Other nationalities 818.0 or 1.6 per cent.

SOURCE: V. I. Naulko, *Etnichnyi sklad naselennia Ukrainskoi RSR* (Kiev, 1965), 79. *Itogi vsesoiuznoi perepisi naseleniia 1959 goda, Ukrainskaia SSR* (Moscow, 1963), 168; *Itogi vsesoiuznoi perepisi naseleniia 1970 goda,* (Moscow, 1973), 4: 152: *Naselenie SSSR* (Moscow, 1980), 28; *Vestnik statistiki,* no. 8 (1980): 64ff.

Between 1926 and 1959 the ethnic minorities living in Ukraine decreased in size. The Jewish population fell from 2,491,900 in 1926 to 840,300 in 1959 as a result of the Nazi occupation, whereas most of the Poles were resettled in Poland after the Second World War. The German minority, which stood at 624,900 in 1926, had been reduced to 23,100 by 1959—partly as a result of deportation to the eastern regions of the USSR and partly as a result of forced repatriation during the Second World War (see Table 6.6).

The war itself had a catastrophic effect on the demographic structure of the Ukrainian SSR. Whereas in 1940 the population of Ukraine (excluding Transcarpathia) was 41.3 million, in 1950 it had fallen to 36.6 million, a decrease of 13.1 per cent. The prewar level was not reached until 1959. Based on a 1960 population of 42.5 million, the growth rate for the preceding twenty years was only 0.4 million.[12] According to a Soviet source, the total war loss was 3.3 million people (excluding military personnel), while 2.1 million were deported for work in the German Reich.[13] These figures exclude those Ukrainians deported to labour camps after the war. Few Soviet nations suffered a demographic catastrophe as great as that of the Ukrainians. Moreover, as Table 6.7 shows, the natural

TABLE 6.7   **Ukraine: Natural Population Growth 1913–78 (per 1000 of Population)**

Year	Births	Deaths	Natural Growth
1913[a]	44.1	25.2	18.9
1926[b]	42.1	18.1	24.0
1940	27.3	14.3	13.0
1950	22.8	8.5	14.3
1960	20.5	6.9	13.6
1970	15.2	8.9	6.3
1975	15.1	10.0	5.1
1978	14.7	10.7	4.0

[a] Excluding the western oblasts.
[b] Within the 1926 borders of the Ukrainian SSR.

SOURCE: *Naselenie soiuznykh respublik* (Moscow 1977), 69. S. I. Bruk, "Etnodemograficheskie protsessy v SSSR," *Istoriia SSSR*, no. 5 (1980): 24ff.

population growth of the Ukrainian SSR suffered further serious setbacks in the postwar period.

The 1960s and 1970s have witnessed a steady increase in Ukraine's urban population. By 1966 over half the population resided in urban areas, and this proportion grew to 61 per cent by 1979 (see Table 6.8). The Ukrainians, once a minority in urban centres, emerged as a majority in 1959, but the number of urban Russians living in Ukraine increased from 5.7 to 7.1 million between 1959 and 1970 (see Table 6.9). Russian immigration into Ukraine was focused on Ukraine's five most industrially

TABLE 6.8 Changes in the Urban Population of Ukraine 1913–78

Year	Population Estimates as per 1 January (millions)			Percentage of Total Population	
	Total	Urban	Rural	Urban	Rural
1913[a] (pre-Sept. 1939 borders)	27.2	5.5	21.7	20	80
1913[a] (pre-Sept. 1939 borders)	35.2	6.8	28.4	19	81
1926[b] (pre-Sept. 1939 borders)	29.5	5.7	23.8	19	81
1939[b] (including western oblasts)	40.5	13.6	26.9	34	66
1959[b]	41.9	19.2	22.7	46	54
1966	45.5	23.3	22.2	51	49
1970[b]	47.1	25.7	21.4	55	45
1975	48.8	28.7	20.1	59	41
1979 (Census)	49.7	30.5	19.2	61	39

[a] At year's end.
[b] Census figures.

SOURCE: *Narodnoe khoziaistvo Ukrainskoi SSR: Iubileinyi statisticheskii ezhegodnik* (Kiev, 1977), 9; *Naselenie SSSR* (Moscow, 1980), 8.

TABLE 6.9 Ukrainian SSR: Ethnic Structure of the Urban Population 1926–70

Nationality	1926		1959		1970	
	1000s	per cent	1000s	per cent	1000s	per cent
Ukrainians	2,976.2	40.4	11,781.7	61.5	16,164.3	62.9
Russians	1,586.1	21.5	5,726.5	30.0	7,112.3	30.0
Jews	1,834.6	24.9	810.0	4.3	764.2	3.0
Belorussians	39.8	0.5	213.0	1.1	295.2	1.0
Poles	603.4	8.2	163.5	0.8	163.0	0.6
Moldavians }	78.8	1.1	41.4	0.2	71.4	0.4
Romanians }			24.7	0.1	24.7	0.1
Bulgarians	14.2	0.2	58.4	77.0		0.3
Hungarians	27.9	0.4	50.2	53.8		0.2
Greeks	20.2	0.3	54.2	0.3	68.6	0.3
Tatars	17.1	0.2	55.8	67.4		0.3
Armenians	16.6	0.2	25.1	0.1	31.1	0.1
Gypsies	—	0.6	22.5	0.1	30.7	0.1

SOURCE: V. I. Naulko, *Etnichnyi sklad naselennia Ukrainskoi RSR* (Kiev, 1965), 89 (data for 1926 and 1959); *Itogi vsesoiuznoi perepisi naseleniia 1970 goda*, 4:158.

TABLE 6.10   Russian Population of Ukraine's Major Industrial oblasts 1979

Oblast	Total Russian population	As percentage of total population of oblast	Increase in Russian population, 1959–79
Dnipropetrovsk	834,579	22.9	199.9
Donetsk	2,211,992	42.9	145.7
Zaporizhzhia	606,280	31.1	227.5
Voroshilovhrad	1,222,037	43.8	146.7
Kharkiv	966,355	31.6	192.1

SOURCE: *Vestnik statistiki*, no. 8 (1980): 65–8.

developed oblasts. In Zaporizhzhia oblast, for example, the number of Russians increased by 227 per cent between 1959 and 1970 (see Table 6.10).

Mixed Marriages: A Demographic Trend with Political Implications

The Soviet Union is one of the few nations of the world where intermarriage is encouraged for political reasons:

> Mixed marriages strengthen the internationalization of daily life. As a rule, all the progressive elements contained in these peoples' way of life become synthesized in international families. The entire form of domestic and familial life becomes internationalized and acquires a composite character. A number of researchers have established that, in the day-to-day life of the Soviet nations and peoples, the international families make it easier to realize the internationalist features of all-Soviet life and to overcome national characteristics. This emerges in an especially beneficial manner in the education of the younger generation. As in-depth sociological studies confirm, the children of mixed families grow up as convinced internationalists.[14]

Mixed marriages between non-Russian peoples are encouraged in order to weaken their national awareness. Marriages between Russians and representatives of other Slavic peoples (especially Belorussians and Ukrainians) are also encouraged to further assimilation and Russification. Marriages between Russians and representatives of the Soviet Central Asian peoples (a fairly rare occurrence) are discouraged only if there is a danger of the Russian being assimilated—a real risk in rural areas where Russian is not the language of day-to-day communication and the children of such marriages are likely to identify themselves with the indigenous nation. In 1970 almost 30 per cent of all marriages in Ukraine's urban centres were between members of different nationalities (see Table 6.11). Articles in youth magazines, Komsomol lectures and party meetings propagate these mixed marriages. Thus a quarter of all children born in Ukraine's urban centres in 1959 had non-Ukrainian fathers (see Table 6.12).

TABLE 6.11 **Ukraine: Number of Ethnically Mixed Marriages 1959–70 (in per cent)**

	1959	1970
Total Population	15.0	19.7
Urban Population	26.3	29.6
Rural Population	5.8	7.8

SOURCE: V. A. Shpiliuk, *Mezhrespublikanskaia migratsiia i sblizheniie natsii v SSSR* (Lviv, 1975), 150.

TABLE 6.12 **Ukrainian SSR: Number of Children with Non-Ukrainian Fathers 1959**

	Total per 100 births	Urban population	Rural population
Total population	19.5	32.3	8.6
Ukrainians	12.0	24.7	4.1
Russians	45.4	46.7	40.8
Belorussians	68.6	74.7	55.3
Poles	54.5	70.0	41.5
Bulgarians	28.6	61.2	16.1
Chechens	48.7	70.5	37.4
Moldavians	26.1	61.7	15.8
Jews	20.6	20.4	26.1
Kazakhs	34.8	37.3	24.5
Armenians	49.9	54.0	28.9

SOURCE: V. I. Naulko, *Etnichnyi sklad naselennia Ukrainskoi RSR* (Kiev, 1965), 110.

Nations and Language

The policy of "voluntary Russification" has had a marked influence on non-Russians living outside their national republics. At the time of the 1926 census there were 7.9 million Ukrainians living outside the Ukrainian SSR.[15] The corresponding figures for the 1959, 1970 and 1979 censuses were 5.1, 5.5 and 5.9 million. The largest group (over 3.6 million) was living in the RSFSR. Of Ukrainians outside the republic, 3.3 million or 55.3 per cent considered Russian their native language (1959), including those in regions where Ukrainians lived in compact communities. Immediately after the October Revolution, Ukrainians living in the RSFSR had their own schools and cultural institutions, but these were later closed.

In 1956 the Ukrainian press published reports about Ukrainian families who had moved into the Irkutsk region at the beginning of the twentieth century in search of "land and a better lot." The authors of these reports were surprised that these families still spoke Ukrainian, cultivated Ukrainian traditions and were profoundly interested in the cultural life of their homeland. Local Russian radio stations and newspapers also gave the expatriate Ukrainian families considerable publicity. Radio Irkutsk even broadcast recitals of local Ukrainian choirs and the Siminsk district newspaper published a whole page in Ukrainian under the headline "A Ukrainian Village in Siberia."[16]

Such reports can be misleading, however. Ukrainians living in the eastern regions of the USSR have frequently protested the lack of Ukrainian cultural and social institutions. For example, Vasyl Lobko and nine other Ukrainians asked the Presidium of the CC CPU, the Ukrainian Council of Ministers and the Ukrainian Supreme Soviet in January 1964 for "the implementation of Lenin's legacy on the broad use of Ukrainian in all institutions, manufacturing, commercial and transport enterprises, etc." They requested "the restoration in the regions with a large Ukrainian community (Kuban, Siberia, the Far East, Kazakhstan) of those Ukrainian institutions (schools, clubs, libraries, theatres, etc.) abolished under Stalin and Kaganovich, and to establish new facilities there, especially since the Ukrainian population in these regions has increased in recent years."[17] It is also reported that in Siberia, minority groups such as the Ukrainians, Belorussians, Latvians and Moldavians had difficulty obtaining publications in their national languages.

While Khrushchev was still in power, many representatives of the national minorities in the eastern regions of the USSR (especially Ukrainians, Belorussians and Balts) evidently petitioned the governments of the national republics to establish native-language schools or courses and various cultural services. Shelest put forward a scheme to maintain cultural contacts between the Ukrainian SSR and Ukrainians living in other parts of the Soviet Union. The idea was that Ukrainian institutions (universities, schools, factories) would become the patrons of Ukrainian groups in other republics and begin a cultural exchange. During the virgin-lands campaign, Ukrainian institutions spontaneously established a cultural service for their compatriots in Kazakhstan. But Brezhnev banned such actions. Instead, party theorists even developed a "dispersion" [*rasselenie*] thesis, which argued that expatriation made a major contribution to the "internationalization" of the republics. The creation of nationally mixed workers' collectives on major construction projects was seen as a step in this direction.

Soviet statisticians pay considerable attention to the analysis of "dispersion," but this appears to be little more than a euphemism for Russian immigration to non-Russian republics. Thus, between 1960 and 1971, an annual average of 150,000 Russians left the RSFSR to settle in non-Russian regions.[18] Upon arrival, they find no lack of Russian cultural facilities and, in many cases, enjoy a privileged status. Non-Russians who leave their native republic, however, become subject to pressures for

Russification. As noted by E. V. Tadevosian, a party spokesman on nationality policy: "The great Russian people—first among our country's equal nations—plays the leading role in the creation and development of the Soviet multinational state, in the formation and consolidation of the multinational Soviet community."[19]

Integral to Russification is the establishment of the Russian language as a "second mother tongue." Consequently, fluency in Russian is a prerequisite for social and professional advancement. According to the census results, mother-tongue retention by Ukrainians dropped from 94 per cent in 1959 to 89 per cent by 1970, whereas the percentage of Ukrainians giving Russian as their mother-tongue increased from 6.5 to 10.9 over the same period (see Table 6.13). The 1970 and 1979 censuses

TABLE 6.13 Mother-Tongue Identification of Ukrainians and Russians in Ukraine 1959–79[a]

	Total Population	Per cent giving Ukrainian as mother tongue	Per cent giving Russian as mother tongue
1959			
Ukrainians	32,158,493	93.5	6.5
Urban	11,781,476	84.7	15.3
Rural	20,376,743	98.6	1.3
Russians	7,090,813	1.8	98.1
Urban	5,726,476	1.1	98.9
Rural	1,364,337	5.1	94.9
1970			
Ukrainians	36,283,857	91.4	8.6
Urban	16,164,254	82.8	17.1
Rural	19,119,603	98.7	1.3
Russians	9,126,331	1.5	98.5
Urban	7,712,277	1.1	98.9
Rural	1,414,054	3.7	96.2
1979			
Ukrainians	36,488,951	89.1	10.9
Russians	10,471,602	1.3	98.6

[a] percentage of those identifying language other than Ukrainian or Russian as mother tongue not given.

SOURCE: *Itogi vsesoiuznoi perepisi nasleniia 1959 goda. Ukrainskaia SSR* (Moscow, 1963), 168ff.; *Itogi perepisi naseleniia 1970 goda* (Moscow, 1973), 4: 158ff; *Vestnik statistiki*, no. 8 (1980): 64.

included a new classification: "number of people in a given nationality group who are fluent in the second language of the peoples of their own nation." This group consisted of two categories: those who did not declare the language of their own nation as their native language (although they spoke it fluently); and those who spoke the language of other nations. Thus, in 1970, of the three million Ukrainians who said that Russian was their mother tongue, 50 per cent claimed fluency in Ukrainian. In 1979, of the four million Ukrainians who gave Russian as their mother tongue, 53 per cent indicated fluency in Ukrainian.

According to the 1979 census, 74 per cent of the republic's population either considered Ukrainian their native language or claimed to speak it fluently, but 71.2 per cent had a native or fluent knowledge of Russian.[20] The Soviet authorities maintain that such bilingualism improves communication among the peoples of the USSR. In practice, however, Moscow uses bilingualism to promote Russian and, as many Soviet ethnographers admit, to raise the number of people in the non-Russian republics who consider Russian their native language. As we can see from a comparison of the census figures, 2 million of the 32.1 million Ukrainians gave Russian as their native language in 1959, while almost 4 million of the 36.6 million Ukrainians gave it as their native language in 1979. Thus the post-1953 resistance to Russification has proved largely ineffective. This is corroborated by the 1979 census, which revealed that although 23.9 million Russians were living outside the RSFSR (17.3 per cent of the Russian population), only 3.5 per cent claimed fluency in any of the other languages of the USSR.[21]

Scholarship

After 1953 scholarship began to awake from the dogmatic restrictions of the Stalin period, which had a particularly adverse effect on the social sciences. Cybernetics, for example, had been declared a "bourgeois pseudo-science." This was damaging to Ukraine since Kiev had been an important centre of mathematics since tsarist times. As a result of the efforts of individual scientists, however, Ukraine made great progress after Stalin's death, and the Kiev Cybernetics Institute is now the leading institution in this field in the Soviet Union. Sociology had also been condemned by party theorists, who declared that this field was already adequately covered by historical materialism. This attitude, which was perpetuated not only by Stalin, but also ideologists such as Suslov, persisted after 1953.

In Ukraine policies restricting scholarship had a particularly devastating impact on the historiography of Ukraine and the the CPU, and on Ukrainian literature and linguistics. To counter this, two movements developed in the republic after 1953: the "movement for the enrichment of Ukrainian history and literature" and the "movement for the rights of the Ukrainian language." Although these movements met some resistance, there were some positive changes in science during this period. This trend continued until after Shelest's fall. One institution that benefited from this resurgence was the Ukrainian Academy of Sciences, the development of which took two main directions: a constant increase in the number of institutes (and, correspondingly, the number of research areas); and an increase in the output of the academy's publishing house, "Naukova dumka" (Scientific Thought). After 1953 the academy moved into a phase of "Ukrainization," and Ukrainian became the scholarly language in both the social sciences and the technical disciplines. New Ukrainian-language journals appeared, and contributions from Russian authors were translated into Ukrainian. The *Visnyk Akademii nauk Ukrainskoi RSR* (Bulletin of the Academy of Sciences of the Ukrainian SSR) and other academy journals published only résumés in Russian. Prior to Shelest's fall, the articles were translated into Russian at the request of the authorities and sent to Moscow. By 1969 the Ukrainian Academy of Sciences was publishing 30 journals, of which 15 were Ukrainian-language publications, 4 published articles in Ukrainian and Russian, and 11 were Russian-language journals.[22]

By the 1970s, however, almost all the academy's technical journals appeared in Russian. Consequently, in 1975, a mere 7.3 per cent of books and pamphlets published in Ukraine in engineering, industry, communications and economics were in the Ukrainian language (see Table 6.14). Moreover, in March 1977, President B. Ie. Paton declared that the publication of scientific periodicals in the language of the individual republics impeded the development of science in the Soviet Union.[23] His comments have been reflected by the Russification of periodical research papers published by the universities, and of *Ekonomichna heohrafiia*, which deals exclusively with the economic problems of the Ukrainian SSR. "Naukova dumka" now publishes all anthologies devoted to technical subjects in Russian.

Furthermore, there has been a radical change in the contents and character of periodicals devoted to the social sciences. From 1957–65 *Ukrainskyi istorychnyi zhurnal* published some informative articles on Ukrainian history. After 1965, however, the journal began to publish mediocre articles of a propagandistic nature. The lively and well-edited *Filosofska dumka* (Philosophical thought) suffered a similar fate. The most recent (1977) edition of *Ocherki istorii Kommunisticheskoi partii Ukrainy* (Outlines of the History of the Communist Party of Ukraine) was also inferior in quality to its predecessors. However, Ukrainian historians are limited by the Soviet interpretation of history, in which historical events are used to justify the present situation. Major political figures such as Khrushchev are omitted from Soviet works.

The most notable Ukrainian scholarly publications over the past twenty-five years have been the dictionaries. Having covered the first half of the alphabet in two volumes, 1953 and 1958, the *Ukrainsko-rosiiskyi slovnyk* (Ukrainian-Russian Dictionary) published *four* volumes on the second half of the alphabet between 1961 and 1963. Recently, there have appeared (in single volumes) a Russian-Ukrainian dictionary (1971), a Ukrainian-Russian dictionary (1975), and a Ukrainian orthographic dictionary (1977). Another achievement was the *Slovnyk ukrainskoi movy* (Dictionary of the Ukrainian Language) (1980) compiled by the Ukrainian Academy of Sciences. The publication of dictionaries of Western languages

TABLE 6.14 Scholarly Books and Tracts Published in Ukraine 1955–75

Subjects	Total		In Ukrainian		In Russian	
	Titles	Copies	Titles	Copies	Titles	Copies
Natural Sciences and Mathematics						
1955	300	10,782	177	10,443	100	286
1965	670	17,275	257	14,212	287	2,925
1970	734	16,225	228	13,649	427	2,418
1975	1,066	16,531	189	12,699	773	3,489
Engineering, Industry, Communications, Communal Economy						
1955	966	4,487	176	1,854	790	2,633
1965	2,160	9,053	170	2,186	2,300	6,852
1970	2,805	9,894	277	3,754	2,514	6,116
1975	2,820	17,101	205	4,566	2,612	13,118
Agriculture						
1955	824	6,390	458	4,233	364	2,155
1965	680	3,841	420	3,040	259	800
1970	628	3,622	367	2,692	255	911
1975	874	5,165	356	3,254	516	1,909

Health and Medicine						
1955	380	5,054	121	3,443	257	1,607
1965	431	4,699	101	3,229	330	1,470
1970	387	2,464	69	1,060	313	1,383
1975	384	3,925	64	1,471	319	2,419
Physical Culture and Sport						
1955	70	496	26	201	44	295
1965	56	996	20	244	36	752
1970	55	379	22	304	33	75
1975	42	554	17	320	25	334
Linguistics						
1955	158	10,487	79	6,585	36	2,414
1965	283	12,690	104	7,101	38	2,809
1970	264	17,434	79	10,661	44	4,700
1975	264	13,565	74	8,102	57	3,118
Literary History and Criticism						
1955	109	4,606	81	3,694	27	912
1965	113	5,362	107	3,715	22	1,640
1970	112	4,052	85	3,475	22	451

SOURCE: *Pechat SSSR v 1955 godu* (Moscow, 1956), 60ff; for 1970, *ibid.*, 15ff; for 1975, *ibid.*, 32ff; *Presa Ukrainskoi RSR 1918–1975* (Kharkiv, 1976), 48ff.

is, however, inadequate. There is a shortage of Ukrainian-German, Ukrainian-English and technical dictionaries. Three Soviet publications of note are: the seventeen-volume *Ukrainska radianska entsyklopediia* (Ukrainian Soviet Encyclopedia), (1959–65, with a second edition begun in 1978); the four-volume *Radianska entsyklopediia istorii Ukrainy* (Soviet Encyclopedia of Ukrainian History) (1961–72); and the eight-volume *Istoriia ukrainskoi literatury* (History of Ukrainian Literature) (1967–71).

A major highlight was the two-volume *Entsyklopediia kibernetyky* (Encyclopedia of Cybernetics) (1972–4), published simultaneously in Ukrainian and Russian. The Ukrainian edition effectively refutes the Soviet thesis that the Soviet nationality groups do not need their own national scientific languages. Other major Ukrainian-language works published in 1953–78 were the five-volume *Istoriia ukrainskoho mystetstva* (History of Ukrainian Art) (1967–77), and the 27-volume *Istoriia mist i sil Ukrainskoi RSR* (History of the Towns and Villages of the Ukrainian SSR), published by the editorial board of the *Ukrainian Soviet Encyclopedia*.

But generally, the situation in publishing left much to be desired. Ivan Dziuba recalled that such monumental works as *Istoriia rusov* (History of the Russes) and the Cossack chronicles were available under the tsarist regime, but banned in the contemporary period. He noted, moreover, that Soviet publishers had not reissued the monumental collections of Ukrainian folklore compiled in the nineteenth century. Concerning forbidden literature, the authorities applied double standards. The works of Bunin, for example, an author whose attitude to the Soviet regime was far from positive, have been published in Russia, whereas those of Vynnychenko have never been reissued, and are not allowed in Ukraine. As Dziuba put it: "What will become of the history of Ukrainian literature without Vynnychenko?"

In a 1969 article which was reprinted in *Ukrainskyi visnyk*, V. I. Kumpanenko, a Ukrainian living in Moscow and a specialist in publishing matters, analyzed the Ukrainian Academy of Sciences' publishing record in that year. In Kumpanenko's opinion, "the Ukrainian language is now experiencing a profound crisis in [the field of] scholarship."[24] He noted that the academy planned to publish 375 titles in 1969, of which 163 or 43 per cent were in Ukrainian; and 212 or 57 per cent in Russian. He also stated that 6 of the 9 academy departments and 19 of the 44 institutes had no publications in the Ukrainian language. The 19 included the Institute of Electric Welding, which was directed by academy president B. I. Paton, and the Institute of Cybernetics, directed by vice-president V. M. Glushkov. "The general impression arises that, in the ocean of the Ukrainian people, several islands of scientists have taken shape—islands that are apart from the people and populated with persons who do not want to communicate with the people in its native tongue, who do not want to propagate scientific knowledge in this language."[25]

Kumpanenko also noted that "Such branches of science as mathematics, physics and chemistry...have a low threshold of tolerance for the Ukrainian language. Eighty-five to 92 per cent of the books appear in Russian." He concluded that the rejection of Ukrainian as a language of scientific expression made it virtually impossible to speak of a "Ukrainian science." As a footnote to Kumpanenko's remarks, it should be mentioned that the Urozhai publishing house, which specializes in agricultural literature, began publishing almost exclusively in Russian in the 1970s. This measure was evidently designed to condition the republic's agronomists, most of whom are Ukrainians, to use the Russian language in their discipline. Urozhai's programme for 1979 listed nine works that promised to be of considerable importance for Ukrainian agriculture, all of which appeared in Russian.

The Ukrainian Academy of Sciences is required to enhance co-operation between science and production and to promote the development of the productive forces in the Ukrainian SSR. Despite the setbacks of recent years, the academy can note some achievements. It has, for example, developed a "complex programme for scientific-technical progress in the Ukrainian SSR for 1976–90 and in the year 2000." Since this is an all-Soviet undertaking, the stress is on projects with all-Soviet implications. Questions concerning Ukraine itself tend to be considered "regional problems," but that does not negate their significance for the republic.

An important indicator of the Soviet strategy for the sciences is the national composition of the scholarly community. In 1975, 67 per cent of scholars (in all disciplines) in the USSR, and 62 per cent of all graduate students were Russians. According to the 1970 census, Russians constituted little more than 50 per cent of the Soviet population. Ukrainians, who represented 19 per cent of the USSR's population in 1970, made up only 11 per cent of the USSR's scholarly community and 12 per cent of the total number of graduate students.[26]

Education

In 1955–6 Ukraine had 29,361 elementary, seven-year and secondary schools. Of these, 4,008 used Russian as the language of instruction, while the remaining 25,353 employed "languages of other nationalities," i.e., Ukrainian and the languages of a few national minorities.[27] A 1967 reference work stated that "Ukraine has schools for the children of other nationalities at which lessons are held in Russian, Moldavian, Polish, Hungarian and other languages. Ukrainian has been made a compulsory subject at all schools in Ukraine because it is the state language of the Ukrainian SSR."[28] But in fact, Ukrainian is not *officially* considered to be the state language of the republic.

Following the revelations of the Ukrainian Canadian ex-communist John Kolasky concerning discrimination against the Ukrainian language in the USSR, the Soviet authorities published a booklet entitled *Narodna osvita v Ukrainskii RSR* (General Education in the Ukrainian SSR) in 1969. Intended for foreign consumption, it maintained that the principle of education in one's native language was being implemented consistently in the Ukrainian SSR. Ukrainian, the booklet said, was the language of instruction in 28,000 general schools and was a compulsory subject at schools where the language of instruction was Russian or another tongue. The authors declared, in response to Kolasky, that 95 per cent of the 1,737 general schools in Lviv oblast used Ukrainian as the language of instruction. Generally, however, Kolasky's study was hard to refute because it was based on Soviet statistics and original documents, and reproductions of school signs and posters. Furthermore, Kolasky analyzed educational policies in other republics. Concerning conditions at specialized secondary and higher educational establishments, where the language of instruction is usually Russian, all the authors could do was juggle statistics and draw comparisons with the distant past (compare Table 6.15).[29]

TABLE 6.15 Ukraine: Language of Instruction in Establishments of Higher Education 1914–71

	1914–15	1940–1	1960–1	1965–6	1969–70	1970–1
Total	27	173	135	132	138	138
Lectures held in Ukrainian	—	173	135	132	138	138
Lectures held in Russian	27	173	135	132	138	138
Number of Students (1000s)	35.2	196.8	417.7	690.1	804.1	806.6

SOURCE: Iu. D. Desheriev, *Zakonomernosti razvitiia literaturnykh iazykov narodov SSSR v sovetskuiu epokhu* (Moscow, 1967), 73. This source gives the number of students of Ukrainian nationality as 426,900 in 1962–3 and 674,000 in 1970–1.

A study prepared by the USSR Academy of Sciences confirmed the gradual Russification of the Ukrainian school system. It noted that the number of Ukrainian children educated in their native language in 1972 fell to 93.8 per cent of the 1965 level, whereas the number educated in Russian increased by 10.4 per cent. Only in Belorussia was the decline in native-language instruction at a worse level.[30]

In an article entitled "Under Chauvinist Pressure," *Ukrainskyi visnyk* no. 6 noted that:

— At the beginning of 1969–70, although listed as a compulsory subject in the curriculum, Ukrainian was not taught at Kievan schools on the grounds that there were not enough qualified teachers. The situation was particularly

precarious in Darnytsia District (Kiev's biggest industrial area), Dniprovsk District and the Central Lenin District.
— The Kiev city soviet refused to call in Ukrainian language teachers from the suburbs. Graduates of the philological faculty of Kiev State University were hired as teachers in 1970–1, but this was not enough to solve the problem.
— At Kievan schools where the official language of instruction is Ukrainian, several subjects were taught in Russian. A number of teachers, including older staff, refused to instruct in Ukrainian. It was their practice to talk to each other and with the pupils in Russian during the rest periods.

Ukrainskyi visnyk listed several schools officially designated "Ukrainian" in which instruction was carried out in Russian. Only the signboards were written in Ukrainian and few teachers taught in the native language.

Moreover, the Ukrainian schools are usually housed in old and dilapidated buildings. This alone is enough to deter some parents from sending their children there. As a result the number of pupils in these schools is relatively small, while the Russian schools are overcrowded—even in those districts of Kiev with a predominantly Ukrainian population. In conclusion, *Ukrainskyi visnyk* stated:

We may draw the conclusion that the process of Russification . . . is making continuous advances in the Ukrainian school system. Contrary to all placatory declarations, this process is not developing automatically: it is being consciously directed and stimulated by the further Russification of pre-school facilities, higher education, the state institutions and cultural life. Perhaps the situation could be changed if the public at large, if the citizens were to learn about the true state of affairs and oppose the chauvinistic anti-Leninist course in the Ukrainian school system by organized protests. The school problem must be seen in the context of the demands for organizing the whole of cultural and administrative-state life in Ukraine.[31]

Higher and specialized secondary education in Ukraine was also beset by problems. Ukrainians were restricted from entering these institutions, which accounts for the relatively low number of Ukrainian specialists employed in the republic's economy. In 1970, for example, although Russians accounted for only 19 per cent of the population, they made up 33 per cent of the 813,026 students enrolled in the republic's specialized secondary schools. Ukrainians formed only 54 per cent of the total number of students registered in these schools.[32] Table 6.16 shows the comparative size of the Russian and Ukrainian student contingents at all higher educational establishments in the Soviet Union in 1970–1 and 1974–5. A breakdown of the Ukrainian figure indicates that over 487,300 Ukrainian undergraduates were studying in the republic itself in 1970–1 and 134,000 in other parts of the USSR. Of the latter group, 101,773 were studying in

TABLE 6.16   **Number of Students at All Soviet Higher Education Establishments 1970–5**

	1970–1		1974–5	
	Thousands	Per cent	Thousands	Per cent
Total	4,506.6	100.0	4,751.6	100.0
Russians	2,729.0	59.6	2,834.8	59.7
Ukrainians	621.2	13.6	640.0	13.5

SOURCE: *Narodnoe obrazovanie, nauka i kultura v SSSR* (Moscow, 1971), 282.

the RSFSR. At the same time, the 167,390 Russians studying in Ukraine accounted for 34.3 per cent of all students at the republic's higher educational establishments.[33]

Table 6.17 reveals that students at Ukrainian higher educational establishments had a better supply of Ukrainian-language textbooks in 1953 than in 1975. The number of Russian textbooks exceeded that of Ukrainian textbooks in 1958, when the ratio was 207:199. This situation was a result of Khrushchev's school reform, which was designed to promote Russian-language usage in Ukraine. By 1960, there were in total in the republic 960,000 Russian-language and 779,000 Ukrainian-language textbooks.[34] The trend has continued and indicates the progress of Russification in higher education. In other national republics, Russification has made less headway, although it has penetrated strongly in Belorussia, Moldavia and Latvia.

TABLE 6.17   **Textbooks Intended for Use in Higher Education in Ukraine 1953–75**

			In Ukrainian		In Russian	
Year	Titles	Copies (1000s)	Titles	Copies (1000s)	Titles	Copies (1000s)
1953	140	574	94	394	46	180
1960	618	1,801	198	779	392	960
1965	813	2,239	232	928	526	981
1970	460	1,322	168	486	263	702
1974	599	1,515	147	463	417	962
1975	644	1,820	112	348	502	1,308

SOURCE: *Presa Ukrainskoi RSR 1918–1975* (Kiev, 1976), 93.

Religion

The theoretical status of religion, according to the constitution of the USSR, is as follows:

> *Article 52.* The citizens of the USSR are guaranteed freedom of conscience, that is, the right to have or not to have any religion, to conduct religious rites or to conduct atheist propaganda. It is forbidden to incite enmity and hatred in connection with religious beliefs.

In the USSR the church is separated from the state, and the schools are separated from the church.

The state's relations with the church are handled by the Council of Religious Affairs, which is attached to the USSR Council of Ministers. There are similar councils dealing with local religious affairs in many of the union republics. The Central Asian republics, where Islam is widespread, are the most homogeneous region of the USSR from the viewpoint of religion. The Orthodox Church predominates in the Slavic republics.

Since 1953, religious organizations have managed to enlarge their sphere of influence and a number of sects have spread to all parts of the Soviet Union. Many believe that contrary to Soviet assertions, there has been a religious revival in recent years, both inside and outside the church. From 1953–78 believers often showed great courage in defending their rights and protesting against religious persecution in the USSR. During the 1960s organized believers often rejected rapprochement with the political opposition, arguing that they were not interested in secular goals. But in the second half of the 1970s many religious activists recognized that the defence of freedom of conscience and the defence of national rights are both integral parts of the protection of human rights. As a result, such prominent representatives of the human-rights movement as Academician Andrei Sakharov are now among the foremost defenders of religious freedom.

In Ukraine, in contrast to some Soviet republics, there are close links between religion and nationality problems. Ukrainian Orthodox believers seek independence from the Russian church. A number of them revealed their former membership in the "Ukrainian Autocephalous Church," an autonomous national church that had also sought independence from the Russian Orthodox Church and favoured the use of the Ukrainian language in religious services. It was liquidated as a "counter-revolutionary" organization.[35]

Many Ukrainians suffered from the 1945 decision (probably adopted on Stalin's initiative) to liquidate the Greek Catholic (Uniate) Church in Western Ukraine. As a preliminary to this, the authorities accused the church of collaborating with the Nazi occupation forces. One of the main targets of attack was Metropolitan Sheptytsky, who remained popular long after his death in 1944. The Soviet defamation campaign linked the current events in the Greek Catholic Church with the historical "Union of Brest" (1596), under which part of the Church in Western Ukraine recognized the Pope. The Soviet authorities began pressing for the return of the Greek Catholic Church to the fold of Orthodoxy. The campaign culminated in March 1946, when a synod of the Greek Catholic Church convened in Lviv to proclaim the end of the 350-year union with Rome and the return to the Russian Orthodox Church. The latter automatically acquired the entire property of the Greek Catholic Church. The Greek Catholic Church of Transcarpathia suffered the same fate in 1949.

The priests and believers who resisted this campaign were arrested and, for the most part, deported to the Asian part of the USSR. All bishops who refused to break with Rome were imprisoned. Metropolitan Slipy, Primate of the Ukrainian Greek Catholic Church, was able to leave the USSR in February 1963. The events of the late 1940s still have repercussions in Ukrainian religious life today, and the Greek Catholic community has been forced underground.

The Soviet authorities have introduced "socialist" customs and ritual ceremonies designed to usurp religious rites and use Ukraine as a testing ground for these innovations. They send delegations to Ukraine from other parts of the USSR and from East European countries to discuss the efficacy of these experiments. The Ukrainian Council of Ministers has established a special "Commission for Soviet Traditions, Holidays and Rites" and similar commissions exist in all the Soviet executive committees down to the village level. The forty members of the commission attached to the Council of Ministers include representatives of all the ministries, the civil service, the scientific and artistic unions, the major public organizations, and those who have received specialist training in this area.

The first Soviet commercial enterprise for the organization of Soviet "rites" and "ceremonies" ranging from birthday celebrations to funerals—*Sviato*—was established in Kiev. Similar establishments have since been opened in Donetsk, Dnipropetrovsk and Zaporizhzhia. The Soviet authorities give special attention to the organization of funerals: now being planned are special halls of mourning where the bereaved can pay their last respects to the accompaniment of orchestral music and hear a funeral speech delivered by a professional orator. Such halls are under construction at a large number of cemeteries.

Traditionally the authorities have been opposed to religious customs. But they have also tried to abolish age-old customs that have little to do with religion. For example, in the late 1960s and early 1970s, Kiev saw a revival of the old New Year custom of singing *shchedrivky*. Groups of young people in traditional Ukrainian costume went from house to house, singing these old folksongs.[36] In 1971 over 20 of these groups (*vatahy*) were organized. The authorities decided that this custom contradicted the principles of "Soviet culture" and ordered the militia to intervene. The singers, most of them Kiev University students, were treated as "hooligans" and subjected to reprisals. The authorities are also trying to restrict performances of old Ukrainian music on the traditional folk instrument, the *bandura*. Thus the "rapprochement of the Soviet peoples" has been extended to include the elimination of folk culture, which has little to do with religion.

The Russian Orthodox Church

The Russian Orthodox Church is the strongest church in the republic. It is led by Metropolitan Filaret of Kiev and Galicia, Exarch of Ukraine (Mikhailo Antonovych Denysenko), who was born on 28 January 1928 in Blahodatne, Donbas, and studied at the Theological Academy in Moscow. After being ordained a monk in 1950, he occupied a series of church posts in Ukraine. The church's official periodical is *Pravoslavnyi visnyk* (formerly *Eparkhialnyi visnyk*). First published in 1946 in Lviv, it was moved to Kiev in 1970. In the opinion of Metropolitan Mykolai of Lviv and Ternopil, since the move to Kiev the style of the monthly has been consonant with the standards of literary Ukrainian.[37]

According to Exarch Filaret, the Ukrainian Orthodox Church possesses eighteen eparchies headed by metropolitans, archbishops and bishops. There is a theological seminary in Odessa, two monasteries and seven convents, including the famous *Pochaivska Lavra*.[38] The church has problems in Western Ukraine, where the traditions of the Greek Catholic Church have remained. The *Zhurnal Moskovskoi Patriarkhii* admitted this, while maintaining that this loyalty is limited to the older generation of priests, who are gradually being replaced by younger men schooled in Moscow, Leningrad and Odessa "in the spirit of true loyalty to the Orthodox Church and the Fatherland."[39]

In addition to articles on historical and theological subjects, the *Pravoslavnyi visnyk* provides information about church life in Ukraine and the foreign activities of the Ukrainian Exarchate. Although the journal is written in Ukrainian, the official administrative language of the Russian Orthodox Church in Ukraine is Russian. Sermons are preached either in Russian or Ukrainian, depending on the locality: sermons in Ukrainian are a rarity in the churches of Kiev, for example.

The Russian Orthodox Church is one of the least persecuted religious organizations in the Soviet Union. Co-operation between the church and the authorities is relatively good, because the Moscow Patriarchy is usually willing to make concessions to the state. This has led to considerable unrest among believers and to the establishment in Moscow of the unofficial "Christian Committee for the Defence of the Rights of Believers in the Soviet Union." The committee is headed by Father Gleb Iakunin, monk-deacon, Varsonofii Chaibulin and Viktor Kapitanchuk, its secretary. It has documented the persecution of the adherents of various Christian faiths—the Russian Orthodox, the Catholic, the Baptist and other churches. In their appeal of 27 December 1977, the members of the committee declared:

Orthodoxy was the state religion in our country throughout the centuries. The representatives of the Orthodox Church frequently used methods of brute force to limit the religious freedom of other religions. Since we consider the use of force against dissidents or the members of other faiths contradictory to the spirit of Christianity, we deem it our duty to take the initiative in defence of the religious freedom of all believers in our country, regardless of their religion."[40]

The increasing anti-religious propaganda in Ukraine in the late 1950s also affected the Russian Orthodox Church. A number of priests were tried on charges such as the embezzlement of church funds, selling votive candles and maintaining contacts with banned religious organizations. One priest was accused of collaborating with a group of former "Petliurite officers and nationalists."[41] Indicative of the methods used by the authorities to incriminate priests was *Pravda*'s reprimanding of the militia in Kherson for permitting the wife of a priest to sell eggs on the kolkhoz market. The eggs concerned had been given to the priest as a present, declared *Pravda*, and thus could not be considered legal ware.[42] Such methods are still in use today.

Despite the placatory attitude of the Russian Orthodox Church, the KGB keeps a close watch on its activities. Two aspects of the church disturb the authorities. First, its tightly knit hierarchical structure: the subordination of the deacon to the priest, the priest to the dean, etc.[43] This structure also makes infiltration by the KGB difficult.

Second, some Ukrainian priests and believers maintain a spiritual allegiance to Rome or identify themselves with the banned Ukrainian Autocephalous Orthodox Church. Occasionally, Orthodox priests have united with political dissidents and thus have suffered legal reprisals. One well-known case is that of Vasyl Romaniuk, an Orthodox Ukrainian priest born in 1925, who was arrested in 1942 and sentenced to a ten-year term. He was rearrested in 1972 when he spoke out in defence of Valentyn Moroz and sentenced to two years' imprisonment, five years in labour camps and three years' internal exile. Romaniuk has written several letters, appeals and protests to various secular and clerical authorities, including Pope Paul VI. He is one of the best loved political prisoners in Ukraine.[44]

The Evangelical Christian Baptists

The second-largest legal religious organization in the USSR is the Church of the Evangelical Christian Baptists. It is directed by the All-Union Council of Evangelical Christian Baptists [*Vsesoiuznyi Sovet Evangelskikh khristian-baptistov*] under the chairmanship of Ilia Ivanov. At the local level the organization of Baptist activities is handled by senior (or elder) presbyters and their assistants, who are elected at meetings of the church community. The church headquarters are in Moscow and it has an official bimonthly publication, *Bratskii vestnik* (Fraternal Messenger).

The Baptists have a sizable number of religious communities in Ukraine, but it is difficult to determine their exact number. They are most common in the rural areas, but they also inhabit larger urban settlements and cities. *Bratskii vestnik* reports, for example, that there are Baptist communities in almost all towns in Donetsk oblast, including Donetsk itself. In some parts of Ukraine over half the local Baptist communities support the breakaway Council of Churches (see below).

The traditions and teachings of the Baptist Church give it more independence than the Russian Orthodox Church enjoys. Its communities seem to have a greater sense of solidarity and are more active. One explanation for this is that:

> The absence of the hierarchy as giver of grace gives the Baptist greater personal responsibility toward God, making a thorough knowledge of the Holy Scripture as the sole authoritative guide for daily life a *sine qua non*. The zealous and talented preachers benefit from this thorough knowledge, and they have the courage to go on preaching outside the prayer-house, when they meet friends or strike up casual acquaintances. Their sermons are close to reality and are easily understood in the midst of the sombre and godless everyday reality of the Soviet Union. They awaken interest in the Christian way of life, a circumstance that is leading to a steady growth in the size of their communities."[45]

The Council of Churches of the Evangelical Christian Baptists

In 1961 a schism occurred in the Soviet Baptist Church. Dissident Baptists broke with the officially tolerated All-Union Council of Evangelical Christian Baptists and formed an "Initiative Group" (the *initsiativniki*). The split was formalized with the creation of the "Council of Churches" (*Sovet Tserkvei*). The new body established statutes and called on its adherents to register their religious affiliation as required by Soviet law. The Soviet authorities, which considered the Council of Churches an illegal organization, refused to accept its members' registration applications, even though the required formalities had been met. Thereupon the *initsiativniki* organized an All-Union Congress of Evangelical Christian Baptists, led by G. K. Kruchkov. Some officially registered Baptist communities then declared their allegiance to the Council of Churches, to which the Soviets responded with a wave of arrests.

The families of the persecuted founded the Council of the Relatives of Arrested Evangelical Christian Baptists, which quickly developed into one of the most active religious opposition groups in the USSR. It began publishing a bulletin, which appears at regular intervals. Some copies were reproduced by primitive typographical methods while others appeared in printed booklet form. The volume and accuracy of the information in the bulletin reflect the group's solidarity and degree of organization. The

Council of Relatives has held regular congresses. The second of these, held in Kiev on 12–13 December 1970, adopted an "Appeal to All Christians in the World" that described the persecution of the Baptist community. According to this document, 524 servants of God, including 44 sisters, had been arrested for their religious convictions between 1961 and 1970. Eight of them had died under torture. Further, the authorities had reportedly confiscated 2,840 religious books and pamphlets. Almost 400 people had been sentenced to 15 days' imprisonment for attending prayer meetings. The documents suggest that a high percentage of Ukrainian Baptists recognized the unofficial church, and that a large proportion of the prisoners were Ukrainians.

The adherents of the Council of Churches consider their organization legal and hold their prayer meetings openly. They are prolific writers of letters, protests and appeals to the Soviet authorities (both local and central) and to such international bodies as the United Nations. They also organized a mass protest against the murder of a Baptist called Biblenko, who was killed on 13 September 1975 when he left his house to attend a Thanksgiving service in Dnipropetrovsk. The Baptists organize these Thanksgiving services throughout the Soviet Union, despite frequent disruptions by the authorities.

One of the most prominent Evangelical Christian Baptists is the Kievan Georgii Petrovych Vins, who was arrested in May 1966 and sentenced to three years in labour camps. A *samvydav* document describes how the authorities continued to hound and harass him in the camps and in his later exile, gradually reducing him to an invalid incapable of work. Vins' son Petro became equally prominent. Besides being an active church leader he joined the Ukrainian Helsinki Group and campaigned for the observance of civil rights and religious freedom. He was arrested and given a one-year sentence.[46] Both Georgii and Petro Vins were allowed to leave the USSR in 1979.

The Roman Catholic Church

There are no Roman Catholic bishops in the Ukrainian SSR, and most of the Roman Catholic churches have been requisitioned "for civilian use." However, several dozen churches and chapels remain open and are a spiritual refuge for Roman Catholics of Polish, Hungarian and Ukrainian nationality. According to a 1978 issue of the Paris-based Polish weekly *Kultura*, there were six Roman Catholic priests in Vinnytsia oblast, three in Zhytomyr, five in Khmelnytsky, and one in Chernivtsi, Ternopil, Odessa and Ivano-Frankivsk oblasts respectively. Most of the priests were elderly. There is no recognized Roman Catholic community in Volyn, although local Catholics are reportedly trying to establish one. In 1960, it is said, the Roman Catholic Church in Transcarpathia, serving the Hungarian minority, had over 26 churches and 22 priests.[47] These numbers are probably fairly accurate, since the Soviet leadership has to show some consideration for Catholics in Hungary. At the time of the 1970 census, there were evidently about 158,000 Hungarians in Transcarpathia.

The Greek Catholic Church

During the de-Stalinization campaign of the mid-1950s, many Ukrainians hoped that the decision to dissolve the Greek Catholic Church of 1946 would be reversed. Evidently this question was discussed; Beria reportedly considered the restoration of the church seriously and made contact with Metropolitan Slipy, who was then under arrest, in order to prepare the ground. Instead, however, the propaganda campaign against the Greek Catholic Church was intensified. Numerous publications carried articles criticizing the church. One of the main targets was the former Metropolitan, Sheptytsky, whom the authorities tried to depict (falsely) as a "Nazi collaborator" and a supporter of the Organization of Ukrainian Nationalists (OUN).

A film entitled "Ivanna," which was shown throughout Ukraine in 1960, played a major role in the anti-Sheptytsky campaign. Its purpose was to prove that the late Metropolitan had sympathized with Hitler and worked with the Gestapo. But one critic, writing in the journal *Mystetstvo* (Art), declared that the film had a negative psychological effect on the audience. The director, he said, could have achieved a greater effect with a more moderate approach. As it was, "Ivanna" had failed to achieve the desired result.[48] The film's leading lady, Inna Burdutchenko, was burned to death during the filming of a scene in which she was supposed to escape from a blazing house. Some Greek Catholics saw this as "divine punishment." The Supreme Court of the Ukrainian SSR blamed the film's producer A. A. Sliusarenko for the fatal accident and (on 24 April 1961) sentenced him to five years' imprisonment, after which he was forbidden to exercise his profession for a further five years. His co-defendants also received prison sentences.

Around this time the Soviet press published an increasing number of reports on the Greek Catholic Church's alleged contacts with the Vatican. A "specialist" on this subject, D. Pokhylevich, wrote in *Komunist Ukrainy* that, unwilling to yield its influence in Ukraine, the Vatican was working with Bandera's nationalist organization to undermine the Russian Orthodox Church. He also claimed that after the Second World War, the Catholic church had supported the Ukrainian nationalist movement, even permitting it to use churches and cloisters for arms caches. Although this was a thing of the past, wrote Pokhylevich, "We must not forget that not all Uniate priests have broken with Rome. Some of them are still active among the faithful, trying to 'save their souls' in conversations with a pronounced anti-Soviet content, seeking to give religious instruction to children, and manufacturing various 'miracles'."[49]

There were several reports on the "church of the Catacombs" (as the Greek Catholic Church in Ukraine is sometimes called) in the second half of the 1960s. In 1963 the Moscow illustrated weekly *Ogonek* described the Ukrainian Catholic cloisters in Lviv as an illegal but well-organized secret society. Referring to the cloister in Muchna Street, *Ogonek* said: "This building is a real cloister. The cells, whose walls are decorated with icons and crucifixes, are inhabited by ten nuns with their mother superior. One untenanted room is the chapel." According to the weekly, the cloisters were run by Catholic orders, such as the Order of the Sisters of St. Mary, the Order of St. Vincent and the Order of St. Basil, and Uniate priests held regular religious services in them. *Ogonek* denounced the cloisters as centres for the distribution of prayer books, icons, crucifixes and other votive objects. It also accused them of maintaining contacts with "foreign countries."[50]

The *Ukrainian Herald* has published authenticated personal accounts of the events during the incorporation of the Catholic Church into the Russian Orthodox Church. One such account is provided by a letter sent by H. Budzynsky to the Prosecutor-General of the USSR on 25 March 1966. Budzynsky describes the merger as an extension of tsarist religious policy.[51] The persecution of the Greek Catholic Church has also been documented in the Moscow samizdat journal *Chronicle of Current Events* and publicized in appeals issued by the "Christian Committee for the Defence of the Rights of Believers in the USSR."

Today, the Greek Catholic Church continues its underground existence as the Church of the Catacombs and the number of active priests is reportedly very large. Some experts estimate that there are at least 300–350 working under the authority of their primate in Rome, Iosyf Slipy.[52] In addition to the Church of the Catacombs, many Orthodox priests have retained a spiritual allegiance to the Pope, while others have taken up civilian professions and continue to celebrate the sacraments in private.

The Jewish Community

The Jewish community is scattered throughout the Ukrainian SSR. There is no precise information on the number of synagogues in the republic. The deputy chairman of the Council of Religious Affairs in the USSR is quoted (by the *Chronicle of Current Events*) as saying that of the 5,000 synagogues that used to exist in the USSR only 200 were still standing in 1976. Of these only 92 were said to be officially registered as synagogues. In addition, there are few rabbis in the Soviet Union. There is a large synagogue in Kiev, but it is not always open.[53] In the 1960s the Soviets began a propaganda campaign against the Jewish faith, and attacked especially the Talmud and other religious practices.

The Religious Sects

A detailed account of the religious sects in the USSR was given by the deputy chairman of the Council of Religious Affairs attached to the USSR Council of Ministers, Furov, in a lecture delivered in May 1976. According to Furov, there were some 4,000 sects in the Soviet Union with a total membership of 400,000. Furov noted that 1,200 of these sects were illegal and were "anti-Soviet" in nature. He included the Baptist Council of Churches [*initsiativniki*] in this group, despite its open work and efforts to become registered.[54]

Of the Ukrainian sects, the Jehovah's Witnesses had a sizable following between 1953 and 1978, but declined as a result of state reprisals. Nonetheless, it continues to operate underground and issues a Ukrainian version of the *Watchtower* at sporadic intervals. Some issues are printed in Siberia, others in Moldavia. The *Pokutnyky* [Penitents], who derive their name from the word *pokuta* [penitence], are a specifically Ukrainian sect. The *Ukrainian Herald* described the arrest of members of this sect, following a schism in the Greek Catholic Church:

> The *Pokutnyky* believe that they must do penance for Ukraine's national misfortune. They refuse to work for the state as long as it is not Ukrainian. They issue a variety of documents, etc. They are invariably sentenced as "parasites." Regardless of our attitude to the ideas of the *Pokutnyky*, we must view them as political prisoners.[55]

The sect has evidently survived the dragnet of the KGB.

The Pentecostalists [*piatydesiatnyky*] are fairly widespread in Ukraine. The Soviet press began to focus on this sect in the 1960s because its members refused to perform military service. In June 1962, the security organs arrested Pentecostalists throughout Ukraine. A Kharkiv court sentenced their leaders to terms of imprisonment ranging from one-and-a-half to five years and, in many cases, confiscation of property. The Soviet press denounced the Pentecostalists' "barbaric" religious practices, claiming that they were detrimental to health. The authorities were particularly incensed by the sect's refusal to send its children to school.[56] Other Pentecostalists were tried in Pochaiv (Western Ukraine), a well-known place of pilgrimage for Orthodox believers. Six of the leaders received sentences of three to five years for trying to persuade Young Pioneers and Komsomol members to boycott official cultural events.[57]

The sect's refusal to perform military service was based on the commandment "Thou shalt not kill," which was interpreted as an interdiction against resistance to aggression in any form, inasmuch as everything that happens is God's will and must be borne with fortitude. Soviet propagandists were especially irked by the claim of some Pentecostalists that the Nazi invasion of the Soviet Union in 1941 had been "God's punishment" for the evil of communism. The propagandists claimed that these preachers had even called "the struggle of Soviet patriots against Hitler's occupation an act against the will of God."[58] Like the Baptists of the Council of Churches, the Pentecostalists make no effort to conceal their beliefs, and have also tried to obtain official recognition. In the 1970s, the authorities carried out further reprisals against the Pentecostalists. Many were arrested and deported on the grounds that they had engaged in religious propaganda at their places of work. Today most sect members live in poverty and have little chance of finding work. Their large families render their situation particularly acute. Thus many are trying to emigrate, in concert with the Baptists of the Council of Churches.

Another religous sect with a considerable following in Ukraine is the All-Union Church of the True and Free Seventh-Day Adventists [*Vsesoiuznaia tserkov vernykh i svobodnykh adventistov sedmogo dnia*]. This sect celebrates the sabbath on Saturday with readings from the Bible, hymn-singing and sermons. The members reject formality in favour of improvised prayer and seek communion with God by weeping and moaning during their orisons. They also oppose military service, although less firmly than the Pentecostalists. Indeed, the Fifth Congress of the Seventh-Day Adventists in 1974 ruled that service in the Red Army did not contradict Holy Writ and that military service was a personal matter. The sect was split by the formation of a group of "Reform Adventists" who categorically refused to perform military service and rejected all forms of entertainment (theatre and movie-going, reading fiction, watching television). The authorities have persecuted the Seventh-Day Adventists rigorously, arresting their leaders as thieves and parasites.[59] The elderly head of the Adventist Church, V. A. Shelkov, recently died in prison after spending 23 years in prisons, labour camps and internal exile.[60]

The repression of religion by the authorities in Ukraine and the Soviet Union as a whole has grown more acute during the 25-year span covered by this study. Nevertheless, religious organizations have increased in numbers and gained some public acceptance. But the authorities are alarmed also by the spread of religiosity outside organized religion—in the intelligentsia and among urban youth and scientists, for example. Many persons with no church affiliations have openly disputed the official thesis that religious belief is a sign of backwardness.

For all their achievements, science and technology are always confronted with inexplicable phenomena. This in itself creates the gnoseological basis of belief. The primitive arguments of Soviet "scientific atheism" only tend to encourage this development; they are unable to provide satisfactory answers to the questions posed by searching young minds. It is not surprising, then, that the Bible is so widely read in the Soviet Union.

Notes

1. See *Sovremennye etnicheskie protsessy v SSSR* (Moscow, 1977), 131.
2. *Rabochii klass razvitogo sotsialisticheskogo obshchestva* (Moscow, 1974), 68.
3. *Itogi vsesoiuznoi perepisi naseleniia 1970 goda* (Moscow, 1972–4), 5: 216.
4. "Turbota pro kadry-zakon zhyttia partii," *Ukrainskyi istorychnyi zhurnal*, no. 2 (1979): 9.
5. I. I. Serov, *Sovetskaia obshchenatsionalnaia gordost* (Minsk, 1981), 61.
6. Cf. V. A. Shpiliuk, *Mezhrespublikanskaia migratsiia i sblizhenie natsii v SSSR* (Lviv, 1975).
7. *Osnovnye problemy ratsionalnogo ispolzovaniia trudovykh resursov v SSSR* (Moscow, 1971), 318ff.
8. *Ibid.*, 317.
9. *Ibid.*
10. *Ibid.*, 318.
11. *Sovremennye etnicheskie protsessy v SSSR*, 487.
12. *Naselenie soiuznykh respublik* (Moscow, 1977), 67.
13. *Ibid.*
14. Shpiliuk, *Mezhrespublikanskaia migratsiia*, 150.
15. *Vsesoiuznaia perepis naseleniia 17.12.1926. Vypusk IV. Narodnost i rodnoi iazyk naseleniia SSSR* (Moscow, 1928), 6.
16. *Radianska Ukraina*, 2 November 1956.
17. V. Lobko et al., "Nashi propozytsii," (Kiev, 1964) *Arkhiv Samizdata* 18 (1973).
18. *Osnovnye problemy ratsionalnogo ispolzovaniia trudovykh resursov v SSSR* (Moscow, 1971), 317.
19. E. V. Tadevosian, "Sovetskii narod—novaia istoricheskaia obshchnost liudei," *Voprosy istorii KPSS*, no. 5 (1972): 25.
20. *Vestnik statistiki*, no. 8 (1980): 64, 152ff.
21. *Sovremennye etnicheskie protsessy v SSSR*, 487; *Naselenie SSSR*, 23, 27.
22. *Akademiia nauk Ukrainskoi RSR* (Kiev, 1969), 266ff.
23. S. Iu. Protsiuk, "Bumerang rusyfikatsii," *Ukrainske slovo*, 26 March 1978; *Vestnik Akademii nauk SSSR*, no. 7 (1977).
24. *Ukrainskyi visnyk*, no. 3 (October 1970): 94ff.
25. *Ibid.*, 95.
26. *Narodnoe obrazovanie, nauka i kultura v SSSR* (Moscow, 1977), 308, 313.
27. *Kulturnoe stroitelstvo* (Moscow, 1956), 186.
28. *Ukraina za 50 rokiv* (Kiev, 1967), 215.
29. O. Dzeverin, O. Savchenko, and M. Smal, *Narodna osvita v Ukrainskii RSR: Realni fakty i natsionalistychni vyhadky* (Kiev, 1969).
30. *Sovremennye etnicheskie protsessy v SSSR*, 270.
31. *Ukrainskyi visnyk*, no. 6 (1972): 72.
32. Calculated from *Narodnoe obrazovanie, nauka i kultura v SSSR* (Moscow, 1971), 205ff.
33. *Ibid.*, 196ff.
34. *Presa Ukrainskoi RSR 1918–1975* (Kiev, 1976), 93.

35. V. K. Tancher, *Russkoe pravoslavie* (Kiev, 1977), 43.
36. *Ukrainskyi visnyk*, no. 6, 29.
37. *Zhurnal Moskovskoi Patriarkhii*, no. 9 (1978): 12.
38. *Ibid.*, no. 5 (1976): 4ff.
39. *Ibid.*, no. 9 (1976): 11.
40. *Khristianskii komitet zashchity prav veruiushchikh v SSSR. Dokumenty* (Frankfurt, 1978).
41. *Pravda Ukrainy*, 16 June 1959.
42. *Pravda*, 11 June 1959.
43. Tancher, *Russkoe pravoslavie*, 45.
44. Cf. *Religion und Atheismus in der UdSSR* (Munich, July 1978), 1.
45. *Ibid.*, (January-February 1977), 11.
46. Cf. *Khronika zashchity prav v SSSR* (New York), no. 25 (July-September 1977).
47. "Kościół katolicki w ZSSR," *Kultura*, no. 5 (1978). There was no information about the Roman Catholic Church in Lviv. According to private information at least two churches are open in this city.
48. *Mystetstvo*, no. 1 (1960).
49. D. Pokhylevich, "Uniatstvo i ioho reaktsiina rol," *Komunist Ukrainy*, no. 7 (July 1959).
50. *Ogonek*, no. 46 (1963).
51. *Ukrainskyi visnyk*, no. 1-2, 64ff.
52. Cf. B. R. Bociurkiw, "Die Katakombenkirche in der Ukraine," *Der Fels*, no. 5 (May 1977): 148.
53. "Religiia v SSSR. Doklad Furova," *Khronika tekushchikh sobytii*, no. 41 (New York, 1976): 7.
54. *Ibid.*
55. *Ukrainskyi visnyk*, no. 3 (October 1970): 76.
56. See *Radianska Ukraina*, 19 June 1962.
57. *Ibid.*, 24 June 1962.
58. O. I. Pervomaisky, *Khto taki piatydesiatnyky (triasuny)* (Kiev, 1961), 18ff.
59. See P. Z. Kozik, *Khto taki adventysty* (Kiev, 1961), and *Khronika tekushchikh sobytii*, no. 48 (14 March 1978).
60. *Khronika tekushchikh sobytii*, no. 47 (30 November 1977), 55.

Conclusion

The tears shed in the streets of Kiev over Stalin's death are a disturbing testimony to the results of Soviet propaganda. For all the dissension, suspicion, fear and lack of solidarity that beset Soviet society, there was a widespread servile loyalty to the dictator. This attitude was prevalent among all ranks of society. The mood changed dramatically in September 1953 when Khrushchev—a man who had twice headed the Communist Party of Ukraine—was elected first secretary of the CPSU Central Committee. Many Ukrainian party members expected him to speak out in Ukraine's interest, and felt obligated to give him maximum support. Khrushchev, in turn, called dozens of Ukrainian party officials to Moscow, and awarded them with responsible positions.

One effect of Khrushchev's rise was to strengthen the self-confidence and self-awareness of the Ukrainian party organization. Ukrainian officials were emboldened to lobby for Ukrainian interests, to strive for a greater role in the USSR hierarchy. More opportunities were available to promote the interests of the republic, and Khrushchev allowed the republics more say in their own affairs, particularly in the economic sphere. The growing influence of the Ukrainian party organization was parallelled by a partial rebirth of "public opinion," a process that received additional impetus from the Twentieth CPSU Congress and was most marked among the republic's student youth, intelligentsia and young workers. In Ukraine many people demanded the elimination of the consequences of the personality cult in nationality policy, as well as more national and cultural rights.

By the late 1950s, however, the situation had changed. Attacks on Ukrainian rights such as the school reforms of 1958 exemplified this. At the same time, Khrushchev lost the loyalty and support of Ukrainians through his contradictory and sometimes haphazard economic experiments. Opponents of Khrushchev's policies both in Moscow and the union republics gradually consolidated their forces. In Ukraine they included such party ideologists as Malanchuk, who was strongly influenced by Suslov, and a large section of the republican KGB, whose personnel (especially in the provinces) had hardly changed since Stalin's time. These two groups played on the thesis that the reformists were being manipulated and exploited by "foreign foes."

What sort of political opposition existed in Ukraine? First there was the lingering political influence of the Organization of Ukrainian Nationalists (OUN) and the Ukrainian Insurgent Army (UPA), which the security organizations had reportedly destroyed by the early 1950s. Second, in the late 1950s, a new political opposition developed. This·was a result of the socio-economic conditions existing in the USSR after 1953 rather than a sequel of the events that occurred before and during the Second World War. Its representatives renounced terrorism as a means of achieving political ends. Unlike the political opposition in the RSFSR, the Ukrainian opposition rejected the creation of clandestine political parties; instead, it wanted to operate within the framework of Soviet law. The authorities were informed of its plans and actions, and most of the important documents it issued bore its members' signatures and addresses. This openness won them recognition and sympathy among the population.

One of the central demands of this opposition was for the use of the Ukrainian language in private and public life. Seeing Russification as the worst threat to Ukraine, it campaigned for the "enrichment of Ukrainian literature and history." It rejected nationalistic antagonism and considered its aims fully consonant with Lenin's programme. Although Kiev (especially its university) was the centre of opposition, the movement spread to all parts of Ukraine. Eventually, this opposition was also repressed, first by propaganda and later though threats, intimidation, psychological terror and physical reprisals. An increasing number of dissidents were sent to prison, labour camps and special psychiatric clinics.

The problems of the Moscow-Ukraine relationship were reflected in the leadership of the Ukrainian party organization. Shelest could only slow the centripetal forces in his own domain. Although they appreciated a loyal party official, Brezhnev and his supporters needed a man in Ukraine who had no scruples about subordinating the republic's interests to those of the Soviet state. They were convinced that Shcherbytsky had exactly the qualities they needed.

Another feature of the postwar years which affected both Ukraine and the entire Soviet Union was the party's efforts to wrest control of the political system from the security organs. Initially the Soviet party organs were hindered by a rigid ideology, the inability to cast off obsolete dogmas, and inertia in the face of change. But Stalin's death allowed the absorption of new ideas, which permitted the party to regain total political control of Soviet society and turn the security organs from its master into its servant.

After the Twenty-second CPSU Congress in 1961, the expansion of the union republics' economic rights was ended in favour of a return to centralism. The number of all-union ministries was increased and many union-republican and republican ministries were dissolved. This process culminated with the adoption of the new Constitution of the USSR in October 1977, which treats the Soviet economy as a single entity.

In the sphere of language the main problem facing the Soviet leadership has been to get the non-Russian peoples to learn and use Russian with the minimum of persuasion. Accordingly, the Kremlin must have been somewhat alarmed by the situation in Ukraine in the early 1960s. Many linguists, and not only the proponents of Russification, detected a strong increase in the use of Ukrainian compared with the 1950s. They also observed fewer differences between colloquial and literary usage. This phenomenon was the fruition of the movement for the greater use of the Ukrainian language that had built up in the republic after 1953, initially among students but later among other sections of the population. This did not imply rejection of bilingualism; the difference was that many Ukrainian linguists now believed that this question could be resolved without detriment to their mother tongue.

The policy of Russification had as its secondary objective the reduction of interest in the learning of other languages, thus limiting the possibility of communication with other peoples. This policy is being implemented throughout the Soviet Union with a huge outlay in human and financial resources. Ukraine has been a testing ground for this. The most intensive research into bilingualism has been conducted there, notably at the O. O. Potebnia Institute for the Study of Language of the Ukrainian Academy of Sciences and at the faculties of Russian and Ukrainian at most of the republic's universities. Measures have been taken in Ukraine to improve the teaching and learning of Russian at general schools and teachers' training colleges. The Soviet authorities have made this a key pedagogical priority and political task. In Ukraine the emphasis is on Russian instruction starting in the first grade at schools where the language of instruction is Ukrainian, Hungarian, Moldavian or Polish. On the basis of an experiment begun in 1977, Russian was made a permanent part of the first-grade curriculum after 1980–1.

The drive to increase the use of Russian sparked protests among nationally conscious Ukrainians. This aggrandizement of the Russian language has created privileges for the Russians who live in the national republics. Already enjoying a special status, these Russians find their situation enhanced by the elevation of their language. They tend to consider themselves "bearers of civilization," an attitude that encourages them to look down on the "natives" of the republics in which they live.

Prospects

Soviet society is in many ways divided. The extent of the opposition to central policies reflects the changed situation that emerged after Stalin's death. Yet the present Soviet leadership is making every effort to accelerate the integration of the "Soviet people," a policy that entails the curtailment of the rights of the non-Russian republics, to rob them of their national identity, of their national language. The authorities try to mask this process—a most blatant violation of human rights—with such terms as "rapprochement" and "internationalism." The Soviet leaders are pursuing a utopian goal with repressive methods.

Nevertheless, the last twenty-five years of Ukrainian history are not entirely black. The Ukrainian people's self-awareness and sense of national identity is greater now than in 1953, and they are at the forefront of the world-wide struggle for the realization of human rights.

Index